CHILD RIGHTS AND YOUNG LIVES
Theoretical Issues and Empirical Studies

CHILD RIGHTS AND YOUNG LIVES

Theoretical Issues and Empirical Studies

Edited by

Prof. D. Sarada

&

Dr. N. Rajani

DISCOVERY PUBLISHING HOUSE PVT. LTD.

NEW DELHI-110 002

Reprinted - 2018

First Published - 2009

ISBN: 978-81-8356-435-9

Child Rights and Young Lives

Published by:

DISCOVERY PUBLISHING HOUSE PVT. LTD.
4383/4B, Ansari Road, Darya Ganj
New Delhi-110 002 (India)
Phone: +91-11-23279245, 43596064-65
Fax: +91-11-23253475
E-mail: discoverypublishinghouse@gmail.com
sales@discoverypublishinggroup.com
web: www.discoverypublishinggroup.com

Printed at:
Infinity Imaging Systems
Delhi

Foreword

In the process of development, human material counts much, as it is both the means as well as the end of all development processes. If the human being counts, as Pandit Nehru rightly observes "he counts much more as a child than as a grown-up". Children are generally loved everywhere, though this sentiment of affection they enjoy does not assure them needed rights and care which is their due. There is a growing feeling that child care deserves much more support than what it is today realizing the child as a potential human resource. The traditional thinking of listing the child development programmes as mere welfare programmes must change and investment in children is to be taken as investment in human resource development. R. Debre, the founder of the International Children's Centre, Paris has said "the child is a modern invention". The observation though appears to be paradoxical, yet it indicates the value of child as potential human resource for the growth of a nation.

However, it is encouraging to note that some committed social reformers and non-governmental agencies have chosen to address the issues of child rights with a holistic approach. The Basic Education (Wardha System) as advocated by Gandhiji had a concern for child rights and through the help of "eyes, ears and tongue" create a natural interest in acquiring required skills for self reliance. Gandhi desired active involvement of students in awareness building and rural reconstruction which in modern terminology is termed as extension education. Srinikethan Experiment of Ravindranath Togore had focused on child rights and child welfare through health and education programmes. The training facilities for boys and girls in kitchen gardening, poultry, dairy, carpentry and other crafts paved the way for child rights in acquiring skills needed for happy life.

The Declaration of the Rights of child as adopted by the U.N. General Assembly in 1959 is a single major step in the direction of policy measures. Based on the recommendations of the duly constituted committee, under the chairmanship of Shri Ganga Saran Sinha, the Government of India proclaimed the National Policy Resolution in August 1974, declaring that "the Nation's Children are a supremely important asset, their nurture and solicitude are our responsibility". The policy lays down that the "the state shall provide adequate services to children both before and after birth and through the period of growth to ensure their full physical, mental and social development". Indian Constitution has provisions for the care, protection and prevention of exploitation of children. Article 24 of the Constitution prohibits employment of children below the age of 14 years in any factory or mine or in any other hazardous employment. The Directive Principles of State Policy in the Constitution direct the state (Article 39) that the tender age of children is not abused and forced by economic necessity to enter avocations unsuited to their age or strength. Article 45 lays down that the State shall endeavour to provide free and compulsory education for children upto the age of 14 years.

The issues relating to child rights and child care are no doubt addressed through series of initiatives, but they are not tackled effectively. Disappointingly there are basic handicaps in well understanding the issues of child rights and child welfare: statistics with regard to child rights are not adequate and reliable so as to draw meaningful conclusions; empirical studies in the area are not adequate; Children below 14 years are the worst sufferers due to malnutrition, hunger and ill health. M.S. Swaminathan states that every third child born in India is characterized by low birth weight (LBW). The LEW children, resulting from the maternal and foetal under nutrition suffer set backs in brain development and several serious health problems in adult life. Such enforced handicaps at birth represent the cruelest form of inequality; girl children continue to be viewed as inferior and remain neglected segment of the society; female literacy, family limitation, nutrition and health services do not receive adequate attention; Literature and Films on child rights continue to be a neglected sector; the extension compound in the curriculum of institutions of higher learning in the direction of child rights and child welfare is yet to receive serious consideration; the role of non-governmental agencies in the direction of child rights is not adequate enough; the media, both electronic and print is not well projecting the rights of children in right perspective; the children of poor category are often bypassed by the Balwadi programme; the school environment in the rural areas is discouraging calling for assured incentive measures such as supply of books, stationary, uniform, and mid-meal of quality and physically and mentally handicaps children's continue to be neglected.

During the planning era schemes addressing the welfare of children include among others, Minimum Needs Programme, Antodaya Scheme, Integrated Child Development Services (ICDS), Training of Rural Youth for Self Employment (TRYSEM) Development of Women and Children in Rural Areas (DWACRA). The Sarva Abhiyan (SSA) is the on going programme (2004-2008) to achieve universal elementary education in a mission mode with funding pattern of 75:25 between the Centre and the State Governments. No doubt, out of these schemes and of the role of non-governmental agencies, significant progress has been achieved in different areas of child welfare. Selected institutions of higher learning are actively engaged in addressing child-related problems through extension education. Much has been done but many areas are yet to be tacked effectively.

Child rights and child care is a wide area touching nearly 40 per cent of the total population of India with complex issues of challenging nature. It becomes really difficult for the schemes initiated by the government to cover all issues relating to child rights. All sections of the society - individuals and institutions of varying nature including institutions of higher learning have a role to play. APJ Abdul Kalam, as a word of both a message and caution, very rightly observes "India should become developed nation by 2020 with the base of its vast human resources. In this task, all must work and all have a role to play. If you are a teacher, in what ever capacity, you have a very special role to play because more than any body else you are shaping generations". He proceeds to state "Teachers should update their own knowledge because the student is only as good as the teacher".

The publication, **"Child Rights and Young Lives: *Theoretical Issues and Empirical Studies*"** is the outcome of wide reading and academic interest of Prof. D. Sarada and Dr. N. Rajani. The work is systematically organized and well presented. The authors of different articles deserve to be congratulated for identifying right themes and well presenting different issues. The themes chosen by different authors are both interesting and challenging. The theoretical issues covered in the first part of the book, present an overview of different issues centered round child rights. The role of International Organisations in safeguarding the child rights such as International Labour Organization (ILO), International Programme for Elimination of Child Labour (IPECL), United Nations International Children's Emergency Fund (UNICEF) and United Nations Educational, Scientific and Cultural Organisation (UNESCO), is well analysed. The different provisions of the constitution of India guaranteeing rights to the children are well presented. The child related schemes initiated from time to time are critically examined and useful suggestions indicated.

Empirical studies cover a wide range of issues and concrete suggestions emerge in each paper. In one paper a case is made out for strengthening the training programme with the component of child rights and thus equipping the Anganwadi workers with required knowledge on child rights. In more than one paper the need for well educating the mothers on matters of child rights is well identified. In a study pertaining to Rural

Primary School Education, reasons for school dropouts are identified and a case is made out for coordinating poverty alleviation programmes with education programmes so as to strengthen the enrollment. Also, in one study it is pointed out that with improved facilities and better home and school environment regular strength of the children can be ensured in primary schools. It is rightly noted that the child rights knowledge, attitude and practice are significantly associated with each other and they are inter related. The need for publication of child rights manual is well pointed out. The pathetic conditions of street children are well identified and the need for active role of the non-government organizations is indicated. Children's behaviour in relation with family background and school environment is studied and remedial measures suggested. Appropriate statistical techniques are applied to strengthen the quality of work. The references cited in each article are well listed and they are a single major source of useful information for further research. Empirical studies cover critical evaluation of selected schemes of child welfare and in so doing gaps in the functioning of the schemes are located and remedial measures indicated.

The conclusions of empirical studies throw out a useful material for policy makers and administrators. The burning issues of critical importance identified in the study that need effective measures include "Street children", "Child Labour, Malnutrition of Pregnant women and Infant child", "Exposure to HIV/AIDS", "Criminality and Domestic Violence", "Drug and alcohol addiction", "Inadequate Information and Poor legal support" and "Inadequacy of media in sensitizing the public issues of child rights". If this publication facilitates effective measures in tackling these burning problems, the purpose of the publication is well served.

I am sure the publication "Child Rights and Young Lives" of the Department of Home Science, Sri Padmavathi Mahila University, Tirupati will contribute to greater clarity in the thinking of administrators and policy makers with regard to programmes covering Child Rights. The editors of the book and authors of different articles deserve appreciation from the readers for well presenting issues of current relevance. I wish the publication a wide circulation stimulating right thinking and action in the direction of covering uncovered areas of child rights and child welfare, ultimately paving the way for better quality of human resource.

Prof. K. Venkata Reddy
Formerly Vice-Chancellor
S.K. University, Anantapur (A.P)

Preface

Child rights and young lives, Theoretical issues and Empirical studies is a compilation of research studies carried out in the department of Home science, Sri Padmavathi Mahila Visvavidyalayam (Tirupati) by post graduate students under the guidance of Dr. D. Sarada and also articles contributed by Dr. D. Sarada and Dr. N. Rajani. The book is a comprehensive document on child rights approach to development programmes, child rights education and research. It serves as a reference book for students, teachers, researchers of various disciplines such as Human Development, social work, women studies, Home science, Education, Nursing , Psychology, Law, Adult and population education. This book is useful to personnel working in child development programmes of Government and NGOs.

—Authors

Contents

List of Contributors

1. *Prof. D. Sarada,* Head, Department of Home Science, Sri Padmavathi Mahila Visvavidyalayam (Women's University), Tirupati – 517 502, Andhra Pradesh.

2. *Dr. N. Rajani,* Assistant Professor, Department of Home Science, Sri Padmavathi Mahila Visvavidyalayam (Women's University), Tirupati – 517 502, Andhra Pradesh.

3. *Ms. T. Mamata,* M.Sc., Department of Home Science, Sri Padmavathi Mahila Visvavidyalayam (Women's University), Tirupati – 517 502, Andhra Pradesh.

4. *Ms. K. Mithila Jyothsna,* M.Sc., Department of Home Science, Sri Padmavathi Mahila Visvavidyalayam (Women's University), Tirupati – 517 502, Andhra Pradesh.

5. *Ms. K. Rajitha,* M.Sc., Department of Home Science, Sri Padmavathi Mahila Visvavidyalayam (Women's University), Tirupati – 517 502, Andhra Pradesh.

6. *Ms. N. Venkatalakshmi Sowjanya,* M.Sc., Department of Home Science, Sri Padmavathi Mahila Visvavidyalayam (Women's University), Tirupati – 517 502, Andhra Pradesh.

7. *Ms. K. Hymavathi,* M.Sc., Department of Home Science, Sri Padmavathi Mahila Visvavidyalayam (Women's University), Tirupati – 517 502, Andhra Pradesh.

8. *Ms. M. Deepa*, M.Sc., Department of Home Science, Sri Padmavathi Mahila Visvavidyalayam (Women's University), Tirupati – 517 502, Andhra Pradesh.
9. *Ms. P. Bharathi*, M.Sc., Department of Home Science, Sri Padmavathi Mahila Visvavidyalayam (Women's University), Tirupati – 517 502, Andhra Pradesh.
10. *Ms. N.C. Krishnaveni*, M.Sc., Department of Home Science, Sri Padmavathi Mahila Visvavidyalayam (Women's University), Tirupati – 517 502, Andhra Pradesh.
11. *Ms. K. Lalitha Kumari*, M.Sc., Department of Home Science, Sri Padmavathi Mahila Visvavidyalayam (Women's University), Tirupati – 517 502, Andhra Pradesh.
12. *Ms. A. Sowmya*, M.Sc., Department of Home Science, Sri Padmavathi Mahila Visvavidyalayam (Women's University), Tirupati – 517 502, Andhra Pradesh.
13. *Ms. T. Manju Bhargavi*, M.Sc., Department of Home Science, Sri Padmavathi Mahila Visvavidyalayam (Women's University), Tirupati – 517 502, Andhra Pradesh.
14. *Ms. S. Anuradha*, M.Sc., Department of Home Science, Sri Padmavathi Mahila Visvavidyalayam (Women's University), Tirupati – 517 502, Andhra Pradesh.

Theoretical Issues

1

Child Rights and Indian Constitution

—Prof. D. Sarada

In November 1990, the Government of India endorsed all the 27 survival and development goals for the year 2000, argued at the world summit for children, and firmly committed to the children of this country that the worst elements of poverty, ill-health, malnutrition, illiteracy and exploitation and unhealthy environment would soon become conditions of the past.

Two years later, in December 1992, the country committed itself once again, this time by ratifying the convention on the rights of the child, the convention is guided by the principle of a "First call for children" a principle that the essential needs of children showed be given highest priority in the allocation of resources at all times. It obligates the state to respect and ensure that children get a fair and equitable deal in society and advocates concrete plan of action by all individuals and agencies – government as well as non-governmental, local, national, regional and international to create an environment in which all children are able to live securely and realise their full potential in life. Such an affirmation is contained in a detailed "National Plan of Action: A Commitment to the child" adopted in 1992 by the Government of India.

The constitution of India reiterates several times over the importance of improving the well-being of children. Article 39 of the Directive Principles of State Policy, for instance, requires that the state shall, in particular, direct its policy towards securing that the health and strength of workers, men and women, and the tender age of children are not abused, and that citizens are not forced by economic necessity to enter avocations unsuited to their age or strength, that children are given opportunities and facilities to develop in a healthy manner and in conditions of freedom and dignity, and that childhood and youth are protected against exploitation and against moral and material abandonment.

Similarly, Article 24 stipulates that no child below the age of 14 years shall be employed to work in any factory or mine or engaged in any other hazardous employment. And according to Article 45, the State shall endeavour to provide free and compulsory education for all children until they complete the age of 14 years. Nearly 25 years later, in 1974, India reaffirmed its constitutional obligations to children in the National Policy for children by declaring that: It shall be the policy of the State to provide adequate services to children, both before and after birth and through the period of growth, ensure their full physical, mental and social development. The state shall progressively increase the scope of such services so that, within a reasonable time, all children in the country enjoy optimum conditions for their balanced growth.

The laws framed in the statute books of India broadly recognised the rights of the child as proclaimed in the Child Rights Convention (CRC). The statute books proclaim that the child is entitled to the equal protection of the laws, that the child shall not suffer from any discrimination, child labour is condemned; the desirability of the child having a healthy environment, nutrition, food and education is recognised. The rights of the child to citizenship, the humane treatment when the child violates the law is also recognised.

The Constitution of India itself guarantees many rights to the child. This is two-fold the Fundamental Rights and the Directive Principles.

Fundamental Rights Enforceable Against the State only through the High Courts and the Supreme Court :

Articles 14-17	:	Right to Equality
Articles 19-22	:	Right to Freedom
Articles 23-24	:	Right against exploitation
Article 25	:	Right to Freedom of Religion
Article 29	:	Cultural and Educational Rights
Article 32	:	Right to Constitutional Remedies

Directive Principles not Enforceable at all.

Article 39	:	Ban on unsuitable work for children, opportunities and facilities for them.
Article 42	:	Maternity relief just conditions of work.
Article 45	:	Free and compulsory education for children till 14 years.
Article 47	:	Right to nutrition and health.

Fundamental Rights

Article 14: Equality of Law: The State shall not deny to any person equality before the law or the equal protection of the laws within the territory of India.

Article 15: Prohibition of Discrimination

1. The state shall not discriminate against any citizen on ground only to religion, race, caste, sex, place of birth or any of them.

2. No citizen shall on grounds only of religion, race, caste, sex, place of birth or any of them, be subject to any disability, liability, restriction or condition with regard

   — to access to shops, public restaurants, hotels and places of public entertainment; or

   — use of wells, tanks, bathing ghats, roads and places of public resort, maintained wholly or partly out of state funds or dedicated to the use of the general public.

3. Nothing in this article shall prevent the state from making any special provision for women and children.

Article 16: Equality of Opportunity in Matters of Public Employment

1. There shall be equality of opportunity for all citizens in matters related to employment or appointment to any office under the state.
2. No citizen shall, on grounds only of religion, race, caste, sex, decent, place of birth, residence or any of them, be ineligible for, or discriminated against, in respect of any employment or office under the state.

Section 4 deals with the powers of the state to make reservations for backward class of citizens.

Article 17: Abolition of Untouchability

Untouchability is abolished and its practice in any form is forbidden. The enforcement of any disability arising out of untouchability shall be an offence punishable in accordance with law.

Article 19: Protection of Certain Rights regarding Freedom of Speech, etc.

All citizens shall have the right

- To freedom of speech and expression
- To assemble peacefully and without arms
- To form associations or unions
- To move freely throughout the territory of India
- To reside and settle in any part of India
- To practice any profession, or to carry on any occupation, trade or business.

Article 21: Protection of Life and Personal Liberty: No person shall be deprived of his life or personal liberty except according to procedure established by law. The Supreme Court has declared the right to education as part of the fundamental right to personal liberty, as without education, life cannot be lived with dignity.

Article 22: Protection Against Arrest and Detention in Certain Cases

1. No person who is arrested shall be detained in custody without being informed, as soon as may be, of the grounds for such arrest, nor shall he be denied the right to consult and be defended by a legal practitioner of his choice.
2. Every person who is arrested and detained in custody shall be produced before the nearest magistrate within a period of 24 hours of such arrested excluding the time necessary for the journey from the place of arrest to the court of the Magistrate, and no such person shall be detained to custody beyond the said period without the authority of a Magistrate (exceptions are aliens and detentions under any law providing for preventive detention).

Article 23: Prohibition of Traffic in Human Beings and Forced Labour: Traffic in human beings and beggary and other similar forms of forced labour are prohibited and any contravention of this provision shall be an offence punishable in accordance with law.

Article 24: Prohibition of Employment of Children in Factories, etc. No child below the age of 14 years shall be employed to work in any factory or mine or engaged in other hazardous employment.

Article 25: Freedom of Conscience and Free Profession, Practice and Propagation of Religion: subject to public order, morality and health and to the other provisions of this part, all persons are equally entitled to freedom of conscience and the right peacefully to profess, practice and propagate religion.

Article 29 (1): Freedom to conserve their distinct language, script or culture.

Article 32: Remedies for enforcement of rights conferred by this part. The right to move the Supreme Court by appropriate proceedings for the enforcement of the rights conferred by this part is guaranteed.

Directive Principles

Article 37

The provisions in this part shall not be enforceable by any court, but the principles there in laid down are fundamental in the governance of the country, and it shall be the duty of the state to apply these principles in making laws.

Article 39 (e)

The state shall ensure that the health and strength of workers, men and women, and the tender age of children are not abused and that citizens are not forced by economic necessity to enter avocations unsuited to their age or strength.

Article 39 (f)

That children are given opportunities and facilities to develop in a healthy manner and in conditions of freedom and dignity and that childhood and youth are protected against exploitation and against moral and material abandonment.

Article 42

The state shall make provision for securing just and humane conditions of work and for maternity relief.

Article 45

Provision for free and compulsory education for children: The state shall endeavour to provide, within a period of 10 years from the commencement of this constitution, for free and compulsory education for all children until they complete the age of 14 years.

Article 47

Duty of the state to raise the level of nutrition and the standard of living and to improve public health: The state shall regard the raising of the level of nutrition and the standard of living of its people and the improvement of public health as among its primary duties.

The rights perspective has practical implications for public policy on child development services. First, this perspective is the main foundation of the demand for "Universal" child development services. Indeed, one implication of the rights approach is that all children are entitled to certain "opportunities and facilities" (as the Constitution puts it) that do not have to be justified on a case by case basis, let alone submitted to cost benefit tests.

Thus the Indian constitution made provisions for the welfare of children well before the declaration of child rights by the United Nations. The Indian Government has launched several welfare programmes for children to fulfill the promises made in the constitution of India. Good intentions will now have to be matched with the political will to act and fortified by changes in Individual and National attitudes and priorities.

REFERENCES

1. Devi, L., 1999: *Policies and Programmes Related to Child Development*. Published by Anmol Publications, New Delhi, pp. 384-386.

2. Gupta, S., 1996: *Rights of the Child Workers*. Published by Ministry of Social Justice and Empowerment, Vol. XXXVIII(124), New Delhi, pp. 1-3.

3. Hoover, D., 1998, cited by Pramila Pandit Barooah, 1999: *Handbook of Child*. Published by Concept Publishing Company, New Delhi.

4. Meherdale, A., 1997: *Law and Child Labour: A Case for Protecting Children's Rights*. The Journal of Social Change, Vol. 27(33), pp. 132-146.

5. Mehta, P.L., 1996: *Child Labour and the Law*. Published by Deep and Deep Publications, New Delhi.

6. Muthuswamy, 2000: *Rights of the Children*. The Journal of Social Welfare, Vol. 46(10), pp. 15-17.

7. Pandey, R., 1973: *Street Children of Kanpur*. Published by National Labour Institute, New Delhi, p. 1.

8. Singh, O., 1995: *Child Development Issues, Policies and Programmes*. Published by Kanishka Publishers, Vol.3, New Delhi, pp. 339-341.

2

Child Rights Convention and the World's Children

—Prof. D. Sarada

Children have no political power, they do not vote and their opinions carry littler weight with governments. They are therefore totally dependent on their parents or guardians to act in their best interest and to protect their rights.

For many children in the world today, that protection is manifestly not enough. Millions of boys and girls are physically or sexually abused or economically exploited, by the families that are supposed to provide them with security and love. In an even larger number of cases, children are denied their rights by forces beyond the family's control-by war and natural disaster, by unemployment, poverty, and their parent's lack of education. In our times, governments are still recruiting children to fight wars, employers are still exploiting the children of the desperately poor in fields and factories, and national and international economic forces are still allowed to inflict permanent mental and physical damage on young children, who, no matter what the external circumstances, have a special right to protection for their growing minds and bodies.

To support families, or to compensate for their failings, there is a need for broader social and legislative consensus on what is and what is not acceptable in the treatment of the young. And it was to help in the creation of such a consensus that the idea of an International convention on the rights of the child was first proposed by the government of Poland, during the International year of the child (1979). Since them, the delegates of some forty governments have been meeting regularly to try to draft such a convention in the form of a legal agreement which will be binding on all states by which it is ratified.

Negotiating a detailed agreement across many different political and cultural systems has not always been easy, but from it all a consensus has emerged in the form of a draft text.

Now the International approach to children has changed dramatically once again. The idea that children have special needs have given way to the conviction that children have rights, the same full spectrum of rights as adults, civil and political, social, cultural and economic. Adults have to accept this concept of child rights and reorient themselves to assist children in utilising their rights.

The convention on the rights of the child, entered into international law on 2nd September 1990, nine months after the conventions' adoption by the United National General Assembly. Since then the convention has been ratified (as of mid-September 1996) by all countries except the Cook Islands, Oman, Somalia, Switzerland, the United Arab Emirates and the United States, making it the most widely ratified human rights treaty in history.

The convention has produced a profound change that is already beginning to have substantive effects on the world's attitude towards it's children. Once a country ratifies, it is obliged in law to undertake all appropriate measures to assist parents and other responsible parties in fulfilling their obligations to children under the convention. Now, 96 per cent of the world's children live in states that are legally obligated to protect children's rights.

A statement of the child's rights is a statement of adult responsibilities. It is the responsibility of all adults, of governments and of the International Community, to create and maintain the circumstances in which families themselves can protect the rights of the child. If families fail their children, or if circumstances such as war or disaster or absolutely poverty prevent families from protecting their children's rights, then governments and the International community again have the responsibility of quickly rebuilding the essential walls of physical and mental protection around the vulnerable years of childhood (UNICEF, 1989).

The convention draws attention to four sets of civil, political, social and economical and cultural rights of every child. These include:

The Right to Survival

Which includes the right to life, the highest attainable standard of health, nutrition and adequate standards of living. It also includes the right to a name and a nationality.

The Right to Protection

Which included freedom from all forms of exploitation, abuse, inhuman or degrading treatment and neglect, including the right to special protection in situations of emergency and armed conflicts.

The Right to Development

Which includes the right to education, support for early childhood development and care, social security and the right to leisure, recreation and cultural activities.

The Right to Participation

Which includes respect for the views of the child, freedom of expression, access to appropriate information, and freedom of thought, conscience and religion.

The Rights of the Child

The preamble recalls the basic principles of the United Nations and specific provisions of certain relevant human right treaties and proclamations; reaffirms the fact that children, because of their vulnerability need special care and protection; and places special emphasis on the primary caring and protective responsibility of the family, the need for the legal and other protection of the child before and after birth, the importance of respect for the cultural values of the child's community, and the vital role of international cooperation in achieving the realisation of children's rights.

Article–1

Definition of a Child: All persons under 18, unless by law majority is attained at an earlier age.

Article–2

Non-Discrimination: The principle that all rights apply to all children without exception, and the states obligation to protect children from any form of discrimination. The states must not violate any right and must take positive action to promote them all.

Article–3

Best interests of the Child: All the actions concerning the child should take full account of his/her best interests. The state is to provide adequate care when parents and other responsible fail to do so.

Article–4

Implementation of Rights: The states obligation to translate the rights in the convention into reality.

Article–5

Parental Guidance and the Child's Evolving Capacities: The state's duty to respect the rights and responsibilities of parents and the wider family to provide guidance appropriate to the child's evolving capabilities.

Article–6

Survival and Development: The inherent right to life, and the State's obligation to ensure the child's survival and development.

Article–7

Nationality: The right to have a name from birth and to be granted a nationality.

Article–8

Preservation of Identity: The state's obligation to protect and, if necessary, re-establish the basic aspects of a child's identity (name, nationality and family name).

Article–9

Separation from Parents: The child's right to live with his/her parents, unless this is deemed incompatible with his/her interests, the rights to maintain contact with both parents if separated from one or both; the duties of States in cases where such separation results from State action.

Article–10

Family Reunification: The right of the children and parents to leave any country and to enter their own in order to reunited or to maintain the child-parent relationship.

Article–11

Illicit Transfer and Non-return: The states obligation to try to prevent and remedy the kidnapping or retention of children abroad by a parent or third party.

Article–12

The Child's Opinion

The child's right to express an opinion, and to have that opinion taken into account in any matter or procedure affecting the child.

Article–13

Freedom of Expression

The child's right to obtain and make known information, and to express his/her views, unless this would violate the rights of others.

Article–14

Freedom of Thought, Conscience and Religion

The child's right to freedom of thought, conscience and religion, subject to appropriate parental guidance and national law.

Article–15

Freedom of Association

The right of children to meet with others and to join or setup associations, unless the fact of doing so violates the rights of others.

Article–16

Protection of Privacy

The right to protection from interference with privacy, family, home and correspondence, and from libel/slander.

Article–17

Access to Appropriate Information

The role of the media in disseminating information to children that is consistent with moral well-being and knowledge and understanding among peoples, and respects the child's cultural backgrounds, the state is to take measures to encourage this and to protect the children from harmful materials.

Article–18

Parental Responsibilities

The Principle that both parents have joint primary responsibility for bringing up their children, and that state should support them in this risk.

Article–19

Protection from Abuse and Neglect

The State's obligation to protect children from all forms of maltreatment perpetrate by parents or others responsible for their care, and to undertake preventive and treatment programmes in this regard.

Article–20

Protection of Children without Families

The state's obligation to provide special protection for children deprived of their family environment and to ensure that appropriate alternative family care or institutional placement is made available to them, taking into account the child's cultural background.

Article–21

Adoption

In the countries where adoption is recognised and/or allowed, it shall only be carried out in the best interests of the child, with all necessary safeguards for given child and authorisation by the competent authorities.

Article–22

Refugee Children

Special protection to be granted to children who are refugees or seeking refugee status, and the state's obligation to cooperate with competent organisations providing such protection and assistance.

Article–23

Handicapped Children

The right of handicapped children to special care, education and training designed to help them to achieve the greatest possible self-reliance and to lead a full and active life in society.

Article–24

Health and Health Services

The right to the highest level of health possible and access to health and medical services, with special emphasis on primary and preventive healthcare, public health education and the diminution of infant mortality. It is the state's obligation to work towards the abolition of harmful traditional practices. Emphasis is laid on the need for international cooperation to ensure this right.

Article–25

Periodic Review of Placement

The right of children placed by the state of reasons for care, protection or treatment to have all aspects of that placement evaluated regularly.

Article–26

Social Security

The right of children to benefit from social security.

Article–27

Standard of Living

The right of children to benefit from an adequate standard of living, the primary responsibility of parents to provide this, and the states' duty to ensure that this responsibility can be fulfilled, and then fulfill, where necessary through the recovery of maintenance.

Article–28

Education

The child's right to education, and the state's duty to ensure that primary education at least is made free and compulsory. Administration of school discipline is to reflect the child's human dignity. Emphasis is laid on the need for international cooperation to ensure this right.

Article–29

Aims of Education

The state's recognition that education be directed at developing the child's personality and talents, preparing the child for active life as an adult, fostering respect for basic human rights and developing respect for the child's own cultural and national values and those of others.

Article–30

Children of Minorities and Indigenous Populations

The right of children of the minority communities and indigenous populations to enjoy their own culture and to practice their own religion and language.

Article–31

Leisure, Recreation and Cultural Activities

The right of children to leisure, play and participation in cultural/artistic activities.

Article–32

Child Labour

The state's obligation to protect children from engaging in work that constitutes a threat to their health, education and development, to set minimum ages for employment, and to regulate conditions for employment.

Article–33

Drug Abuse

The child's right to protect from the use of narcotic and psychotropic drugs and from being involved in their production or distribution.

Article–34

Sexual Exploitation

The child's right to protection from sexual exploitation and abuse, including prostitution and involvement in pornography.

Article–35

Sale, Trafficking and abduction

The states obligation to make every effort to prevent sale, trafficking and abduction of children.

Article–36

Other forms of Exploitation

The child's right to protection from all other forms of exploitation not covered in Articles 32, 33, 34 and 35.

Article–37

Torture and Deprivation of Liberty

The prohibition to torture, cruel treatment or punishment, capital punishment, life imprisonment, and unlawful arrest or deprivation of liberty. The principles of appropriate treatment, separation from detained adults, contact with family and to legal and other assistance.

Article–38

Armed Conflicts

The obligation of states to respect and ensure respect for humanitarian law as it applies to children. The principle that no child under 15 takes a direct part in hostilities or be recruited into the armed forces, and that all children affected by armed conflict benefit from protection and care.

Article–39

Rehabilitative Care

The states obligation to ensure that child victims of farmed conflicts, torture, neglect, maltreatment or exploitation receive appropriate treatment for their recovery and social reintegration.

Article–40

Administration of Juvenile Justice

The rights of children alleged or recognised as having committed an offence to respect for their human rights and, in particular, to benefit from all aspects of the due process of law, including legal or other assistance in preparing and presenting their defence. The principle that recourse to judicial proceedings and institutional placement should be avoided wherever possible and appropriate.

Article–41

Respect for Existing Standards

The principle that if any standards in national law or other applicable international instruments are higher than those of this convention, it is the higher standard that applies.

Article 42-45

Implementation and Entry into Force

The provisions of Article 42-45 notably for see:

1. The state's obligation to make the rights contained in this convention widely known to both adults and children.
2. The setting up of committee on the rights of child composed of ten experts, which will consider reports that state parties to the convention are to submit two years after ratification and every five years thereafter. The convention enters into force.
3. States parties are to make their reports widely available to the general public.
4. The committee may propose that special studies be undertaken on specific issues relating to the rights of the child, and may make its evaluation known to each state party concerned as well as to the UN General Assembly.
5. In order to "Foster the effective implementation of the convention and to encourage International Cooperation" the specialised agencies of the UN (such as ILO, WHO, UNESCO) and UNICEF would be able to attend the meetings of the committee. Together with any other body recognised as "Competent", including NGOs in consultative status with UN and UN organs such as UNHC, they can submit pertinent information to the committee and be asked to advise on the Optional Implementation of convention.

The convention recognises that not all governments have the resources necessary to ensure all economic, social and cultural rights immediately. But it commits them to make those rights a priority and to ensure them to the maximum extent of available resources.

Fulfilling their obligations sometimes requires states to make fundamental changes in national laws, institutions, plans, policies and practices to bring them into line with the principles of the convention. The drafters of the convention recognised, real change in the lives of children will come about only when social attitudes and ethics progressively change to conform with laws and principles. And when, as actors in the process, children themselves known enough about their rights to claim them.

The official monitor of this process of change is the committee on the rights of the child. Governments are obliged to report to the committee within two years of ratification, and every five years thereafter, specifying the steps taken to change national laws and formulate policies and actions.

The committee, made up of 10 experts, gathers evidence from Non-governmental Organizations (NGOs) and Inter Governmental Organisations including UNICEF, and these groups may prepare alternative reports to that of government (panel 1). The committee and the government then meet to discuss the country's child rights efforts and the steps necessary to overcome difficulties.

The reporting process has proved dynamic and constructive, with the dialogue established helping to advance children's rights. Unfortunately however, many countries have missed their reporting deadlines, 28 of them by as much as three years, as a September, 1996 (UNICEF, 1997).

The process of implementing the convention still remains in its infancy but, as we have noted, the international treaty for children is already beginning to make an impact. As reported in 1996 in UNICEF's annual publication, the progress of nations, of the 43 countries whose reports had been reviewed at the time, 14 had incorporated the principles of the convention into their constitutions and 35 had passed new laws or amended existing laws to conform to the convention. And 13 had built the convention into curricula or courses to begin the key process of educating children about their rights. Around the world, teachers, lawyers, police officials, judges and care givens and being trained in the principles and application of the convention.

Child Rights encompassed all the needs of child to grow as a healthy and productive individual, policies, strategies, programmes, delivery services should aim at fulfillment of Child Rights. The stake holders of these activities should be trained to do so.

A World Fit for Children

The message from the Children's Forum, delivered to the UN General Assembly Special Session on children by under-18 delegates on 8th May, 2002 reflects children's demand for a world fit for children, because a world fit for children is a world fit for everyone. Because the world's children are the victims of exploitation and abuse, street children, the children of war, the victims and orphans of HIV/AIDS, are denied good quality education and healthcare, are victims of political, economic, cultural, religious and environmental discrimination and they are children whose voices are not being heard it is time they are taken into account.

The children's Forum further stated that, in this world:

We are the world's children;

We are the victims of exploitation and abuse;

We are street children;

We are the children of war;

We are the victims and orphans of HIV/AIDS;

We are denied good quality education and healthcare;

We are victims of political, economic, cultural, religious and environmental discrimination;

We are children whose voices are not being heard, it is time we are taken into account;

We want a world fit for children, because a world fit for us is a world fit for everyone.

In this world,

We see respect for the rights of the child:

- governments and adults having a real and effective commitment to the principle of children's rights and applying the Convention on the Rights of the Child to all children;
- safe, secure and healthy environments for children in families, communities and nations.

We see an end to exploitation, abuse and violence:

- laws that protect children from exploitation and abuse being implemented and respected by all;
- centres and programmes that help to rebuild the lives of victimised children.

We see an end to war:

- world leaders resolving conflict through peaceful dialogue instead of using force;
- child refugees and child victims of war protected in every way and having the same opportunities as all other children.
- disarmament, elimination of the arms trade and an end to the use of child soldiers.

We see the provision of healthcare:

- affordable and accessible life-saving drugs and treatment for all children;
- strong and accountable partnership established among all to promote better health for children.

We see the eradication of HIV/AIDS:

- educational systems that include HIV prevention programmes;
- free testing and counselling centres;
- information about HIV/AIDS freely available to the public;

- orphans of AIDS and children living with HIV/AIDS cared for and enjoying the same opportunities as all other children.

We see the protection of the environment:

- conservation and rescue of natural resources;
- awareness of the need to live in environments that are healthy and favourable to our development;
- accessible surroundings for children with special needs.

We see an end to the vicious cycle of poverty:

- anti-poverty committees that bring about transparency in expenditure and give attention to the needs of all children;
- cancellation of the debt that impedes progress for children.

We see the provision of education:

- equal opportunities and access to quality education that is free and compulsory;
- school environments in which children feel happy about learning;
- education for life that goes beyond the academic and includes lessons in understanding, human rights, peace, acceptance and active citizenship.

We see the active participation of children:

- raised awareness and respect among people of all ages about every child's right to full and meaningful participation, in the spirit of the Convention on the Rights of the Child;
- children actively involved in decision-making at all levels and in planning, implementing, monitoring and evaluating all matters affecting the rights of the child.

We pledge an equal partnership in this fight for children's rights. And while we promise to support the actions you take on behalf of children; we also ask for your commitment and support in the actions we are taking—because the children of the world are misunderstood.

We are not the sources of problems; we are the resources that are needed to solve them.

We are not expenses; we are investments.

We are not just young people; we are people and citizens of this world.

Until others accept their responsibility to us, we will fight for our rights.

We have the will, the knowledge, the sensitivity and the dedication.

We promise that as adults we will defend children's rights with the same passion that we have now as children.

We promise to treat each other with dignity and respect.

We promise to be open and sensitive to our differences.

We are the children of the world, and despite our different backgrounds, we share a common reality.

We are united by our struggle to make the world a better place for all.

You call us the future, but we are also the present.

Thus the convention on rights of the child brought extraordinary change in the outlook of people towards children's needs, problems, services and development in the light of their rights as human beings.

The convention requires families, societies, governments and the international community to take action designed to fulfill the rights of all children in a sustainable, participatory and non-discriminatory manner. In practical terms, this means that the poorest, most vulnerable and often the most neglected children in all societies, rich and poor, must have first call on resources and efforts.

REFERENCES

1. Brenner, B., 1970, cited by Laxmi Devi (1998): *Encyclopaedia of Child and Family Welfare*, Published by Anmol Publications, Vol. 5, New Delhi, pp. 111.

2. Desai, M., Montiem, A. and Narayan, L., 1998: *Child Rights*. The Indian Journal of Social Work, Part-I, Vol. 59.

3. Devi, L., 1998: *Encyclopaedia of Child and Family Welfare*. Published by Anmol Publications, Vol. 5, New Delhi, pp. 111, 366.

4. UNICEF Carol Bellamy (1997) "*The State of the World's Children*", Published by Oxford University Press, U.K., pp. 9-14.

5. Gupta, S., 1996: *Rights of the Child Workers*. Published by Ministry of Social Justice and Empowerment, Vol. XXXVIII(124), New Delhi, pp. 1-3.

6. Muthuswamy, 2000: Rights of the Children. The Journal of Social Welfare, Vol. 46(10), pp. 15-17.

3

Child Rights and Capabilities of Families

—Dr. N. Rajani

Although infancy and childhood occupy only a small fraction of life span, they are the most crucial years in determining and influencing the personality of adulthood. The needs of children have to be fulfilled at the right time as the childhood is for today and it cannot be made to wait till tomorrow. The following poem of Gabriel Mistral well explains the urgency of children's needs fulfillment:

We are guilty of many errors and faults.

But our worst crime is abandoning the children.

Neglecting the foundation of life.

Many of the things we need can wait; the child cannot.

Right now is the time his bones are being formed,

His blood is being made

And his senses are being developed

to him we cannot answer

"Tomorrow"

His name is Today......

Dare we answer "Tomorrow"?

Meeting the basic needs of children is a crucial function of the family. Caring for children remains the most generally recognised basic responsibility of families, because the human infant needs a great deal of care in order to survive. Human Development requires emotional involvement and interaction with the child as well as physical care. Even when young children begin to play with other children outside the home, the family remains the most important socialising influence. Young children's attitudes towards people, things and life in general are patterned by their family life. Children brought up in democratic homes generally make better adjustments to outsiders and have lesser behavioural problems. Parenting is important even after the preschool age, during childhood, adolescence and beyond. Without adequate training and support, this responsibility can be too heavy a burden for many parents, particularly those who are separated from the support systems of extended family or kin. In many cultures, the old traditions of child care are no longer practised. Moreover owing to the absence of an extended family structure, the older relatives are not able to transfer their knowledge or offer support to younger generation. Parental education on child needs, care and rights is therefore needed most urgently when the children are small.

Almost all the world's population live in family units, but their structure or form vary not only from society to society but also within a society. The family thus, is an institution found in all human societies in one structural form or the other. It is a Universal grooming whether it be nuclear, compound or extended. In all human societies provision must be made for biological and social reproduction, if the society is to continue.

The growth and development of children depends on their families capabilities to perform familial functions effectively and their abilities to meet the child's needs. The families' failure to perform their functions or fulfill their familial obligations towards their children due to economic, social and other reasons subjects children of such families to psychological, social and economic stress. Which not only affects the all-round development of children but also manifests into social and behavioural problems of national and international concern.

Universally children have rights to family:

(a) every child has the right to be reared by his or her children;

(b) every parent has the duty to rear his or her children;

(c) every adult has the right to marry and found a family.

The reasons for failure of families to function effectively can be categorised as:

1. Changes in Family structure and environment.

2. Changes in livelihood opportunities and migration.

1. Changes in Family Structure and Environment

Several onslaughts continues to prove its usefulness in moulding our children into productive citizens. In India the family as a system underwent several changes due to urbanisation, industrialisation, westernisation and technological advances and other associated phenomena. The families are caught to the process of continuous change, which resulted in restructuring of families redefining the rules, norms and values. These transitions were marked by changes in occupational patterns, family roles and responsibilities, decision making patterns, work distribution patterns, status of women and girl children and family equilibrium. Thus the traditional families underwent structural changes affecting normal family life, making the children the worst sufferers. In India irrespective of place of residence (urban, rural, tribal), the number of large families have drastically reduced and most of the families are smaller and of nuclear type. The small families are in need of dependable social support systems to assist them in child care and other familial functions as they are not self-sufficient. In absence of family support systems the problem families may become dysfunctional jeopardising their own and their children's future. It is the States responsibility to establish or assist the families to establish reliable and dependable family support systems to fulfill the rights of children.

2. Changes in Livelihood Opportunities and Migration

The state of poor families in rural and tribal areas are alarming due to drastic changes in employment structures and livelihood opportunities. In India major percentage of people living in rural and tribal areas continue to live on agriculture and allied occupations. The undue importance given to information and other technology and foreign trade by the policy makers and planners has led to minimised investments and subsidies to crucial areas like irrigation, power generation, agriculture, animal husbandry, small scale and rural industries. This shift in priorities displaced many rural artisans, farmers, fishing communities and people engaged in other traditional occupation. The rural poor, tribal and indigenous populations are unable to avail the opportunities available in the field of technology due to lack of required skills. On the other hand they are forced to migrate to urban areas and depend on manual labour for their livelihood. Unemployment and underemployment has reduced the purchasing power of people making them even more poor and their children even more vulnerable. Migration of one or both the parents with or without families has placed them in conditions where they are unable to take care of their children. In absence of adult members/ parents the children are left either alone or in the care of elderly. The physical conditions in rural and tribal areas are also not favourable to these children that is continuous drought, water scarcity, lack of infrastructure, in sanitary conditions, outbreak of epidemics and endemics are making people even more weaker physically and economically. Such a situation has made them even more susceptible to exploitation of traffickers and middle men. The children from these distressed families are the victims of abuse, forced labour, streetism and exploitation.

The child's vulnerability to exploitation lies in his or her family circumstances. The majority of exploited children are either from marginalised families in cities, destitute and poor families in the country or children of indigenous groups. Contributing to their vulnerability everywhere is the absence of an adequate social and economic safety net to catch families or children in difficulty before they caught by the traffickers.

The child rights convention proclaims the right to protection, which includes freedom from all forms of exploitation, abuse, inhuman or degrading treatment and neglect, including the right to special protection in situations of emergency and armed conflicts. Thus, provision of safety measures and services for protection of vulnerable children is the responsibility of the State. The Government may fulfill these rights of children by strengthening families capabilities, providing supportive services through Government departments, agencies or by funding Non-Governmental Organisations. Effectiveness of such services can only be ensured through close monitoring and evaluation.

Clearly much remains to be done to strengthen families and to find effective ways to support their main functions. Families can and do function to the benefit of their members. Empowering social policy and participatory approaches extend that range of functioning, and family policy becomes another family resource. Public services that support and strengthen the family in the performance of its functions need a strong preventive focus, building on strengths rather than reacting to weaknesses.

A decade ago the United Nations General Assembly proclaimed and observed 1994 as the International year of the Family. The theme of the year was "Family: resources and responsibilities in a changing world".

1. The following principles underlined the International Year of Family (IYF).

(a) The family constitutes the basic unit of society and therefore warrants special attention. Hence, the widest possible protection and assistance should be accorded to families so that they may fully assume their responsibilities within the community, pursuant to the provisions of the Universal Declaration of Human Rights, the International

Covenants on Human Rights, the Declaration on Social Progress and Development; and the Convention on the Elimination of All Forms of Discrimination Against Women;

(b) Families assume diverse forms and functions from one country to another, and within each national society. These express the diversity of individual preferences and societal conditions. Consequently, the International Year of the Family encompasses and addresses the needs of all families;

(c) Activities for IYF will seek to promote the basic human rights and fundamental freedoms accorded to all individuals by the set of internationally agreed instruments formulated under the aegis of the United Nations, whatever the status of each individual within the family, and whatever the form and condition of that family;

(d) Policies will aim at fostering equality between women and men within families and to bring about a fuller sharing of domestic responsibilities and employment opportunities;

(e) Activities for TIYF will be undertaken at all levels – local, national, regional and international; however, their primary focus will be at the local and national levels;

(f) Programmes should support families in the discharge of their functions, rather than provide substitutes for such functions. They should promote the inherent strengths of families, including their great capacity for self-reliance, and stimulate self-sustaining activities on their behalf. They should give expression to an integrated perspective of families, their members, community and society;

(g) IYF will constitute an event within a continuing process. Measures will be needed to ensure appropriate evaluation of progress made and obstacles encountered both prior to and during IYF, in order to ensure its success and adequate follow-up.

2. The objectives of IYF were to stimulate local, national and international actions as part of a sustained long-term effort to:

(a) Increase awareness of family issues among Governments as well as in the private sector. IYF would serve to highlight the importance of families; increase a better understanding of their functions and problems; promote knowledge of the economic, social and demographic processes affecting families and their members; and focus attention upon the rights and responsibilities of all family members;

(b) Strengthen national institutions to formulate, implement and monitor policies in respect of families;

(c) Stimulate efforts to respond to problems affecting, and affected by, the situation of families;

(d) Enhance the effectiveness of local, regional and national efforts to carryout specific programmes concerning families by generating new activities and strengthening existing ones;

(e) Improve the collaboration among national and international non-governmental organisations in support of multi-sectoral activities.

(f) Build upon the results of international activities concerning women, children, youth, the aged, the disabled as well as other major events of concern to the family or its individual members.

3. Major family concerns of IYF programmes:

(a) The manner in which families form, establish patterns of behaviour, function and evolve, as well as their relationships with the local community, reflect societal values and expectations and, to some degree, individual choice. Societal values regarding the functions and roles of families differ both among, and within, countries. Similarly, views on the extent to which the community, Government, should intervene and influence the decisions made in individual families also vary according to differing interpretations of what is good for society. Nevertheless, several international legal norms governing the rights of individual family members have been adopted, and most countries have subscribed to their standards. These norms include the Convention on the Elimination of All Forms of Discrimination Against Women and the Convention on the Rights of the Child;

(b) In United Nations instruments, the family is referred to as the basic unit of society; it is appreciated for the important socio-economic functions that it performs. In spite of the many changes in society that have altered its role and functions, it continues to provide the natural framework for the emotional, financial and material support essential to the growth and development of its members, particularly infants and children, and for the care of other dependants, including the elderly, disabled and infirm. The family remains a vital means of preserving and transmitting cultural values. In the broader sense, it can, and often does, educate, train, motivate and support its individual members, thereby investing in their future growth an acting as vital resources for development;

(c) Nevertheless, changes in social structure, in part a result of economic modernisation and the ensuing pressures of development, have in many societies changed the nature of what is considered a family. With economic development and the spread of new forms of economic activity, family based subsistence labour is, to a large extent, being replaced by work for wages, specialisation of labour and concentration of activities in a work place which is removed from the home. Improvements in communication, transport and access to information have allowed individuals increased contact with ideas and behavioural norms beyond their traditional spheres. Formal education has also introduced many new concepts. Greater number of people, both in urban and rural areas, are becoming more aware of opportunities for different life-styles and are also more likely to make individual decisions without the approval of extended family members. Although not universal, there has been a general trend towards reduced family size and increased emphasis on the "nuclear family";

(d) These changes are generally accepted as positive: they provide evidence that individuals are exerting more and more control over their own destinies and are enjoying additional opportunities for more diversified lives. As a result, however, many people now feel less responsible for family relationships. In addition, the ability of many families to meet their basic needs has been weakened by circumstances beyond their control. The result is a reduced ability or willingness on the part of many families to meet the basic needs of some of their members. This has meant that "outsiders", whether from private or government agencies, international organisations or charities, have had to make up the difference, often at great cost;

(e) The fact that, in different places, these changes have taken place at different times, at different speeds and to a different extent, has important policy implications. It has meant that there are many different types of family structures, with different strengths and weaknesses. It has also meant that, both within and among countries, any image of what constitutes the "ideal family" will differ greatly. Policies affecting the family should seek to avoid promoting, implicitly or explicitly, a single, ideal image of the family;

(f) While, in the positive sense, families are capable of playing an important role as agents of development and constructive change in society, the negative aspects of society including social problems, exploitation and abuse, are also often evident within family relationships. When family expectations and commitments are expressed in the context of unequal family relationships, individual initiative and personal development may be hindered;

(g) In short, there is no simple view of the family and no easy definition of family policy; to some degree, all policies affect families. Yet, despite the major changes most societies have undergone in recent decades, policies and programmes still tend to be based on concepts and family models that may no longer reflect reality. Accordingly, while general trends may be known, there seems to be a great need to use whatever knowledge is available to create more relevant and appropriate policies directed at their family, while recognising that many policies that are seemingly of no great relevance may indeed have unseen or long-range implications;

(h) Institutional capabilities should, therefore, be strengthened. The first goal might be to encourage organisations and agencies, whether governmental or non-governmental, national or international, to recognise that their decisions and actions will usually have an impact on how families will be formed, whether they will survive or not, and how well they function as nurturers and providers. The second goal might then be to improve the formulation and implementation of "family-sensitive" policies, assuming that they can be generally agreed in a society, and to devise appropriate means to deal with a range of specific problems related to the family as a unit;

(i) Furthermore, the effects of economic change on family structure and on families' abilities to discharge their functions need to be better understood. Interestingly, both positive and negative economic change would seem to have a strong impact on the family. In many countries, in recent years, economic retrenchment, structural adjustment programmes and the costs associated with government provision of social welfare services have resulted in cutbacks in services. Increasing burdens are placed on families, and particularly on female members. The results has often been to weaken the fabric of family unity. Varying effects on the family have been attributed to such diverse phenomena as migration, agrarian change, urbanisation and population growth. Social changes will continue and families will continue to evolve, perhaps in unpredictable ways. The family is not static and policy must continually evolve as well, if it is to remain relevant and effective.

4. Other substantive considerations regarding families as a part of IYF

(a) Family offers a basis for a holistic approach a variety of social policy and development issues. On the basis of views and suggestions made by Governments and various concerned organisations, the following general considerations regarding families can be suggested, which should be viewed as indicative and not, by any measure, exhaustive;

Families as agents for protecting human values, cultural identity and historical continuity.

(b) Families are important vehicles for preserving and transmitting cultural values: however efforts to preserve the best of the past may be seen also as perpetrating attitudes that have, at times, worked to the detriment of society and some family members, notably women. In the context of social change, families must also become the medium for promoting new values and behaviour consistent with the rights of individual family members as established by various United Nations instruments;

Family resources, responsibilities and intra-familial support systems.

(c) Support between related family units and among family members within a single unit includes emotional, financial and material assistance essential to the growth and development of infants and children and for the care of other dependent members such as the elderly, disabled and sick. Other aspects of intra-familial support relate to the sharing of home-making responsibilities, the socialising of children and the provision of child-care, whether within the home or outside. Infra-familial support may include assistance from the young to the old or from the old to the young. Similarly, it may be between the able-bodies and the infirm. Such support has great importance for policy-makers, who may need to understand the extent to which a family can be viewed as a real resource and the extent to which it cannot. A better understanding could enable the design of more effective policy interventions to reinforce the ability of families to assist their members;

Work and familial responsibilities.

(d) Many families, especially single-parent and female-headed families, find the constant need to balance work and familial responsibilities to be among the most demanding daily aspects of life. Greater attention may need to be given to the reduction in the stress caused by this need. Both parents must be enabled to meet, with the assistance of social support systems, their mutual responsibilities to work and to the family. This calls for a climate in which parents may take time to meet the educational, health or other needs of their children without sacrificing income, work benefits, entitlements career advancement. Approaches adopted in this regard have included maternity leave; public, community and private facilities for providing child care at work, near work or near home; day care for children and older adults; nursing care for the elderly or infirm; and flexible work schedules. It is essential that parents not be penalised in terms of job security, seniority or promotions for meeting familial obligations;

Families in poverty, destitution and other marginal situations.

(e) Poor families are exposed to forces driving them apart, resulting in migration, growing numbers of street children and homeless persons. The destitution of a family implies the non-operation of a basic support system within society, with the result that familial responsibilities are then transferred to communal and national institutions. Further attention is needed on the impact on families of urbanisation and social effects of economic adjustment. Approaches adopted to address these problems have included a variety of income security measures, including income maintenance schemes, family and child allowances, child support measures, sickness and medical insurances, disability payments, unemployment insurance, tax deductions, exemptions and credits. Other measures, especially in developing countries, may be required;

Families as income-generating enterprises

(f) Many family units, especially in developing countries, function as income-generating enterprises. This income-generating function is often crucial for their survival, particularly for the very poor and female-headed families. Increased attention may need to be given to encouraging their self-reliance by such means as credit, technical assistance, training, use of cooperative and marketing assistance;

Education

(g) The family constitutes a context of informal education, a base from which members seek formal education, and should provide a supportive environment for learning. Literacy has a dramatic effect on the dissemination of ideas and the ability of families to adopt new approaches, technologies and forms of organisation conducive to positive social change. Often affected by early school leaving or dropping out, literacy is a prime conditioner of the ability of families to adapt, survive ad even thrive in rapidly changing circumstances. Attention should also be given to promoting equal educational opportunities for girls and young women;

Health

(h) Questions relating to various aspects of health, such as nutrition, food security, clean water and vaccinations, are of crucial relevance to development strategies; they are of direct concern to families because off, for instance, their contribution to familial well-being, children's physical and intellectual growth, reduction of gender discrimination in providing nutrition and health care, the diminution of maternal morbidity and mortality, optimal labour force participation and the prevention of disabilities. Increased attention may be called for to promoting the role of families in meeting the health requirements of all their members and in primary health care, child and maternal health and food security;

Fertility and family planning

(i) Familial well-being may depend in large measure on the ability of families to make informed and sensitive choices concerning fertility. Such choices are important in diminishing maternal and infant morbidity and mortality, especially when mothers are under 18 or over 35 years of age. Full, informed and joint participation in family planning decisions by both spouses appears to be essential to a responsible choice and a wider sharing of familial roles and responsibilities. Increased efforts may be required to ensure adequate family life education concerning reproduction, sexuality, birth spacing, the impact of the Acquired Immuno Deficiency Syndrome (AIDS), parenting skills and responsibilities, as well as access in rural and urban areas to family planning and fertility services. Family life education is required also to promote a deeper understanding of responsibilities in a familial and interpersonal context, as well as the promotion of family values;

Individual Family Members

Men

(j) The well-being of families, the achieving of equal opportunities for women and the sharing of roles by men and women require new perspectives, concepts, patterns of partnership and sharing within families; it therefore seems necessary that major attention should be given to examining and fostering new roles and responsibilities for men. Wider access to family life education, paternity and parental leave and other incentives could be provided to encourage and enable fathers to play wider new roles, especially with regard to home-making, child care, child growth and development, family planning as well as more responsible paternity;

Women

(k) The Year should support and extend recommendations regarding women as contained in the various international instruments and strategies, particularly the Nairobi Forward-looking Strategies for the Advancement of Women and the Convention on the Elimination of All Forms of Discrimination Against Women. Affected as women are by continuing social, economic, cultural and political upheavals and pressures, they should be enabled explore new opportunities for education and employment and to balance work and familial responsibilities;

Children

(l) Issues related to infants and children attract the closest attention from Governments and organisations in the context of family concerns. IYF should promote increased attention being given to those issues, particularly to the implementation of the Convention on the Rights of the Child and the World Declaration of the Survival, Protection and Development of Children, adopted by the World Summit for Children;

Youth

(m) The increasing proportion of youth in many countries suggests the need for adequate educational opportunities to reduce the drop-out rate and increase enrolment ratios, for expanding employment opportunities to provide the basis for family life as well as for family life education. Increased attention may be given to the role of families in the education, guidance and socialisation of young people and in facilitating their transition from adolescence to responsible adulthood and the world of work;

Elderly

(n) The increasing proportions of elderly in most countries have called to the attention of Governments the need to give more consideration to: enabling families to provide economic, material and emotional support for the elderly; supporting care-givers; enabling the elderly to remain in the community as long as possible; and extending the productivity and contributions of the elderly to the community;

Disabled persons

(o) IYF could further the implementation of the World Programme of Action concerning Disabled Persons by enhancing family resources for: (a) prevention of disabilities through family planning, nutrition intervention, accident reduction programmes, and early detection of impairment; (b) rehabilitation of disabled persons; and (c) equalisation of opportunities for the disabled. IYF should stimulate and enable: (a) the participation of disabled persons and their families in decisions concerning care, treatment, and rehabilitation, as well as subsequent living and employment arrangements; (b) counselling, social support and guidance for disabled persons and their families, especially the mentally ill; and (c) the full exercise by disabled persons and their families of the rights, benefits and services available to them;

Criminality and domestic violence

(p) Families offer valuable resources for the prevention of crime and delinquency. An important issue is the prevention of domestic violence. Linkages between the equality of family life and the prevention of violence within the family, including spouse abuse and the abuse of children and the elderly, incest and juvenile delinquency, have long been acknowledged, but need further attention;

Substance abuse

(q) Drug and alcohol abuse, more widely observed and understood than in the past, often arise from and result in a disintegrated family life. Far more effort is required to achieve a greater measure of prevention and rehabilitation of the victims and to make use of the resources offered by the family in this regard;

Social welfare services

(r) The United Nations, Guiding Principles for Developmental Social Welfare Policies and Programmes in the Near Future called for social welfare policies for meeting the needs of families, as well as those of their individual members. Policies and programmes based on assessments of family patterns, model and functions should take into account: the right of women to participate in economic activity; the limited capacity of some families, especially single-parent families, to take on additional responsibilities, such as care for the aged or the disabled; the importance of making family planning information, education and methods universally available; and the need for prevention of violence and abuse as well as immediate protection and assistance for family members who are abused. Designation of the family as an entity to which support might be given more effectively than to its disadvantaged members may be means to enhance the impact of social welfare services;

Policies for families

(s) Consideration should be given to the possible establishment of national policies for families and the improvement of existing ones. Early steps in this process would be the identification of principles as to family qualities and functions that should guide the process of policy formulation. Assessment of the positive and negative impacts on families of other policies needs to be undertaken.

Family law

(t) Family is a most pervasive form of family policy and varies according to the legal system and policies adopted different countries. IYF should facilitate global exchange of information by national legal institutes, associations and societies and encourage legal reform, as appropriate. Analyses of family laws and the values that they reflect could yield information as to the basic social, cultural and political assumptions and values undergirding national laws as they apply to families;

Research and data collection

(u) To enable a wider understanding of family structures, their formation and dissolution, and their functions, attention needs to be given to the clarification of concepts and terminology as they relate to the individual family member, family types and households. Similarly, indicators should be identified that relate to the condition of families and especially the impact of development on families, which would permit the collection of statistical data, the establishment of data banks, data networks, the exchange of data, and the identification of statistical trends related to families. Research institutes, research consortia and universities, especially in developing countries, should be enabled to undertake analyses of relevant topics such as family structures, family formation and dissolution, family functions, domestic violence, roles and responsibilities, family types, criteria for identification of families in trouble, identification needs of families, families as resources, intra-familial support and resource transfers, and relationships of families to other social structures.

5. **Consideration of specific family issues part of IYF**

1. Since issues that influence the situation of families vary from one country and region to another, local and national authorities and organisations should establish their own priority issues. The following categorisation of issues may suggest a starting point for the identification of local and national priorities.

Issue one

Strengthening the family's ability to meet its own needs

2. The family remains a primary source of nurturing, as well as a conduit for the transmission of values, culture and information, particularly to children and young people. The family should, therefore, be aided and encouraged to fulfill these important functions for the benefit of all society. For example, even limited government expenditure to educate and encourage adults to practice appropriate

parenting techniques, whereby responsibility for child-rearing is shared by both parents, can result in vastly improve health, education and socialisation of children, thus lowering the overall costs of social services. Attention may be given to:

(a) encouraging families to recognise the health requirements of members and enhancing their ability to provide primary health care in the home, by providing information on pre-natal and maternal health care, the spacing of births, proper nutrition, ways to improve food storage and preparation and the importance of having access to clean water supplies;

(b) encouraging families to recognise the importance of education for all family members – especially women and girls – and enhancing their involvement in the provision of formal and informal educational opportunities;

(c) acknowledging that the ability of families to provide adequate care for their older members may be put under strain, and the families who are taking care of the older generation at home may need extra resources; at the same time, the fact should be recognised that elderly family members often have an important position within the family structure and in decision-making, and the contribution they make to the family and the community should be encouraged;

(d) providing more information to strengthen families' capacity to prevent disabilities, to detect impairment at an early stage, and to provide basic rehabilitation of disabled persons; families may be supported in these endeavours by government assurance of the equalisation of opportunities for persons with disabilities, thereby encouraging their better integration into the community;

(e) providing assistance and information to families to encourage prevention of violence in the home and of delinquency, crime, drug and alcohol abuse, irresponsible sexuality and the spread of diseases, especially the Acquired Immuno Deficiency Syndrome (AIDS); also assisting in the rehabilitation of addicts, as well as both victims of crime and criminal offenders.

Issue Two

Clarifying and understanding the balance between how the family can satisfy its needs and what it can expect through public provision of services

- Changes in economic conditions have altered and indeed, at times, undermined the ability of families to meet their needs as a unit and as individuals. This may create stress or alienation for the individual, may further weaken family relationships, or may increase the demand for public services.

- At the same time, a trend towards limiting public provision of social services has placed additional burden on families, and on female members in particular, to meet basic family needs. This may cause families to assume direct responsibility for providing needed services or it may require them to assume additional financial commitments to pay for services previously provided free.

- When making decisions about providing or cutting back services, Governments should consider how these decisions will affect families, directly or indirectly. When serves are reduced, apparent savings of public expenditure may conceal great costs in terms of private deprivation, as families struggle to satisfy their needs; likewise, investments in serves may be squandered if they fail to take into account the considerations that influence families' ability and willingness to partake of them.

Issue Three

Recognizing the effect of societal on family relationships and acknowledging that government policy intervention may be needed to counter resulting negative behaviour or exploitation in the family

➢ Because of the intimate nature of family relationships, negative behaviour or exploitation may be tolerated within families. In line with the concepts of equality between women and men and the rights of all individual family members social policy may seek to educate and inform family behaviour to discourage anti-social or detrimental practices. Such policy might involve:

(a) education and activities to foster equality between women and men, including equality in their roles as spouses and parents, thereby improving the status of women in the context of the Nairobi Forward-looking Strategies for the Advancement of Women and the Convention on the Elimination of All Forms of Discrimination Against Women; furthermore, information and education might encourage a more equitable distribution of family resources and more flexible sharing of household and parental responsibilities in order to improve opportunities for women within and outside the family;

(b) information, legal support and counselling to assist in the prevention of all forms of exploitation, violence and abuse of family members, both physical and psychological;

(c) assistance and encouragement to families to nurture and protect children and facilitate the transition from adolescence to responsible adulthood and the world of work, in the context of the World Declaration on the Survival, Protection and Development of Children and the Plan of Action for Implementing the Declaration in the 1990s, adopted by the World Summit for Children, and the Convention on the Rights of the Child;

(d) education to encourage and develop values and behaviour patterns that contribute to responsible citizenship, ensure equal rights for all, discourage discrimination and protect the environment.

A child must be treated with respect and dignity within the family and be given proper nurturance and support for developing its talents and resources in order to become an adult who helps create and participate in a democratic society. If democratic social structures are to be created, they must be built upon democratic family structures and experiences. "Building' the smallest democracy at the heart of society means that society sits on a foundation of common values, beliefs and behaviour that are learned in the family. The values, ideas and forms of behaviour of democracy must be taught and modelled in families in order to create sustainable democratic societies. Several ancient cultures that have been able to build sustainable democratic societies did so by first building capable and democratic families.

REFERENCES

1. Arvindrani, D.N., 1990: *Family and Child Welfare*. Published by Ashish Publishing House, New Delhi.
2. Brenner, B., 1970, cited by Laxmi Devi (1998): *Encyclopaedia of Child and Family Welfare*, Published by Anmol Publications, Vol.5, New Delhi, pp. 111.
3. Desai, M., Montiem, A. and Narayan, L., 1998: *Child Rights*. The Indian Journal of Social Work, Part-I, Vol. 59.
4. Devi, L., 1998: *Encyclopaedia of Child and Family Welfare*. Published by Anmol Publications, Vol. 5, New Delhi, pp. 111, 366.
5. Eshleman, Jr., 1974: *The Family: An Introduction*. Published by Allyn and Bacon Inc. Boston.
6. Jha, R., 1998: *Rights of the Child: An Assessment*. The Journal Indian Bar Review, Vol. XXV(4).
7. Saraswathi, T.S. and Kaur, B., 1993: *Human Development and Family Studies in India and Agenda for Research and Policy*. Published by Sage Publications, 1st Edition, New Delhi, pp. 223-253.

4

Child Streetism

—**Prof. D. Sarada**

UNICEF reports that "Millions of other children struggling to survive in close-to-battlefield conditions on the streets of the world's cities from Los Angeles to Sao Paulo to Manila. Guns and knives and fights are chilling parts of daily life. In the US, gang violence, often drug-related, is drawing in ever-younger children. In urban areas around the world, children spend their days begging or cleaning car windows – numbing their pain by inhaling chemical solvents or glue. And in some Latin American countries, businessmen have paid off duty policemen, security guards, or professional killers to eliminate street children they consider a nuisance." (UNICEF The State of World's Children 1996).

The situation of street children in India is no better. Those who escape from the homes due to violence in the families land up in much more difficult circumstances. On the streets, they are much more, insecure and are subjected to torture. Several gangs operate in towns who exploit these children as a means to achieve their ends as they are 'cheap labour' and 'expendable community'. The gangs sell these children as sex workers. They are also asked to work for these 'gangs'. The income generated through the labour of the children is consumed by the 'lords' of the gangs with no end to the sufferings of these children.

Role of Adulthood

The role models of street children are not children of their own age group but people of the street who are in adult roles. The street children copy the life styles of these adults using the language of the adults and also copying their habits such as smoking, gambling etc. They take up adult roles too early – a total eclipse of childhood.

The Deprived Lot

Street life reduces them to a lot deprived of so many things. The deprivation is in terms of nutrition, health, adequate shelter, recreation and facilities for education. They stand deprived of even ordinary pleasures of childhood. So often they grow up as negative personalities or criminal adults as a consequence of many deprivations suffered in early childhood.

The child cannot wait. This means that of all the social challenges, children's needs are the most pressing' (A Chilean poet). Childhood is the time when the person's personality starts taking definite shape. Its like the green twig. Once it has grown in an undesired direction and strengthened, it cannot be brought back to the natural course. It is, therefore, very important that society takes sufficient measures to ensure that its future citizens have ample opportunities for the right growth. If the resources are limited, the crunch must not fall on children. In a society where children are neglected, they tend to grow into irresponsible adults creating various social problems.

The causes that deprive children to streets away from the loving care and security of their homes are varied but in all cases beyond their control. They are a victim of cruel circumstances and social compulsions for no fault of theirs. While they pine for a loving hand or even moments of affectionate concern, the world around them goes on with little care for the unfortunate children who are creatures of the same God. It is not enough that we know why they are on the streets. Social conscience must assert itself to ensure that these children are helped to join the main stream and contribute to social good in a meaningful way of which they are certainly capable.

Causes of Streetism

Ideally, every child should be enjoying the cosy comfort, affection, care and protected environment of the family and, if he or she is in the school-going age, should be attending educational institutions in general or vocational streams. Deviations from this ideal often occur in practice for various reasons such as lack of a family and, if there is one, physical, emotional and other stresses in the family, conditions of poverty preventing pursuit of education and/or requiring participation of the child in income-producing activities, socio-cultural factors hindering the educational process (as, for example, sometimes in the case of the girl-children), inability of the child to perform in school and the resultant sense of frustration leading to dropping-out from the school, bad company and environment that encourages the child to fall prey to evil habits, etc. Not all these factors, each by itself or in conjunction with others, necessarily lead to the child's losing family protection, care and support totally, if at all. Examples are girl children not sent to school due to socio-cultural reasons or children working on family farms or in household enterprises. The children, in such cases, retain more or less in full measure their ties with the family. On the other hand, some maintain just a nominal relationship with the family while others snap all such ties. In all cases, however, the children do invariably get deprived to a degree their right to education and general development as enunciated in the United Nations Convention on the Rights of the Child (Rashmi Agrawal 1999).

Socio-structural Causes

Industrial growth and economic development has not always been uniform throughout a country and has often resulted in imbalances, as for instance, between different regions of the country or between the rural and urban areas in the same region. New industries not only provide new opportunities for employment but also displace traditional workers from their place of work. Workers start migrating from relatively undeveloped regions of the country to the developing regions often leaving their families behind in their traditional homes, as the new work sites have no provision for shelters for families of workers.

Economic Compulsions

Often the earnings of the parents are insufficient to provide for the family's minimum needs. Children have to be sent to work to supplement the family's income. The organised sector doesn't like to employ them. They work at the mercy of the unorganised employers and in many situations end up as self employed persons in the trades like shoe-shining, rag picking and selling etc. 'Captive employment' or 'Bonded labour' is the curse of a number of families. The parents accept lump sum payments from contractors and send their children to work for them. Although they may have agreed to send their children only for specific periods, these children rarely come out of the trap.

The Quality of Education

School dropouts often end up as street-children. The enrolment of children in educational institutions and their dropout rates in India shows that at primary level (Class I to V) 10,8200539 children were enrolled, at middle level 3,99,14,582 children were enrolled around 36.32 per cent of children at primary school level and 52.8 per cent children at middle level dropout this shows the high dropout rate of children from education system. Among several reasons for such high drop-out rates is the poor quality of education in the country. Quite a number of schools are single-teacher schools who have to deal with very large numbers of children at a time. Sometime these teachers are not even trained in dealing with children. To discipline the student population, the teachers depend on 'sticks' and other traditional methods which develop phobia against education among the young minds and they think it is better to run away. Moreover, the teaching methods and learning material do not attract the children, being uninteresting and monotonous. As a consequence, learning is not a pleasure but a persecution to many.

A survey of the conditions that prevail in primary schools conducted by UNESCO and UNICEF (1994) in 14 countries that were least developed showed that there was dearth of proper seating arrangement, text books, chalk, boards etc. For example, one teacher was handling 90 students at a time in Equatorial Guinea. Results show that beating was very common in schools.

Education is a solution to several problems of the country but it has become a problem in itself.

The waves of violence that have swept across the world in recent years have uprooted enormous numbers – at least half of these being children. The displaced children who had fled from their home due to violence are refugees. Sometimes they live with their families but so often they are unaccompanied minors. In Rwanda, at the end of 1994, about 1,14,000 children had been separated from their families. Many of them were unaccompanied minors. As per a survey in Liberia in 1991, it was found that of the 90 per cent of the children studied, half of them had been on the streets as they had got separated from their families (Ressler, Evert M., J.M. Torturui and A. Marcelino, 1993). Even if these children were reunited with their families, it is very likely that they would still be on the streets, may be only in a new setting.

Families are often disentranced as a consequence of natural calamities like floods, droughts, earthquakes etc. The relief operations coming from various sources not only arrive long after the disaster but also are woefully inadequate. There is so much red tape to be gone through before relief becomes operative. As a consequence, children of affected families are often compelled to be on the streets, sometimes, begging for survival. In many cases, streets become their home gradually. Once settled in their new groove, they rarely think of going back even after rehabilitation.

The 'Quality of Parenting' exercises a domineering influence in a child's life. Proper and caring interactions between the parents and the child provide emotional security to the child besides helping him in developing an integrated and wholesome personality. The child starts his first lessons in behaviour patterns inside the home and while living with the family. The parents are his role models with whom he identifies himself. In the absence of parent's adequate role modelling and the caring touch that goes with that, the child find his home a hostile and a threatening place. He wants to escape and run away from it at the first available opportunity.

Yet another factor that often generates hostility towards home and parents among children is the practice of inflicting corporal punishments by the seniors in the family. The role of reasoning with the child is being increasingly appreciated, and corporal punishment is being rejected as a measure for inculcating desirable behaviour patterns. In families where violence is common or coercive methods of rearing children continue to persist, children suffer from trauma which leads to far-reaching consequences. Abandoning home and parents is one of them.

In large sized families, more so if they happened to be economically deprived, parents get little time to devote to their children. Mostly both the father and the mother have to remain away from home for long hours. The children stay at home unattended. There is too little for them to share by way of food and the younger ones in particular do not always get their proper share. The neglected and deprived among the children feel not only insecure but unjustly treated. In some cases the parents may show preference for a younger child in relation to an elder one. In such a situation also one member of the family feels neglected and often turns hostile or starts seeking safer places outside the home. The places may turn out to be the worst choice but by then the damage has been done.

'Broken Homes' are yet another reason why children run away from home.

Children living with a single parent or worst still a stepfather or a stepmother are most prone to emotional hang-ups and suffer from a feeling of neglect that may drive them out in search of some place where they may be better accepted.

Problems of Street Children

Prolonged life on the streets makes street children more prone to acquire bad habits at an early age. They first run errands for their seniors in many of the anti-social activities but soon become a part of the system doing things on their own. They start using tobacco, alcohol and indulge in gambling. They are exposed to many more social evils like prostitution and drug trafficking. Often addicted to bad habits, they resort to stealing for their indulgences. Anti-social habits and crime so often become a part of their personality. Their behaviour starts conforming only to the world they live in. They acquire a value system which is not the same as applicable to the rest of the people. Their activities may be regarded as anti-social by the police or other authorities but to them there is no other escape. Begging may be a social vice or a criminal offence but to them it is a job and even an occupation. Pestering foreign tourists may be undesirable from the view point of national image but the street child knows that he has much better chances of a handsome day's earning if he targets the foreign tourist rather than picking rags and selling them. The police may think of them as potential baggage lifters and hound them out periodically from waiting halls in railway stations. But the street child finds no reason why he should be picked up when there is no other place where he could find a night's shelter. Stealing is an undesirable social behaviour but the deprived street child knows that this is his only chance of a big return. He gambles when he has surplus money for he knows that even if he wants to save, there is the risk of the money being snatched by some elder member of his group. The compulsions of life in the streets are different from the ones for children living in normal homes. As such, the street child develops a variety of undesirable attitudes, which as per his perception are both necessary and normal. In his own peer group he is accepted. Sometimes the seniors among them initiate them into vices or anti-social habits. Once addicted, the new entrants are exploited by the older members. Such habits, if they persist for long, tend to drive children into the world of crime. In the absence of any counselling or escape to a better environment, some of them in the long run start working for more organised criminal gangs.

Constant physical and mental strain and living in environment least protected against health hazards makes street children highly prone to infectious diseases. Lack of proper medical care often leads them to permanent deformities or disabilities. These children are exposed to accidents and other occupational hazards. At a very tender age, they start consuming tobacco, alcohol or even drugs which retards their physical growth. Child abuse in terms of prostitution makes the children high risk carriers of sexually transmitted diseases including AIDS. Many children suffer from bronchitis, asthma and even tuberculosis due to continued exposure to dust and other pollutants. Several kinds of skin diseases like scabies and ulcers are common among street children. They pick up infection while collecting used papers, tins, plastics and rags from garbage dumps. The growth of their height and weight is thwarted as they carry heavy loads on their heads and backs. Eating disorders and malnutrition also develop as so often these children feed on leftovers and that too at odd times. Exposure to toxic substances, work or road accidents, psychological disturbance and other damaging effects are all too common (Levin, 1983, 1984).

Malnutrition

Surviving on streets, street children have no scope for getting two square meals everyday. Reliance on junk and discarded, often stale, food does not provide enough calorific nutrition necessary for their physical growth. In some cases where the children are employed in hard manual work, the calorific requirements are still more. But their earnings are too meagre to enable them to replenish the lost energy, leave aside the demands of body growth at this age. UNICEF reports that "A mildly malnourished child has twice the risk of dying from common childhood diseases as an adequately nourished child. A moderately malnourished child's mortality risk triples and for a severely malnourished child the risk death is 10 times great."

Low Individual Skills

Survival on streets denies street children all opportunities and facilities for the identification and development of their specialised skills and potentialities. All the abilities of the child remain limited to doing petty jobs for earning bread the whole day.

Needed Social Interventions

Interventions are activities/programme undertaken to either speed up and increasing the pace of development or to alleviate the problem in hand. In the sex of street children the main focus is on reduce the number of children and release them from the clutches of girls such as child abuse, prostitution, sustance, serious communicable diseases.

Macro Level Strategies

Social situation of the street and working children need to be tackled at two levels; macro and micro, simultaneously and together with a close follow-up and continuous monitoring of the trends and ground level tendencies. Both macro and micro levels are organically linked and inseparable. The macro level intervention will sharply reduce the magnitude of the problem category called the street and working child (SWC).

It will strike at the roots of the problem, while the micro level intervention as will negotiate with and bring under control the current pressing inequities and hardships being encountered by the Street and Working Children in Gujarat towns and cities.

The macro level interventions should address to following problem areas; the first and foremost area is that of rising unemployment and marginalisation among the poor peasants including the ladless. Factors that push them out of their rural habit should be effectively controlled, and their involuntary migration should be arrested.

Secondly, there should be strengthening of rural development and poverty alleviation programmes including the EGS, NREP etc. To increase the minimum wage of agricultural labourers and take steps towards effective implementation of minimum wages payment or other urgent measures.

Thirdly, a question of urban housing and slums should be dealt with a focus on families living under sub marginal conditions. The urban authority should strain to regulate and implement urban housing norms and provide and maintain basic civil services and amenities in the slums and at concentration points. Their needs of housing, health education, civil supply, recreation etc. should be correctly assessed and services provided with efficient management and delivery systems.

Fourthly, we must carefully watch and monitor the growth and expansion of a tertiary sector including self-employment (TS-SE). Structure and growth of TS-SE should be closely examined and ways found to minimise the hardships of both the owners and workers associated with TS-SE. Aspects which need closer attention are social security measures including wage regulation, occupational health and hygiene, credit support and provision of physical infrastructure.

Fifthly, there is a need for further co-ordinating and strengthening social service sector (SSS). The SSS areas which need attention at the policy level are: Urban health delivery system, primary education including pre-primary and community leadership including awareness of citizenship rights and duties, provision of citizenship rights and duties, provision of basic needs like drinking water, toilet, bath and electricity facility.

And last but not the least significant is networking with the NGO's both at the rural and city level. Effective policy and action framework need be evolved to bring together the NGOs working in the fields of welfare and development of family, mother and child both at rural and urban areas. There are many organisations and groups doing commendable work in the fields of welfare and development of weaker sections in Gujarat Society. Our Street and Working Children largely belong to such weaker and vulnerable sections. Hence involvement and leadership of competent and committed NGOs and Government can make a meaningful dent in the existing situation.

All these six parameters need to be taken up at the highest level in policy formulation; that is State level Planning Commission, Inter-Departmental Co-ordination Committee or the similar bodies vested with sufficient powers. Also the issues need to be discussed and programme evolved through vertical linkages at national level Go-NGO bodies.

Micro Level Strategies

Now about the micro-level structures and programme we envisage two layers of organisation for execution of relevant projects, programme and services for the street and working children in Gujarat. These are: (i) State level executive authority whose work can be assigned to the Directorate of Social Defence (DSD) or Social Welfare (DSW). The DSD or DSW can create a separate cell for the Street and Working Children with appropriate staff structure and facility. Their work content and modalities can be co-ordinated jointly by the DSD/DSW and NGO federation; and (ii) City-level authority or unit which can execute the relevant projects and programme for the benefit of Street and Working Children and their family.

The city-level authority and associated functions can be assigned to the Urban Community Development (UCD) and Urban Basic Services (UBS) departments of municipal corporation in respective cities or a separate arrangement can be conceived. The basic desiderate should be: familiarity with the street and working children situation, sustained experience, sensitivity and competence of handling such critical mass; and ensure legitimacy and acceptance of such critical mass; group/ organisation/body by the Street and working children and themselves excessive delusion of these norms should be carefully avoided to ensure success and foreclose possibility of mid-term failures and setbacks. This decision as to which group or agency can be relied upon to handle the city level execution of the Street and Working Children project should be taken by state level co-ordination committee. The street and working children in the SBAR region display similarities and also differences. We have carefully identified them in the text. The city level executive cell can take note of these variations and can also utilise their own field insights to evolve specific programmes and activities after due consideration of locality specific and work/job specific conditionalities. Designing a set programmes at the city level is indeed a delicate task requiring much deeper probe in the specifies of local situation motivation and mobilisation efforts at the family and working children level and NGO's self-critical and experimental outlook towards the whole project.

It is better to start with limited number of localities and limited target population, gain experience and understanding assess critically the strengths and limitations of the programme implemented; apply appropriate mid-term correctives in design and processes of the programme and then proceed further. Such flexible, innovative style and perspective can yield results, we believe.

Since we have to work for them and with them, we need to argue, discuss and decipher together the meaning and relevance of invidious distinction between child coolie and child rag-picker, between child domestic servant and a child beggar. That is how their thinking and consciousness is structured. This may create obstacles in bringing them together under common programme or activity. And unless they come together by underscoring their commonalities and ignoring their supposed high and low statuses embodied through mainstream socialisation; a lasting impact may elude us (Punelakar, 1993).

Institutionalization Vs "Child" Rescue Centres

A child's best situation is at home with relatives, in most cases... but that is not always the case. Your "CHILD" centres are more like a home than anything else.

Important

It should be noted that one does not, in any way, condone "institutionalisation" of children, especially street children. Although the "Child" system utilises "Semi-residential and residential" Rescue centres, the projects themselves, under guidance, and can leave whenever they like. The mood in the centres must be like a home atmosphere, at all times. For firsthand experience of how it is implemented, successfully, please visit the SKCV children's Trust centres in Vijayawada, A.P., India.

The five phases that this manual takes you through, step by step are :

- Establishing your credentials
- Night rescue centres
- Rescue centres for working children
- Residential rehabilitation centres
- Non-forma and formal school and vocational training workshop projects.

BASIC PRINCIPLES OF THE CHILD RESCUE CENTRES

1. To provide security and a home to street children

The sense of security for any young child is most important. A street child also needs a place to call home a small place where he/she can keep his/her belongings, no matter how few, and have the knowledge that the door is always open to him/her.

2. To provide facilities for cleanliness

Basic hygiene can only be taught to a child by those who care. Guidance and information on cleanliness and nutrition are given to all children who avail of any "Child" centre facility.

3. To provide literacy programmes

Most of the children we see daily, working in hotels, mechanic shops, factories... or just picking rags and begging are illiterate, and will stay that way if not given the chance to learn. The 'CHILD' system teaches basic literacy and nurtures their willingness and ability to learn.

4. To provide love and affection

The main problem these poor children is one of rejection. They trust no-one, have faith in no-one and will not ask for help from anyone. They build a defence around themselves that is almost impossible to penetrate. However with constant love and affection, the barrier melts away... and the real nature of the child shines through like a golden ray of warm sunshine.

5. **To provide medical aid and supervision**

   Majority of children on our streets have little or no idea about medical treatment, least of aids, and cannot go to a doctor because they have insufficient money to pay the bills. The result is that most of them just die in some dirty corner somewhere due to malnutrition, dehydration and infection. The 'CHILD' system provides medical care leading to complete health and fitness for their future.

6. **To provide a working model**

   To provide a model example for other organisations and Governments, wanting to run street child assistance programmes so that they can benefit from proven methods, and develop meaningful programmes of their own, without any waste of resources or delay and with limited failure and mistakes.

The review reveals that sufficient thought is being given to the problem of street children covering most of the dimensions. Attempts are being made to rehabilitate the street children. Government and Non-government organisations started undertaking programmes for street children. Funds also started flowing from Government and Non-Government sectors at National and International level for this cause. Commendable suggestions were drawn from Seminar/Conferences/Workshops held at different nations/levels. But there are not many studies conducted focussing their attention on the quality of services provided to street children in rehabilitation centres, which is an important area of research to know what the street child is really getting.

EFFORTS OF GOVERNMENT AND NON-GOVERNMENT ORGANISATIONS

There are three principal agencies which are responding to the problems of street children in India. NGOs, Government, and Municipal Corporations (Rajondra Pandey 1993).

Actions by NGOs

Several non-governmental organisations (NGOs) are involved in programme and service delivery for street children.

Though they are not very large in numbers, they vary in their approaches and strategies. Let us take some examples.

'Bangalore Oniyavara Seva Coota (BOSCO)' is an association for the services of street people. It establishes contacts with street children in areas of concentration in the city, such as bus stands, railway stations, market places, street corners etc. It emphasises on establishing rapport with street children and providing service to them based on their needs. Importance is given on helping the child to return to family.

'Jaya Rajendra Rag Pickers Project', Bangalore, focusses mainly on children who are engaged in rag-picking. Services, such as recreation, non-formal education, health, and return to the family are provided to rag pickers. Attempts are also underway to train them.

'Rag Pickers Education and Development Scheme (REDS)', Bangalore, is also concerned mainly with rag pickers. Attempts have been made to institutionalise rag picking, and towards this end, facilities have been made available for collection of rags, sorting, weighing, packing and selling to major dealers. This has perhaps resulted in the elimination of the middle men who used to exploit such children.

'Vatsalya-Project' of the College of Social Work, Nirmala Nikelan, Bombay, is busy making contacts with groups of street children in the streets of Bombay. The workers of NGO and the volunteers working with street children are provided with benefits of services like recreation, saving, caps, non-formal education, etc.

'Prema Seva Sadan-Open House', Hyderabad, is an open-house accessible to "any or all street children. The workers of the NGO establish contacts with various groups of street children and they are invited to the open-house where facilities for recreation, non-formal education, health, training, etc., are provided.

'Missionaries of Charity (Brothers)', Calcutta, provide very flexible facilities. The entire programme has yet to be structured rigidly. The agency premises are kept open for children on Sundays. Bathing, recreational, medical and meal facilities are provided.

'Ashalaya', Calcutta, is run by Salesian priests. The contacts are made with street children who, later on, come here. They are offered various kinds of services, including non-formal education, recreation, health etc.

'Social Project', Calcutta, operates for the children picking rags from the garbage dumps located on the outskirts of the main city. The NGO provides facilities for primary education in a very informal approach and also runs free dispensary where health services are provided.

'Cochin Project', Cochin, initially started by the Municipal Corporation of Cochin, was handed over to the Salesian priests. The programme continues to have operational link with the Cochin City Corporation.

'Butterflies', New Delhi, concentrates on street children. It sensitizes the people about the problems and plight of street children.

In addition, there are several NGOs engaged in providing services to the child labour in different ways.

Actions by Government

The Ministry of Welfare (Social Defence) is concerned with providing services for destitute children, mainly through support to various centrally sponsored schemes implemented by state governments. But there is no specific inclusion of street children within the different categories of children broadly termed as 'destitute'.

What is true to Central Government's Ministry for Welfare is more true to the Social Welfare Departments and the State Governments in general. They have yet to incorporate street children among the various categories of children for whom the department implements the programme.

Actions by the Municipal Corporations

The street children are primarily a phenomenon of the metropolitan cities. Whatever the sources of their entry in cities, street children end up in urban areas and metropolitan cities. But, as of today, the Municipal Corporations do not have the information about the magnitude and dimensions of the problem of street children and basic services, such as health, recreation etc., are not sensitised with a view to adapt them for facilitating access to the street children.

Action for and by the Community

The public at large and the communities are not aware of the phenomenon of street children. The street children are perceived as pests, rogues, thieves, delinquents and parasites of our society. It fails to recognise them as children who have lost their childhood and are contributing to the city dwellers by providing cheap labour. Media has to play the role of sensitising the public on issues and problems related to street children.

REFERENCES

1. Berger, P. et al., 1973: *The Homeless Mind Modernisation and Consocionsm*, New York Vintage Books.
2. Bellary, C., 1997: *The State World's Children—Focus an Child Labour*, UNICEF Oxford Univ Press.
3. Ghosh, A., 1992: Ministry of Welfare, Government of India and UNICEF *Street Children of Calcutta*, National Labour Institute Sector – 24 NOIDA – 201301.
4. Phillips W.S.K., 1994: *Street Children in India*; Rawat Publications, Jaipur and New Delhi.
5. Panicker R. and Nangia, P., 1992: *Working and Street Children of Delhi*; National Labour Institute UNICEF Study, India.
6. Rajendra Pandey 1993: Indian Institute of Technology, Kanpur, *Street Children of Kanpur: A Situational Analysis*, National Labour Institute Sector 24, NOIDA 20301, India.

5

Child Labour

—Prof. D. Sarada

Child Labour: Origin and Concept

The term "child labour" is a multidimensional and generic term which includes within its purview several categories of workers. Strictly speaking there is distinction between the term 'child labour' and 'child worker'. The former works on full time basis in ways payable after regular interval, child worker on the other hand often attends school regularly and during spare time at home he or she, either assists their parents in domestic work or agricultural pursuits or some other work done by the family and under these circumstances his involvement is on part time basis.

The encyclopaedia of Social Sciences (1959) defines "child labour" as "when the business of wage earning or of participation in self or family support conflicts directly or indirectly with the business of growth and education, the result is child labour". Child labour can be conceived to include children under the age of 15 years in work or employment with the aim of earning a livelihood for themselves or for their families.

Three basic characteristics are included within the concept of child labour. They are :

- The child should be employed in gainful occupation;
- The work to which he is exposed is dangerous; and
- It must deny him, the opportunity of normal physical and mental development.

The term 'Child labour' is not only applied to children working in the industries, but also to the children working in all forms of un-organised non-industrial occupations which are injurious to their physical, moral and social development. A large number of children are employed in unorganised sector and they work as domestic servants, or as workers in hotels, restaurants, canteens, wayside shops and establishments, or as hawkers, newspaper sellers, coolies, shoe shine boys, vendors or helpers in repair shops. The children are taken with their parents in construction work for loading, unloading and breaking of stones etc. Some writers believe that a major sector where children are put to work is begging.

The child labour has existed all over the world in one form or the other. The compulsions of life forced the children to work in houses and in fields. But child labour showed its evil effects only after the industrial revolution in England and thus attracted the attention of social reformers. Cotton factories in London and Yorkshire were perhaps the first in England to engage children coming from families of London and other towns. These children were housed in horribly overcrowded and unsanitary dormitories and were subjected to atrocious treatment at the hands of the employers.

According to the International Labour Organisation (ILO) annual report (1994) some 200 million children in the third world countries are forced to make their own living Asia accounts for about 72 per cent of child labour in the world. India has the dubious distinction of having the largest number of child labourers, and the incidence of child labour is often underestimated. One third of the world's child labour is in India. Again in India working children constitute about 26 per cent of the entire labour force (Satya Sundaram, 1994).

In India, the child labour is mainly employed in large scale in unorganised sectors like beedi and looms, weaving, carpet making, matches, fireworks etc. They work in both agricultural and non-agricultural occupations. Concentration of child labour in organised sector is comparatively low.

The participation of child workers to the total child workers was 42.7 per cent in agriculture followed by 35.9 per cent in cultivation. The manufacturing sector, household industries and other than household industries together accounted for only 8.6 per cent (Census, 1981).

When work is imposed upon the child against his wishes, at the cost of learning and play, which are necessary for the full blown development of his personality, it becomes exploitative in nature and can be considered as labour. This work includes the participation in the production of economic goods and services, including unpaid family work in an economic enterprise, as well as work for pay or profit (Rita Punicker, Parveen Nangia, 1992). There are some types of child labour which are defined as exploitative. "Exploitative child labour" has been defined by ILO as many labour which deprives children of any basic need, including health (David, 1985). It is the exploitative labour which is more harmful to the physical and mental development of the child.

Child labour in Shivakasi are leading a miserable life due to their exploitation by the employers in gross violation of statutory restrictions, in terms of payment of negligible wages, for long working hours and adverse working conditions unsuited to their health and safety. Kothari Smith (1988), a known human rights activist and the editor of Lokyan Bulletin pointed out in her study that the children in the age group of 3½ years to 15 years are made to work for a long span which sometimes extends to 12 hours a day, in degrading and hazardous working conditions.

Age and Sex of Child Labourers

In India children of very young age do work because these children can be hired for work at very cheaper rates. Some of the following studies reveal the age group of child labourers.

Singh et al (1980) conducted a study on the working children in Bombay. The sample comprised of 203 boys and 97 girls. It was found that 71.3 per cent of the working children belonged to the age group of 12-15 years. Ghatak (1981), has conducted these age specified child labour force participation both for urban and rural. He observed that very high participation rate in the higher age group of 10-14 years than that of the age group of 5 to 9 years. Khan (1988), reported that the Shivakasi match factories in Tamil Nadu employ children as small as 3-3½ years.

Kaura and Khan's (1988) study on child labour in Bombay revealed that 24.7 per cent of working children began work between the age of 6 and 9; 48.4 per cent between the age of 13 and 15. One out of every four working children was below the age of 9 years when he/she joined the labour force. Patil (1988) conducted a study on working children in urban India. The survey revealed that among the selected 600 child workers in Bangalore, 79.67 per cent are boys and 65.33 per cent of the child workers are in the age group of 15 and 17 age; at least 10.5 per cent are below the age of 10. The percentage of girls within each age group varies but younger the age group, 41.27 per cent are in the age of below 10 years, 22.67 per cent in the age group of 10-12 years and 16.33 per cent among the teenaged child workers. This suggests that girls start working at an early age than do boys but are withdrawn from employment much earlier than boys.

According to the report of National Institute of Public Co-operation and Child Development (NIPCCD), 1979, the percentage of working children in the age group of 6-9 is 24.7, while in the age group of 10-12 it is maximum i.e., 48.4 and in the higher age group of 13-15 years, it accounts only 26.9.

The Baroda based research organisation, namely the Operations Research Group (ORG, 1980) estimates that two third of child workers in India are in the age group of 12-15 years, out of the remaining one third i.e., 33 per cent are below the age of 10 years. For every 1000 boys at work there are namely 1200 girls. In contrast to this, the ratio of working boys to girls as per the census of India 1981 is 1000: 675 respectively.

Child Labour: Causes and Consequences

It has been the tradition from the very earliest times that children were to perform some work both in the home and in the field. In the olden days, the children of tender age performed some work along with the adults agricultural and machinery or during the manufacturing process, poisonous gases or vapours might be required to work on furnaces maintained at a temperature of 1500 to 1800°C, thereby causing harm to the eyes, lungs and other vital organs of the child labourers. In both types of work, health of the child labourer is adversely affected, and they suffer in terms of physical as well as mental growth and development.

Employer's Views on Child Labour

The employers often advanced their argument that by employing the children they increase the income of children's families and they save them from hunger, lazy and anti social persons. Thus they argued, that it is the feeling to sympathy rather than the desire to exploit children, which play dominant part in employing children. No nation can risk to destroy its children's life, who are the future possibilities of the country's prosperity and development. Due to poverty and other similar reasons children are exposed to inhuman treatment namely, sexual exploitation, doing work even during illness.

Economic Benefits of Children

Benefits which the child labourers bestow upon their parents is of two types. They are direct or actual benefits and perceived benefits.

Direct benefits are which the parents and households receive from their children in the form of regular or irregular cash payments, help or assistance in the house, on the farm and business, old age security, status maintenance and so on. From his study of a Punjab village, Mamdani (1972) conducted that a large family is an asset to peasants, further he stated that children's contributions to the family income is positive because the amount of money or labour they contribute exceeds that which is spent on them. According to Ashok Mitra (1976) the monetary help the working children provide to their parents. in old age are the two reasons for the employment of children in the age group of 5-14 in India.

Perceived benefits are the benefits which parents or other members of the family expect to receive from their children in the form of irregular assistance in the shape of money, food, housing, support in old age, living arrangements with their children etc. Rayappa's study (1979) of child labour in the Chittoor District of A.P. revealed that the demand for child labour did not diminish as long as parents expected high economic benefits from children. Perceived economic benefits may be more realistic than actual benefits.

Causes of Child Labour

Madan (1975) viewed that the children are required to seek employment either to augment the income of their families or to have a gainful occupation in the absence of school going facilities at various places. Gangrade (1978-79) believes that child labour is a product of such factors as customs, traditional attitude, lack of school or reluctance of parents to send their children to school, urbanisation, industrialisation, migration so on.

Thus there are many causes of child labour; but it is fruitful to study some of the principle causes in detail.

(a) Poverty

Poverty is the root cause of the problem of child labour, widespread poverty in developing countries like India, compel children to work in unprotective and exploitative conditions. Poverty and inequity are major causes of child labour and the development is inversely related to the increase of child labour (Boudhiba, 1982; Dogramachi, 1985; Naidu, 1985). To put it in simple words, the countries, states and districts with high illiteracy rates, backwardness in economic development combined with other factors like low rates of school enrollment, malnutrition among children and high proportion of children out of schools have greater incidence of child labour problems.

Punekar (1979) stated that in rural areas employment of children as wage paid labour is mainly to supplement the meager income of chronically poverty stricken rural households. During the agricultural season, child labour which is cheaper than adult labour, is in demand because of the general labour shortage.

Singh (1980) conducted a study in Bombay and reported that a maximum of 63.2 per cent migrated in Bombay due to lack of employment or inadequate family income. When their parents were asked to describe the circumstances under which their children had to enter work life earlier than they described, 59.2 per cent of the respondents mentioned economic reasons, 25.8 per cent idleness of the child and 24 per cent discontinuance of studies.

Centre for Social Research (1984) conducted a study in unorganised sector and found that most of the child workers were under compulsion to work due to poverty. Moreover 95 per cent of them look for employment in match units because of the poor financial conditions of their families and were forced by their parents to supplement the family income.

Jajebhoy and Kulkarni (1986) in their study on the economic value of children and fertility behaviour in Maharashtra indicate that parents value children for their current economic utility.

The work of Saritha (1987) on child workers in the cottage industries of weaving and beedi making at Srikalahasti in Chittoor district of Andhra Pradesh, revealed that the earnings of the children are used to supplement the parents income for maintaining a better status of living.

(b) Parental Background

It is argued that the higher the education of parents, the higher the educational aspirations for their children. Less educated parents tend to place lower value on their children's education and therefore put them to work at an early age (Usha Naidu, 1985).

Acharji, Xavier (1986), Labour Relation Institute, Jemshedpur quoted in her paper on "Child labour in India" that books and stationary are expensive. Will the parent choose between food and clothing, the primary needs or purchase books for the children? For S.C. and S.T. although these are of free of cost, but for all poor families the question posed in immediate supplementary income and to use children as the source rather than postpone to an uncertain date till the completion of education.

Tienda (1980) found in a Peru study that children in Single parent households were most likely to be in the labour force and that for any given age, the birth order of children strongly influence the probability of being economically active, the first child having the highest probability.

(c) Large Family

Large families with comparatively less income may not have the happy notions in their mind. As a result, they may not give sheltered childhood to their children. If a family is limited and well planned there may not be the question of sending their children to the labour market and the children can be carefully educated. But impoverished and illiterate parents think just contrary to this.

Rosenweig, Eversion (1979), Kanbargi, Kulkarni (1985) reported that the poor have larger families but they do not resist an addition to the family for they believe that any addition to the family means an additional earning member. Many studies in India have revealed that the fertility rate among the families of working children particularly from the rural areas is high.

Ah-Eng (1982) conducted a study on 85 child labourers in various small scale industries in urban Penang, Malaysia. The sample ranged from 12-16 years of age and included 26 girls and 59 boys. It was found that all the children were from large families, the average family size being 8 members. Most of the family members had either no education at all (or) between one and six years of schooling.

(d) Illiteracy and Ignorance of Parents

In India, the lower socio-economic groups of population are illiterates. They only think about the present time what they gain by the earning of children. It is their sole concern and worry. They are satisfied with what they gain by the earning of children. It is ignored by them that their children may participate even in educational opportunities, but child labour deprives the children of all the educational opportunities and minimises their chances of vocational training.

The Madras school of social work (George, 1977) conducted a pilot study in Madras, Madurai and Coimbatore and reported that about three-fourth of child workers were found at work to supplement their family income and 23 per cent of others due to death of their parents. And also he revealed that a majority of the children come to join the labour force were from low literacy groups of society. About 44 per cent of the children were found illiterate and 33 per cent upto lower standards only.

A study conducted Chandra and Devi (1979) in 4 villages of Mahidergraph district of Haryana which is the child labour pocket of Haryana, revealed a number of surprising facts. It was found that out of the 200 child labour families selected for this study, 89.5 per cent were illiterates. 6 per cent could read and write and 4.5 per cent could write a little.

Naidu (1981) conducted a study to analyse the inter state variation in the child labour participation rates based on sex, residence and sectoral distribution to identify the demographic and socio-economic factors associated with economic activity rates of children. It was found that overall child labour participation rates were not uniform among the states. It was also found that the majority of child drop-out joined labour force. The proportion of child workers was found to be much lower in urban than in rural areas. The higher the level of urbanisation, the lower the percentage of economically active children. The investigator explained that this inverse association was due to the higher school enrolment and less work opportunities for child workers of child labour.

Other Reasons of Child Labour

The study of Khandekar (1970) indicated that the migrant child labour in Bombay was 81 per cent whereas the locals were only 19 per cent.

Burra (1986) states that adults often fall ill or are disabled because of their involvement in work as young children. Unable to work to their full potential they become dependents on the labour of their own children.

Consequences of Child Labour

Child labour is economically unsound, psychologically disastrous and physically as well as morally dangerous and harmful. It involves the use of labour at its point of lowest productivity and is, therefore, an inefficient utilisation of labour power. Child labour precludes the full enfoldment of child's potentialities. It deprives him of education training and skills which are the necessary pre-requisites of earning power and economic development. Children are the most vulnerable group in any population and in need of the greatest social care. On account of their vulnerability and dependence, they may be exploited, ill-treated and directed into undesirable channels by the scrupulous elements in the community. The state has the duty of affording proper care and protection to children at all times as it is on their physical and mental well-being that the future of the nation depends. However in view of our contemporary economic situation, the total eradication of child labour through legislation does not seem to be an immediate possibility. The only pragmatic alternative, therefore is the dissipation of undesirable conditions and practices attendant to it. (India, Report of a National and Institute of Public Co-operation and Child Development, 1977). This explanation highlights the need for a better understanding of Indian social reality, fewer generalisations, greater conceptual clarity and methodological refinement.

Being exposed to adult life at an early age creates numerous problems for the child labour; working for long hours even during the night, with the least protection from a polluted environment at the place of work and under constant mental and physical strain, the children's growth becomes stunted. They are also exposed to infections, diseases or develop some deformity. Partial deformities are also caused by long hours of work and difficult working conditions. Children especially in the manufacturing sector are more prone to accidents and occupational hazards. Some forms of child exploitation such as prostitution carry the high risk of sexually transmitted diseases and AIDS as well (Khatu, Tamang and Rao, 1993).

Working children are unable top participate in leisure time and recreational activities and, therefore, lose these psycho-social benefits. Children soon pick up habits like smoking and liquor drinking. Some of them also become drug addicts and spend time in gambling, smuggling or similar anti-social activities.

Child labour brings down the wages and keeps adults in a highly insecure employment situation. Low wages and low nutrition together result in malnutrition, combined with hard physical work leads to deterioration of the health of the child worker which ultimately shortens the life-span besides lowering efficiency meanwhile. Change of employment relations is common to child workers also. The predominant reason for changing jobs in case of very young children is the long distance between the place of work and the place of residence. As they frequently change their jobs they do not get mastery over any skill and they remain as unskilled labour.

Although infancy and childhood occupy only a small fraction of the life span, they are the most crucial years in determining and influencing the personality of adulthood.

We need to find out some concrete solutions to their problems and inspite of all our limitations (economic, social, political) we have to put all our efforts to give them their right and a perfect kind of environment for their development so that we can protect this hope (child) of future.

Child Labour: Problems at Work Place

Children work because of the poor economic conditions of their families. Being children, they are exploited. They are given work that is strenuous, hard and tedious. They work for long hours and receive low wages in return. Their working conditions are often very harsh. Therefore the children face several problems in the work place.

In a study conducted by Rita Punicker and Parveen Nangia for UNICEF in Delhi (1992) found that majority of children were in difficult circumstances. Majority of the children spoke of long hours of work which made them tired and so were sometimes careless and a bit slack which usually resulted in employers punishing them by deducting their wages, beating or abusing them. Child workers also spoke of the low wages and sometimes of not being paid wages regularly; Illiterate children were at loss in knowing if they were being paid the right wages or not.

In general the various problems faced by child labourers can be categorised as:

(a) Health Problems

Working children are more susceptible to infections, diseases, including Tuberculosis, if they suffer from malnutrition, anaemia, fatigue and inadequate sleep. The other physical health hazards includes bone lesions and postural deformity, attributable to work such as carpet weaving, embroidery and lifting heavy weights.

(b) Occupation Hazards for the Child Labour

In fact child labour may be exposed to occupational hazards in two forms, in one situation the occupation may not be hazardous in itself; but proves to be dangerous both for the physical and emotional growth of the child particularly due to adverse working conditions such as in case of small scale industries, handlooms and power looms, diamond and metal handicrafts, tea shops, dhabas and other small scale commercial establishments where there is darkness, improper ventilation, damphers etc. All these factors create adverse impact on the health as well as growth and development of the concerned children in spite of the fact that the working conditions do not involve any sort of hazard/danger.

The other situation might be wherein the child labour may be required to work under hazardous process either due to the fact that hazardous material such as poisonous chemicals or other material might be used in the plant. It is in the second content that the child labour is now more generally used. In assessing the nature and extent of social evil, it is necessary to take into account the character of the jobs in which the children are engaged, the dangers to which they have been denied.

Occupational hazards and risks can be enormous. Long hours often lead to accidents, especially when children are working with poorly maintained and dangerous machinery; when overloaded, young growing bodies may suffer from strain since the bone structure especially the spine is soft. In addition, in small workshops and mines, there are increased dangers of tripping resulting in broken bones or head injuries. Child workers in city streets are also under constant threat of injury from traffic accidents and street violence.

(c) Environmental Hazards

The work environment of exploitative workshops often have especially pernicious effects on children's health. Excessive notice can lead to hearing loss, and hot, damp and dusty conditions to the transmission of communicable diseases. Since many workplaces have neither running water nor toilets, gastro-intestinal diseases also flourish. (Lakshapathi, 1993).

Exposure to toxic substances used in manufacturing is extremely dangerous to working children. Some of the documented consequences have included lead poisoning and paralysis caused by the use of toxic glues and chemicals in the absence of adequate ventilation. In addition, the extreme air pollution in more and more cities is damaging to the health of children working and living in the streets.

There are some empirical studies on the working children in urban areas which are concentrated with industrial developments.

Child Labour—Control Measures

The children of the world are innocent, vulnerable and dependent. They are also curious, active and full of hope. Their time should be one of joy and peace, of playing, learning and growing. Their future should be shaped in harmony and co-operation. Their lives should mature, as they broaden, their perspectives are gain new experiences. But for many children the reality of childhood is altogether different.

Measures to protect the child has been taken up at the International plane especially to eradicate the child labour.

Eradication of Child Labour Under the United Nations System

The main purpose of the establishment of a general organisation of states was safeguarding peace and promoting international co-operation.

The Atlantic charter, the united nations declarations, the Moscow declaration, Dumbarton Oaks-conference, Yalta conference of February, 1945, San Francisco conference were responsible for shaping the form of the United Nations. (Parimal, Shah, 1976).

The objectives of the United Nations are set forth in the preamble. Some of the relevant objectives are to reaffirm faith in fundamental human rights and in the dignity and worth of human person, "To establish conditions under which justice and respect for International Law and International obligation can be determined. To promote social progress and better standards of life and large freedom".

To employ international machinery for the promotion of economic and social advancement of all the people. In order to achieve these objectives, United Nations is striving since its inception.

Keeping in view the process of exploitation of the child labour it was recommended in the conference on Human rights that the United Nations must stop giving all a financial support to projects which involves or perpetuate child labour and child servitude. These demands have been made by 5 non-government organisations of India, Pakistan and Bangladesh who have appealed to all importing countries that they should ban import of those goods which have been fully or partly made by the child labour with the object of discouraging the employment of the children, for the preparation of goods and manufacture of products. (Varandani Gursharan, 1994).

It was highlighted in this conference that many of the products exposed by South Asian Countries to other developed countries are generally made by these bonded child labour which mainly include carpets, garments, leather goods, glass products etc. In this context, it was observed by five N.G.O's namely South Asia Coalition on child servitude and bonded labour, Liberation Front of India, Pakistan's bonded labour liberation Front, Nepal's INSECT and Bangladesh's Justice and Peace Commission, highlighting and appealing conditions of child labour in their country such as the conditions of mental torture, beating sexual harassment which reflected "medieval age slavery", it was urged by these organisations that despite constitutional guarantees, legal safeguards and International conventions, exploitations of child labour and a violation of basic "Human rights" continued unabated.

There it was proposed by these organisations that United Nations Human Rights Conference must stop all UN aid support to projects that involve or perpetuate bonded or child labour.

Role of International Labour Organisation (ILO)

The International Labour Organisation was constituted under the Treaty of Versailles, 1919. Improvement of labour standards throughout the world is the basic aim of the I.L.O. It paid particular attention to the protection of children and young persons, the preamble of its constitution enunciates this as one of the objects of I.L.O. The declaration concerning the aims and purposes of the I.L.O. also includes the provision of child welfare as one of the areas for specific action. The I.L.O. has sought to achieve its objective of protecting children by adopting international labour standards in the form of conventions and recommendations.

The I.L.O. has so far adopted 18 conventions mainly in respect of children and young persons concerning their minimum age for entry to employment, medical examination and night work. Besides, the I.L.O. has also adopted 16 recommendations on these topics (Goyal, 1987). These conventions and recommendations, along with many others from the

International labour code. The conventions so far adopted by the I.L.O. specifically for children and young persons can be classified under these broad categories as under:

- Minimum Age conventions;
- Medical Examination conventions; and
- Night work conventions.

I.L.O. on Minimum Age for Admission of Children to Employment

At the very first session of International Labour Conference, in the foundation year of I.L.O. a convention on Minimum age was adopted in 1919 (The minimum Age Industry Convention No.5, 1919). It provides that children under the age of 14 years should not be employed or allowed to work in any public or private industrial undertaking or in any branch there of, other than an undertaking in which members of the same family are employed. The term "Industrial undertaking" under this convention includes mines, quarries, manufacturing industries, construction, maintenance and repairs and transportation of passengers or goods by road or rail or inland water way. This convention was partially revised in 1937, Minimum Age (industry) convention (Revised) No.59 of 1937 and thereby it raised the minimum age from 14 to 15 years for admission to industrial establishments.

In 1920 I.L.O. adopted another convention to protect children working on sea. Minimum Age (Sea) convention No.7 of 1920. It required that children below 14 years should not be allowed to work on 'vessels' except those on which only the family members are employed. "Vessels" the term includes all ships, boats, whatsoever engaged in maritime navigation whether publicly or privately owned, but not ships of war.

In order to lay standards regarding the children working in agricultural fields it adopted a convention in 1921, the Minimum Age (Agriculture) Convention No.10, 1921. It required that children under 14 years should not be employed in private or public agricultural undertakings except outside the hours fixed for school attendance; the employment should not affect the attendance of children at school.

Another convention covering Non-Industrial Employment was adopted in 1932. The Minimum Age (Non Industrial Employment Convention) No. 3 of 1932, which applies to any employment not dealt with convention No. 5, 7 and 10. This specified that children below 14 or above 14 years who are still required by National Laws attend primary school should not be employed in any employment to which convention applies.

In 1973 all the instruments were consolidated into a Single Convention, the minimum Age Convention (No.138) of 1973, which provides that states which ratify it undertake to pursue a national policy designed to ensure the effective abolition of child labour and to raise progressively the minimum age for admission to employment or work to a level consistent with the fullest physical and mental development of young persons.

A recommendation was designed to prohibit employment of children below 16 in coal mines and for allowing employment of young persons between 16 and 18 years under restrictive conditions. The Minimum Age (Coal mines) Recommendations No. 96 of 1953.

I.L.O. on Medical Examination of Children

I.L.O. has adopted 5 conventions for making the medical examinations of young persons, a condition precedent for employment. First convention on medical examination was adopted in 1921, Medical examination of young person (Sea) convention No.16 of 1921. It is applicable to persons working in sea. It states that a young person below 18 years should bear a medical certificate of fitness by authorised doctor for employment on any vessel, other than that on which only family members are employed. Such certificates should be made each year in the continued service.

In order to extend the medical examination to industrial workers, a convention was adopted in 1946. Medical examination of young persons (Industry) convention (No.77) of 1946. It prescribed that children and young persons under 18 years (16 years in India) should not be admitted to employment in an industrial undertaking unless they are found fit for work, by a thorough medical examination and the fitness should be subject to medical examination until he has attained the age of 18 (16 in India) in occupations involving high health risks, medical examination for fitness of employment. Later in 1965 a convention regarding medical examination of young persons doing underground work was adopted.

I.L.O. on Night Work of Children

I.L.O. has made 3 conventions in support of prohibition of night employment by child workers. In the very year of inception a convention on night work of young persons in industry was adopted. Night work of young persons (Industry) convention (No.6) of 1919, which applies to all industrial undertakings such as those relating to mines and quarries manufacturing industries, construction, transport etc., provides that no person below 18 years of age are to be employed during night in any public or private industries undertaking. The term 'Night' here signifies the period of atleast 11 consecutive hours between 8 p.m. to 7 a.m.

The convention is partially revised by another convention adopted in 1948. Night work of young persons (Industry) Revised (No.90) of 1948, which signifies 'night' means a period of atleast 12 consecutive hours from 7 p.m. to 7 p.m.

In 1946 a convention on night work in non-industrial occupations was adopted. Night work (Non-industrial) occupations convention No.79 of 1946.

This I.L.O. through various conventions, recommendations and declarations made rules and guided the member countries for abolition of child labour through various measures.

Role of UNICEF

The UNICEF has played a significant role for improving the condition of child labour and it has been a major funding agency for improving a lot of children in general and child labour, in particular, specially in developing countries. Recently a child labour cell has been created in six participating countries including India whose main function is to work as National Focal agency for documentation advocacy, creating public awards and organising various seminars as well as training programmes. For this purpose UNICEF has sanctioned $ 0.5 million under their master plan of operation for the child labour programmes for the five year period commencing from 1991 to 1995. (Varandani Gursharan, 1994).

In India one such child labour cell has been established at the National Labour Institute at NOIDA, New Delhi with the support of Ministry of Labour, Government of India and UNICEF. The main objectives of the Child Labour Cell are:

- To document and bring out published and unpublished research studies on situations and conditions of children working in various industries and regions of India;
- To develop Audio-visual, video printing communication materials for public education and training of various officials concerned with working children;
- To review existing laws and enforcement machinery concerned with child labour;
- To support and strengthen activities for awareness creation and public education through workshops, conferences, symposia etc;
- To develop national and international network among various institutions, university departments and ministries work on this object of child labour.

Two projects have been implemented on the child labour, namely child labour action and support programme and IPEC programme as a result of studies conducted by the UNICEF. UNICEF in collaboration with some nations has undertaken to combat with child labour and one such nation is India.

In this context, the role of the UNICEF is quite akin to the role of I.L.O. for the elimination of child labour in the sense that UNICEF is also concerned with working children specially those living or working on the streets and the framework of its programme provide for children in particularly difficult circumstances.

International Programme for Elimination of Child Labour (IPEC)

The problem of child labour has become the focus of attention throughout the world and has shown serious repercussions particularly in developing countries including India. An urgent need is being felt to combat with this problem by devising suitable means in each country in consonance with the existing local conditions. It is being increasingly realised that child labour continues to be a problem of multifarious dimensions and it has been highlighted by the International Labour Organisation in their report. the recent international programme on the elimination of child labour that the number of the children working and the scale of their suffering increases year by year and millions of the children are working, many in servitude and under hazardous conditions.

The I.L.O. keeping in view the complexities and intricacies of the problem pertaining to the child labour as well as financial implication involved therein, has decided to launch the international programme for elimination of the child labour (IPEC) which is funded by the substantial grant provided by the German Government.

The initiative for the IPEC sprang from a meeting is born between I.L.O. Director General and the German Labour Minister in September, 1990. It led to the signing of a financial agreement between the German Government and the I.L.O. in December, 1991 for D.M. 50 millions for 5 years.

The intention of the agreement was to support a sustainable and effective global offensive against child labour in which other donor countries would participate, thereby enlarging the scope and area of activities.

The IPEC is flexible to provide for the difference among countries and regions in the nature and extent of child labour and the form and severity of the exploitation as also the degree of commitment and scope for action. An important feature of the IPEC's strategy at the country level is to demonstrate what appears to work and where and what does not and why and consequently to enhance the programme through the development of action models that could be replicated and thus enabled broadening of impact.

In India, 49 action programmes are currently under implementation under IPEC for a total amount of $1.36 millions and directly benefiting 17,000 child workers. A major ongoing action programme has as its objective the training of enforcement officers of the central and state governments in order to make them more effective in the enforcement of the law as relating to child labour. This programme is being implemented by the National Labour Institute through the State Labour Institute.

United Nations Conventions on the Rights of the Child in Elimination of Child Labour

No human rights treaty has had such a positive response as the UN Convention on the Rights of the child. It was adopted by the General Assembly in November 1989 and declares open for ratification or accession by states in early 1990. Today not less than 128 countries are parties to the convention and some 30 others have signed it and thereby indicated their intention to ratify.

The convention of the rights of the child is a unique human rights treaty. It not only protects the child's civil and political rights but also extends protection to the child's economic, social, cultural and humanitarian rights.

The convention provides the legal basis for initiating action to ensure the rights of children in society. The convention states that the rights shall be extended to all children without discrimination of any kind, irrespective of the child's or his or her parent's or legal guardian's race, nationality, colour, sex, language, religion, political or other opinion, nation, social origin, property, disability, birth or other status.

An Appraisal of International Framework on Combating Child Labour

Efforts are being made consistently at the global level as well as at the national level by various international organisations as well as their members in their respective countries to curb the tendencies prevailing among the employers for employing child labour in order to earn maximum profit.

International Labour Organisation, UNICEF, and UNESCO have been making efforts in a co-ordinated and well planned manner to combat the problem of child labour and for that purpose various programmes have been formulated and imposed, in furtherance of its objective these bodies organised a five days Asian Regional Seminar on the subject, "Child Labour with Education and Enforcement of Legislation" which was held in New Delhi from 5th February to 9th February, 1991 wherein a grave concern was expressed on the increasing number of child workers, particularly in Third world countries.

The percentage of child labour, although in a decreasing trend it is not completely abolished in any part of the world, of course, in developed countries, it has decreased to a greater extent in comparison to developing countries.

Legislative Commitments for the Elimination of Child Labour

"A black spot of labour conditions in India is the illegal employment of children".

Children are given low priority during the pre-independence period in India and very few statuses relating to children were enacted. It was only after independence that farmers of the constitution became very conscious of the nation's responsibility towards children. (Helen, Senkar, 1993).

The legislative approach is purely a State action. In fact, the state in India has not lagged behind in legislating. But an analysis of the legislative approach adopted by the State reveals that both the central and state Governments have enacted several legislations both before and after India became a democratic republic in 1950 which have had no or a very little impact on the problem. (Devakirani Patil, 1988).

This state in India became concerned with the problem of child from 1880s.

The first legislative attempt to incorporate provisions relating to employment of children was made by the "Factories - Act 1881". The Factories Act was enacted to regulate the conditions of work of persons employed in factories employing 100 or more persons.

This Act laid down the following conditions:

(i) No child under seven years of age would be employed in any Factory;

(ii) The working hours for children between the age group of seven and twelve were limited to nine hours a day with an interval of one hour for rest; and

(iii) A weekly holiday was given to all children;

(iv) Successive employment (employment in two factories on the same day) was prohibited.

Factories Act was amended in 1891. The minimum age limits for the employment of children was raised to nine and the age of those protected was raised to 14.

In order to provide more facilities to workers employed in factories, the Factories Act has undergone an amendment in 1934. The Factories (Amendment) Act of 1934 reduced the working hours of children from 6-5 per day. In order to consolidate and amend the law regulating labour in factories, the Factories Act, 1948 was passed. The Act prohibits the employment of children below the age of 14 in any factory.

To regulate the conditions of work of labour in mines, the mines Act, 1991 was passed which prohibited employment of children under 12 years. Later the minimum age of employment was raised from 12 to 13 by the Indian Mines Act of 1923.

The provisions were inadequate and in order to benefit the child labour still more, certain provisions are made in "The Mines (Amendment) Act, 1935. It introduced division of children according to age groups and the position which emerged was as follows:

(i) Children under 15 years, employment in mines was prohibited;

(ii) Persons under 15 and 17 years, underground employment was permitted only on production of certificate of physical fitness granted by a qualified medical practitioner.

To amend and to consolidate the law relating to the regulation of labour and safety in mines, the mines Act, 1952 was enacted. (Bhargava, 1993).

To check migration of labourers to districts like Assam, "The Tea districts emigrant Labour Act, 1932" was passed. It provided that no child under 15 should be employed or allowed to migrate unless the child is accompanied by his parents or adult to whom the child is dependent.

With an object to prohibit the pledging of labour of children, "The children (Pledging of Labour Act – 1933)" was passed. It is a check upon the unscrupulous guardian who wants to thrive on the labour of these children and who is not ashamed in punishing his children in bonded labour. The act provides that any agreement to pledge the labour of a child shall be punished with fine of fifty rupees and whatsoever includes a parent or guardian to make an agreement whereby such guardian or parent pledges the labour of child, shall be punished with fine of two hundred rupees.

Later in the year 1938, to implement the convention, adopted by the 23rd session of I.L.O. (1937). "The employment of Children Act, 1938 was passed. It prohibits the children below the age of 15 years to work in any occupation connected with the transport of passengers, goods or mails by railways or connected with a port authority within limits of any port.

"The Merchant Shipping Act, 1958" prohibits children under 15 to be engaged to work in any capacity in any ship except in certain specialised cases. Likewise "Motor transport workers Act, 1961" prohibits the employment of children under 15 years in any motor transport undertaking.

In order to provide for the regulation and control of training of apprentices and for matters connected with, "The Apprentices Act, 1961" was passed. It prohibits the apprentices in ship or training of a person under 14 years.

To provide for the welfare of the workers in Beedi and Cigar establishments and to regulate the conditions of their work and for matters connected there with the Beedi and Cigar Workers (Conditions of employment) Act, 1966 was enacted.

It prohibits

(i) The employment of children under the 14 years in an industrial premises manufacturing beedi and cigar;

(ii) Women or young persons working in any industrial premises except between 6 a.m. and 7 p.m.

Recently to prohibit the engagement of children in certain employments and to regulate the conditions of work of children in certain other establishments "The Child Labour (Prohibition and Regulation) Act, 1986"" was enacted. This act intends to ban the employment of children lie those who have not completed their 14th year in specific occupation and processes.

A Critical Appraisal of Child Labour Prohibition and Regulation Act, 1986

The Indian Government perceives child labour as a necessary evil, a concomitant of property, which cannot be done away unless poverty itself is eradicated from society. Gurupadaswamy Committee on child labour 1979 and Sanat Mehta Committee on 1984 strongly felt the need for a single comprehensive legislation covering all aspects of child labour in various industries. The thinking of these committees found place in the enactment of the child labour (Prohibition and Regulation) Act 1986. This is a step towards concretising the labour conditions of the child work force repeating thereby the employment of children Act 1938. The 1986 Act does not completely ban child labour but only seeks to "Protect" working children (Powan Sharma, 1994).

The problem of child labour is a burning problem of the world which has constantly agitated the minds of jurists, legislators, social thinkers, politicians, economists and philanthropists from times immemorial. From the public platforms the problem of child labour has reached the inner circles of legislative, executive and judicial chambers.

Politically, socially and economically child is the seed of further national growth. They are blooming flowers of the garden society. It is therefore a duty on the part of the members of society to protect these flowers from the damaging effects of exploitation.

Strategies to Combat Child Labour in India

To protect childhood is nothing but to make the child enjoy the period of childhood without any fears or burdens upon him and to provide all these facilities Government of India has adopted a number of policies and it aimed at eradication of child labour completely by 2000 A.D.

National Policy on Child Labour

This approach is essential to prevent exploitation of children by the labour market forces, so as to be in consonance with the constitutional provisions and the U.N. declarations on the Rights of the child, the Government of India adopted the National Policy for children in "August 1974 (Phillips, 1982).

This policy was aimed to form part of the Nations plan for human resource development. The National policy for children set out a policy keeping in view to achieve the goal of providing equal opportunities for development to all children during the period of growth and children's programme should find a prominent part in our National plans for the development of human resources so that our children grow up to become robust citizens. Physically fit, mentally alert and morally health, endowed in with the skills and motivations needed by society.

The National Policy for children set out a policy framework and listed measures to provide the required service for children. It provides, "It shall be the policy of the state to provide adequate service to children both before and after birth and through the period of their growth, to ensure their full physical, mental and social development". The state shall progressively increase the scope of such services so that, within a reasonable time, all children in the country enjoy optimum conditions for their balanced growth. The policy does seem to admit that a child is entitled to enjoy his childhood through play, learning, getting parental emotions, love and nutritional and health care. (Deb Saini, 1994).

National policy envisaged the need for "free and compulsory education for all children upto the age of 14, provisions for health and nutritional programmes and services, providing alternative forms of education for children unable to take full advantage of formal school education for whatever reasons and measures for protecting children against neglect, cruelty and exploitation".

In the National policy for children, it is said, no child under 14 should be permitted to be engaged in any hazardous occupation or be made to undertake heavy work (Sathe, 1994). The Government's policy now laid emphasis on regulation of child labour than concentrating on abolishing it altogether.

The Role of Non-government Organisations

There are several N.G.O's that are active in the various districts to rehabilitate child workers. Most of these organisations approach the issue of elimination of child labour through formal/non-formal education perspectives. There are over one hundred organisations all over Andhra Pradesh which are working for this purpose.

Voluntary organisations most often confine their activities to the group of villages or mandal in which they are established. However, successful they do not themselves replicate the experiences in other districts. It is precisely for this reason that we find that non-Government organisations and its methods typical to itself. There is very little interaction between N.G.O's working for the same cause, in different areas within the States.

Although there are several N.G.O's working towards elimination of child labour, some of them need special mention. Mammidipudi Venkatarangaiah Foundation (MVF) is a trust founded in 1981. It is devoted to rural and community development. Active in Ranga Reddy district, MUF spend considerable time in crating an awareness among the parents and children about the evils of child labour. The staff take a personal approach, in that they meet each family individually.

Every year the organisation runs summer education camps for children in the 6-14 years category. The foundation claimed that it has rehabilitated about 2,000 children until now.

Bhagavantula Charitable Trust (BCT) was started in 1976 at Yalamanchili. It started child labour rehabilitation programme in 1992-93. Elementary education skills such as in poultry keeping, dairying, grafting, toys, candle making are provided to children between the ages 10-14 years. There are nearly 400 children. This is funded by the International Labour Organisations special project called the International programme on the elimination of child labour (IPEC). Most of the young trainers are girls. The trust also makes a provision for stipend during the period of training. The State Governor Mr. Krishna Kanth on 30th May, 1993 inaugurated child literacy and training programme for rehabilitation of child labour organised by the BCT.

The "Jagrithi – ASSIST" project at Rajyavaram, near Markapur of Prakasam district aims to rehabilitate children from the states mines and quarries. ASSEST has organised 5 non-formal vocational training centres in each of the five clusters. As a part of preventive child labour programme, ASSIST has initiated Balwadi centres.

In Chittoor District, Rayalaseema Seva Samithi (RASS) and Peoples Action for Social Service (PASS) Organisations are working for Community development. Apart from running old age homes and orphanages they are working for the cause of street children also.

Remedial Measures to Discourage Child Labour

Lakhs of children in our country are under the silent suffering of labour that is exploitative. Unless something is done urgently to discourage child labour, the pillars of future society will collapse and nothing will remain thereafter. Government has recognised this fact and has undertaken remedial measures to discourage child labour.

A blue print to eliminate all child labour from hazardous industries by the year 2000 had been drawn up and 300 million dollars had been allotted for this purpose by the I.L.O. The meeting of the National Authority of elimination of child labour was held on 11th July, 1995 and it decided to approve programmes to be undertaken during the years involving 34.40 crores of rupees for elimination of child labour. It includes grant in aid schemes, awareness generation programmes, and augmentation of the national child labour through child labour projects.

The Government launched a Rs.850 crores for child labour scheme; under the scheme a two days workshop from September, 13, 1995 was convened on child labour. Collectors of 100 districts identified as having the highest concentration of child labour had an elaborate discussion over the topic. They planned to set up special cells and state level machinery to over see the elimination of child labour.

Compulsory education of the children would make substantial difference in improving a lot of child labourers. By virtue of education, awakening is likely to be created among the child labour and consequently they can be expected to fight united to prevent their exploitation as well as to ensure full development of their potential. The instances of child labourers are the lowest, being only 1.9 per cent of the total children in the state of Kerala, which is mainly due to highest literacy rate of the State in the whole country. This observation go to establish in clear terms that the increased literacy among the children and poor working class is bound to provide an effective measure for regulating the problem of child labour. So many of the states have already started setting special schools for child labourers.

Child Labour and Adolescence

Young people go through a series of biological and psychological changes at the end of childhood, as they enter adolescence, their bodies visibly mature, their roles in society change and the very content and complexity of their thoughts change as well.

The set of biological changes that mark the beginning of adolescence is called puberty. Puberty begins as increased levels of hormones enter the blood stream, in response to signals from the hypothalamus region of the brain. As the levels of growth hormones rise in body, the steadily but slowly growing child seems suddenly to spurt up. It is this growth spurt that to the outside world visibly signals the beginning of puberty; the rate of growth may double with young adolescents growing as much as five inches in their peak year. For boys, the growth spurt usually starts at 12 or 13 and peaks at about 14 years, then tapers off after 16, and finally stops at 18 or 19. For girls the growth spurt starts at 10 or 11, peaks at 12 or 13, and stops at 17 or 18 (Bayer and Bayley, 1976; Faust, 1977; Stolze and Stolze, 1951; Tanner, 1970). But there are wide individual differences in when the growth spurt occurs.

The growth in height results from the final stages of bone maturation. It is at puberty that the epiphyses – the parts of the long bones made of cartilage – finally turn to bone. The muscles, too lengthen and strengthen. Internal organs – lungs, heart, stomach, kidneys – grow to adult size and capacity. Boys particularly, in response to androgens, gain muscle mass, strength and stamina. Their bodies grow more efficient at metabolising lactic acid, the byproduct of strenuous exercise. Girls, in response to estrogen, develop curves as breasts, hips and buttocks grow larger and padded with fat. Puberty conversion on males and females measurable differences in size, shape and strength. But cultural attitudes intensify the effects of these biological differences. When gender – role expectations are such that females are presumed to be more delicate and weaker than males, adolescent girls actually may perform at reduced levels of strength after puberty.

Preliminary findings from a study underway at the National Institute of Mental Health (Nottlelmann and Susman, 1985) suggests that a low level of the sex hormone estradiol may be related to psychological adjustment problems in 9 to 14 years old girls. In boys the link between hormones and behaviour is even clearer and stronger. Boys with high adrenal androgen were more likely to have behaviour problems – rebelliousness, talking back, fighting with classmates or feelings of sadness and confusion. This finding fits with the earlier research showing that when adolescents were given androgen, they become more aggressive (Wolstenholme and O' Connor, 1967).

The effect of hormones on adolescents' behaviour are complicated by social and psychological factors, however, cultural and family attitudes make a difference in whether hormones bring about psychological change. Attitude towards menstruation and toward menarche, for example, affect adolescents anxiety and physical discomfort around their menstrual periods.

Some grew closer to their mothers, even those who had not felt close before, and some focussed more on their relationships with their fathers. In another study in which 3500 adolescent girls were polled, most said that they believed menstruation caused physical pain emotional upheaval, mood swings and disruptions in behaviour and relationships (Ruble, Books, 1977). The girls age at the time, her knowledge and expectations, her personality and the support she receives from her family all influence how she interprets menstruation. Girls who are well prepared both physically and psychologically and who being menstruating at about the same time as most of their friends tend to feel that menstruation is a normal event (Ruble and Brooks – Gunn, 1982).

Adolescents who are attractive and who have a favourable body image are likely to have a generally favourable self-image and to be happier, more socially successful, and more pleased with themselves right-into their adulthood than unattractive adolescents with poor body images (Bwerscheid, Walster, Bohrnsteat, 1973), Jaquish and Savin-williams – 1981). Adolescents' body images are based not only on what their bodies look like at present but on a lifelong accumulation of perceptions and feelings about their appearance.

Because of the physical changes we have disclosed, adolescence ushers in its own special health problems and hazards. Sexual activity brings teenage pregnancies and sexually transmitted diseases. Cigarette smoking, drug use and drinking alcohol become fairly common. Violence, accidents, self-imposed starvation and suicide take adolescents' lives (Scheroeder, Telin, Schroeder, 1982).

(i) All adolescents go through ups and down in their moods and feelings about themselves. Some adolescents feel great storm and stress, others find adolescence a fairly smooth transition to adulthood.

(ii) The early part of adolescence, from age 11 to 16. Typically is when physical and psychological pressure are more intense, when family arguments are most heated, and when adolescents' feelings of self doubt and unhappiness are acute.

(iii) By later adolescence, moodiness, irritability, and self consciousness have eased, and the search for a personal identity intensifies, as old issues of personality resurface from childhood and must be put in order in an emerging sense of self. It takes adolescents time to resolve this identity crisis and to find the necessary roles, work, attitudes, and social connectedness.

(iv) Adolescents face the task of achieving autonomy from their families without removing themselves so far that they feel isolated, enraged, depressed or guilty. They test their parent limits and bristle at their parents attempts to control their behaviour. Conflict between adolescent and parents occurs in every family, although it usually diminishes when the adolescent reaches 18 or so.

(v) Girls are more likely to have problems coping with the conflict between removing emotionally close to their parents and breaking away them boys are. Girls argue with their parents most over emotional issues, whereas boys argue over practical illness like using the family case, going to church, or doing chores around the house.

(vi) Parents continue to influence their children during adolescence. The amount of emotional support they provide influences how successfully adolescent children resolve their identity crises.

(vii) Adolescents spend many happy, sociable and exciting hours with their friends. Although they sometimes feel angry and self-conscious with their friends, they are in conflict with them less often and come to feel more intimate with them than with their parents. As they search out their own identities and test their parents' values against their friends'; adolescent's turn to peers and parents on different issues.

(viii) Few adolescents commit serious crimes. Those who do commit crises are likely to suffer from neurological and psychological problems. Their family relationships may be destructive and violent, and their parents probably do not supervise them adequately.

(ix) When adolescents feel that their problems are hopeless, they may attempt suicide. In this country, more girls attempt suicide than boys, but more boys actually kill themselves.

(x) Many adolescents hold part-time jobs. Work teaches adolescents to be responsible, dependable, punctual and self-reliant. But it may interfere with school grades and with an adolescent's family life.

(xi) The work of adolescence is to develop a coherent sense of personal identity and positive self-esteem, to be autonomous and socially responsible, to enjoy working and to be capable of making mature decisions.

The children engaged in work/labour from a very young age, also travel through regular phases of growth like their counterparts. The child labourers when they reach adolescence and puberty have physiological, psychological, social emotional and physical changes, and need familial support to adjust and adopt to these changes. Depravation of such support from parents and elder members in the family may cause depression and unhappiness among them, which may trigger negative feelings towards family members, especially among boys. Like other children, child labourers may want to enjoy adolescence by being free from familial burdens, which may make them visualise shouldering family responsibilities as a burdensome tasks and carry these feelings into adulthood as they grow, which may affect his/her future family life. Therefore it is essential to educate the child labourers in family life education, so that the present life is accepted and preparations for better future is laid. The child labourer thus can be helped to travel through this difficult face of life with less stress and strain.

The foregoing reveals that efforts are being made on several forms to prevent, control and rehabilitate child labour. From the review of literature, it is very clear that child labour is an outcome of family disequilibrium and incapability of parents to support their children. This situation calls for restoring family equilibrium by strengthening the family members capabilities to fulfill their responsibilities as parents. By doing this, such family feel child labour as a problem can be tackled at micro level.

REFERENCES

Mamdani, (1972), "*The Myth of Population Control*", New York, Monthly Review Press.

Phillips, W.S.K. (1992), *Street Children of Indore* (NOIDA), National Labour Institute, pp. 13.

Sarada, D. (1995), *Family Life Education for Adolescent Girls Through the Non-formal Adult Education Programmes.* Thesis Submitted to SPM,VV, Tirupati.

6

Welfare Programmes for Child Development

—**Dr. N. Rajani**

Childhood is a period of rapid growth and development and the child must get proper stimulation at this stage, so that he can attain optimum development – physically, emotionally, socially and intellectually.

The qualities a person imbibes as a child deepen as he grows and appear in several obvious and subtle ways in his conduct and character as an adult. Therefore, what affects the interests of the children affects the well-being of the entire group, of which the child is but one member on their welfare and satisfaction depends, not only the health and welfare of the community, but the claim of the nation to civilisation itself.

Changing Concept of 'Child Welfare' in the Government

Child welfare is distinct from other aspects of social welfare is an integral part of the economic plan. There is a difference in the concept of social welfare as applied to child welfare on one hand, and applied to adult on the others. Social welfare for an adult is a part of the expenditure, and for the child it is a part of investment.

Since independence in all the five years plan, unfortunately there was not a single group or body existing or working in a co-ordinated way for the different services of child welfare. The services were split up among the various central government ministries, several ministries were dealing with some identical programmes, which were operated through the state governments. Co-ordination was important and necessary and hence a new body called "co-ordination committee on child welfare" was formulated under a resolution.

Programmes relating to child welfare were scattered among Ministries of Community Development and Co-operation, Health Education and Home Affairs. Therefore, Ministry of Education which was concerned with child welfare programmes was given the administrative responsibility for child welfare and also co-ordination of the activities of other ministries and organisations in connection with child welfare.

Under the umbrella of social welfare, child welfare has gone from ministry to ministry like a ping pong ball till the International year of child, when at last a separate ministry of social welfare came into existence which unfortunately was again split in 1985. From 1958-1960, the social welfare was under Ministry of Education.

From 1960-1961, Child welfare was looked often by department of social security, which was under the Ministry of Law and Social Security. From 1961-1964, Child welfare was under the Ministry of Education and was known as the Ministry of Education, Social Welfare and Culture. From 1964-1966, it was again handled by the Ministry of Law and Social Security. From 1966-1969, it was under the Ministry of Planning and handled by the Department of Social Welfare. From 1969-1979, it was handled by the Department of Social Welfare under the Ministry of Education.

In 1979, the Ministry of Social Welfare was established as an independence ministry composing different units for women, children, handicap, research etc. In 1985 beginning it was renamed ministry for Human Resource and Development under a Cabinet Minister. Under this umbrella one State Minister looked after women, welfare and sports youth affairs and child development. Under another State Minister, Department of Education and Culture. Then there was ministry of welfare under a State Minister who looked after children totally and also the handicap, scheduled caste, scheduled tribe, backward class and welfare of the children.

Today child welfare and child development has gained importance and the government as well as public in general have become conscious and aware of its need and priority in planning for the future of our country.

In 1989 – The Ministry of Human Resource and Development was under a Cabinet Minister with State Minister who looked for i) Youth and Sports, ii) Culture and Art and iii) Education.

Ministry of Welfare was made independent under a Cabinet Minister with State Minister looking after totally "women and children" in every aspect.

Child Welfare in India

Prior to independence, there were only small groups of voluntary workers in India, who took care of feeding of needy children and educational facilities for the handicapped in 1920, Balkanji Bari, the first children's organisation was formed in Bombay. In 1924, The Guild of Service started its child welfare services in South India. In 1927, The Children's Aid Society took vagrant children in residential care at Bombay. It was only in 1952 that the Indian Council for Child Welfare was formed, the first national organisation to mobilise voluntary activities in favour of various aspects of children's needs. The Central Social Welfare Board (CSWB) was established in 1953. It was wholly supported by government finance with a small staff at the Centre and in the States and assisted by thousands of unpaid women workers. Childcare programmes and projects, such as, rural balwadis, holiday homes and grants to over 7,000 non-governmental agencies etc., were apart of its programme.

After Independence in 1947, as per the Directive Principles of State Policy in the constitution, the Government laid down its objectives. The Planning Commission was set up in 1950, under the chairmanship of Prime Minister Jawaharlal Nehru and the formulations of Five Year Plans began. The major responsibility for developing child welfare services was placed on voluntary agencies.

The First Plan recognised the need for strengthening of the infrastructure of various national level voluntary agencies working in the field of child development. Maternal and child health services were in the fore front of the health programme during the plan period.

The second plan laid greater stress on services for handicapped children through expansion of institutional programmes and creation of additional facilities like schools for deaf and blind children, scholarship for handicapped children and training teachers for physically and mentally handicapped school children.

The Third Plan stressed the importance of welfare services being community and family oriented. The ICCW started the demonstration projects for child development during this plan. The scheme of Balasevika Training (for running balwadis) was also introduced during this plan period.

The Fourth Plan accorded highest priority to Family Planning Programme, where the schemes for immunisation of children and mother were also implemented. Special funds were earmarked under this plan for institutional and non-institutional services for destitute children.

During the Fifth Plan, Health, Nutrition and Family Planning were integrated for best results and children being a vulnerable group, were provided special attention. During this plan and the subsequent ones, a lot of progress was made through the ICDS scheme.

The National Children's Policy

The National Policy for children adopted by the Government of India in August, 1974 describes children as "supremely important assets". It enjoins on the state the responsibility for their nurture and solicitude. It provides high priority to programmes related to health and nutrition. Under this policy, a National Children's Board was set up to plan, review and co-ordinate services to meet the needs of children. A National Children's Fund (NCF) was also set up in 1979 and it finances voluntary organisations for implementing child welfare programmes.

The National Policy for children, enunciated in August 1974, declares children as "a supremely important asset" of the nation, whose "nurture and solicitude" are the responsibility of the nation. It affirms that it shall be the policy of the state "to provide adequate services to children, both before and after birth through the period of growth, to ensure their full physical, mental and social development".

In pursuance of the National policy for children and recognising that it is in early childhood that the foundations for physical, psychological and social development are laid and that provisions of early childhood services, especially to the weaker and more vulnerable sections of the community, will help to prevent or minimise the wastages arising from infant mortality, morbidity, malnutrition and stagnation in schools. The Government of India started the ICDS scheme in 1975 in 33 pilot projects.

National Health Policy (NHP) 2002

National Health Policy is to achieve an acceptable standard of good health amongst the general population of the country. The approach would be to increase access to the decentralised public health system by establishing new infrastructure in deficient areas, and by upgrading the infrastructure in the existing institutions. Overriding importance would be given to ensuring a more equitable access to health services across the social and geographical expanse of the country. Emphasis will be given to increasing the aggregate public health investment through a substantially increased contribution by the Central Government.

It is expected that this initiative will strengthen the capacity of the public health administration at the State level to render effective service delivery. The contribution of the private sector in providing health services would be much enhanced, particularly for the population group which can afford to pay for services. Primacy will be given to preventive and first-line curative initiatives at the primary health level through increased sectoral share of allocation. Emphasis will be laid on rational use of drugs within the allopathic system. Increased access to tried and tested systems of traditional medicine will be ensured. Within these broad objectives, NHP-2002 will endeavour to achieve the time-bound goals mentioned in the Box.

Goals to be Achieved by 2000-2015

Eradicate Polio and Yaws	2005
Eliminate Leprosy	2005
Eliminate Kala Azar	2010
Eliminate Lymphatic Filariasis	2015
Achieve Zero level growth of HIV/AIDS	2007
Reduce Mortality by 50% on account of TB, Malaria and other vector and Water Borne diseases	2010
Reduce Prevalence of Blindness to 0.5%	2010
Reduce IMR to 30/1000 and MMR to 100/Lakh	2010
Increase Utilisation of Public health facilities from current level of <20 to >75%	2010
Establish an integrated system of surveillance	2005
National Health Accounts and Health Statistics	
Increase health expenditure by Government as a per cent of GDP from the existing 0.9% to 2.0%	2010
Increase share of central grants to constitute at least 25% of total health spending	2010
Increase State Sector Health spending from 5.5% to 7% of the budget	2005
Further increase to 8%	2010

This policy broadly envisages a greater contribution from the Central Budget for the delivery of Public Health services at the State level. Adequate appropriations, steadily rising over the years, would need to be ensured. The possibility of ensuring this by imposing an earmarked health cess has been carefully examined. While it is recognised that the annual budget must accommodate the increasing resource needs of the social sectors, particularly in the health sector, this Policy does not specifically recommend an earmarked health cess, as that would have a tendency of reducing the space available to parliament in making appropriations looking to the circumstances prevailing from time to time.

The policy highlights the expected roles of different participating groups in the health sector. Further, it recognises the fact that, despite all that may be guaranteed by the Central Government for assisting public health programmes, public health services would actually need to be delivered by the State administration, NGOs and other institutions of civil society. The attainment of improved health levels would be significantly dependent on population stabilisation, as also on complementary efforts from other areas of the social sectors – like improved drinking water supply, basic sanitation, minimum nutrition, etc., to ensure that the exposure of the populace to health risks is minimised.

Any expectation of a significant improvement in the quality of health services, and the consequential improved health status of the citizenry, would depend not only on increased financial and material inputs, but also on a more empathetic and committed attitude in the service providers, whether in the private or public sectors. In some measure, this optimistic policy document is based on the understanding that the citizenry is increasingly demanding more by way of quality in health services, and the health delivery system, particularly in the public sector, is being pressed to respond. In this backdrop, it needs to be recognised that any policy in the social sector is critically dependent on the service providers treating their responsibility not as a commercial activity, but as a service, albeit a paid one. In the area of public health, an improved standard of governance is a prerequisite for the success of any health policy.

Reproductive and Child Health Programme

The National Family Planning Programme was started in 1951 as a purely demographic programme. Subsequently the element of public education and extension was included to facilitate outcome under the Family Planning Programme. During the seventies, the Family Planning Programme was focussed mainly on terminal methods and the programme received set back due to rigid implementation of a target based approach. The programme has, however, remained fully voluntary and the main effort of the government has been to provide services on the one hand and to encourage citizens by information, education and communication on the other to use such services.

The experiences gained, within the country and outside, had amply established that health of women in the reproductive age group and of small children (up to 5 years of age) is of crucial importance for effectively tackling the problem of growth of population which led to change in the approach from family planning to family welfare. Since the Seventh Plan implemented during 1984-89, the family welfare programmes have evolved with the focus on the health needs of the women in reproductive age group and of children below the age of 5 years as well as on providing contraceptives and spacing services to the desirous people. The main objective of the family welfare programme for the country has been to stabilise population at a level consistent with the needs of national development.

The Universal Immunisation Programme (UIP) aimed at reduction in mortality and morbidity among infants and younger children due to Vaccine Preventable Diseases, was started in 1985-86. The Oral Rehydration Therapy (ORT) was also started in view of the fact that Diarrhoea was a leading cause of deaths among children. Various other programmes under Maternal and Child Health (MCH) were also implemented during the 7th Plan.

INFANT MORTALITY RATE

INDIA

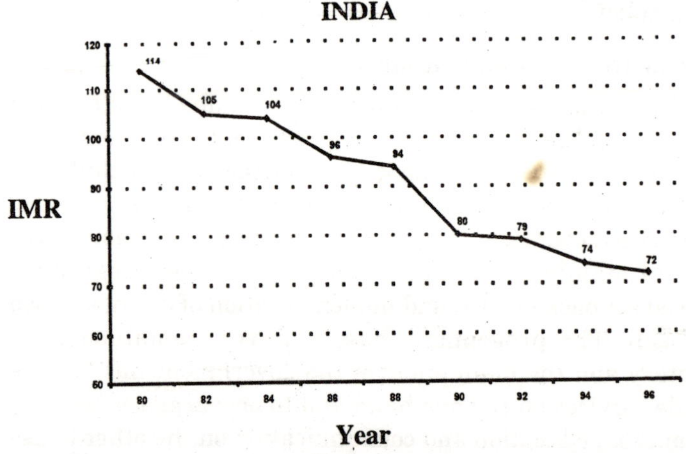

The objectives of all these programmes were convergent and aimed at improving the health of the mothers and young children and to provide them facilities for prevention and treatment of major disease conditions. While these programmes did have a beneficial impact but the separate identity for each programme was causing problems in its effective management and this was also somewhat reducing the outcome. Therefore, in the 90s i.e., in the 8th Plan, these programmes were integrated under Child Survival and Safe Motherhood (CSSM) Programme which was implemented from 1992-93.

Progress made so far

Various programmes have led to substantial improvement in health indicators. The position with regard to some prominent health indicators is depicted in the table:

Indicator	*Past level*	*Current level*
Crude Birth Rate	41.7 (1951-61)	27.4 (1996)
Crude Death Rate	22.8 (1951-61)	8.9 (1996)
Infant Mortality Rate	146 (1951-61)	72 (1996)
Maternal Mortality Rate	NA	4.37 (1991-92)

(Contd...)

Indicator	*Past level*	*Current level*
Life Expectancy at Birth (Years) Est.		
Male	37.1 (1951)	62.4 (1996-2001)
Female	36.1 (1951)	63.4 (1996-2001)
Total Fertility Rate	6.0 (1951)	3.5 (1994)
Effective Couple Protection Rate	10.4 (1970-71)	45.4 (31.3.97)
Immunisation Status* (% coverage) for Pregnant Women		
TT	40 (1985-86)	80 (1997-98)
For Infant		
BCG	29 (1985-86)	96 (1997-98)
Measles	44 (1987-88)	83 (1997-98)
DPT	41 (1985-86)	90 (1997-98)
Polio	36 (1985-86)	90 (1997-98)

NA: Not available Relevant year in parentheses

* Universal Immunisation was started in (1985-86).

CRUDE BIRTH RATE: INDIA

BIRTH RATE PER 1000 POPULATION

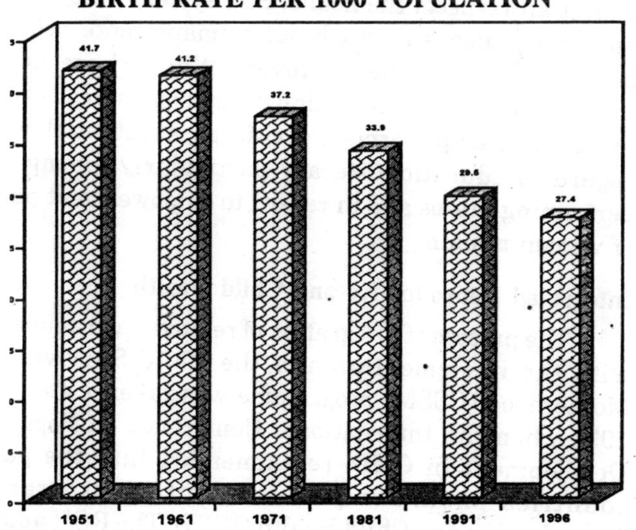

However, the position it not uniform all over the country. Whereas the States like Kerala, Tamil Nadu, Goa, Maharashtra and Punjab have achieved a considerably higher level, the States like Uttar Pradesh, Madhya Pradesh, Bihar, Rajasthan, Jharkand, Assam and Orissa are performing at levels much below the national level. This has been a matter of great concern because some of these States also happen to be very populous and unless performance in these States improve, the national performance will continue to remain depressed. The deficiencies in implementation of the maternal and child health services have been responsible for a high incidence of maternal mortality and child/infant mortality and low health status of women and children. Poor prospect of health and life of the children is one of the prominent factors leading to birth of more children per family.

The results at ground level are influenced by a number of factors like investment for the programme at National/State level, efficiency of the State, health system and response of the people. Allocation for resources for Family Welfare Programme in the past has not been commensurate with the size of the job. This is a severe handicap particularly when it is noted that in almost all respects the health care system needs upgradation and that it needs to reach out to many more people for the national goals to be achieved. While there is a steady improvement due to economic development, spread of education/literacy and empowerment of citizens, substantial problems in regard to education/literacy particularly among the weak performing States and in regard to empowerment particularly of women remain.

Integrated Reproductive and Child Health

The process of integration of related programmes initiated with the implementation of the Child Survival and Safe Motherhood (CSSM) programme was taken a step further in 1994 when the International Conference on Population and Development in Cairo recommended that the participant countries should implement unified programmes for Reproduction and Child Health (RCH). The RCH approach has been defined as "People have the ability to reproduce and regulate their fertility, women are able to go through pregnancy and child birth safely, the outcome of pregnancies is successful in terms of maternal and infant survival and well being and couples are able to have sexual relations free of fear of pregnancy and of contracting diseases".

This concept is in keeping with the evolution of an integrated approach to the programmes aimed at improving the heath status of young women and children which has been going on in the country. It is obviously sensible that integrated RCH Programme, would help in reducing the cost of inputs to some extent because overlapping of expenditure would not longer be necessary and integrated implementation would optimise outcome at the field level. During the 9th Plan, the RCH programme accordingly, integrates all the related programmes of the 8th Plan. The concept of RCH is to provide need based, client centred, demand driven, high quality and integrated RCH services to the beneficiaries. The RCH Programme is a composite programme incorporating the inputs of the Government of India as well as funding support from external donor agencies including World Bank and the European Commission.

It is legitimate right of the citizen to be able to experience sound Reproductive and Child Health and therefore, the RCH Programme will seek to provide relevant services for assuring reproductive and child health to all citizens. However, RCH is even more relevant for obtaining the objective of stable population for the country. The overall objective since the beginning has been that the population of the country should be stabilised at a level consistent with the requirement of national development. It is now established that parents keep the family size small if they are assured about the health and longevity of the children and there is no better assurance of good health and longevity of children than health care for the mothers and for young children. Therefore, by ensuring small families RCH Programme also ensures stable population in the medium and long-term, though in the short-term, population is controlled by use of spacing methods and terminal methods for avoiding unwanted pregnancies. Therefore, the overall strategy of the Government of India (Department of Family Welfare) is to strive for obtaining reproductive and child health arrangements for the whole of the country's population and for simultaneously promoting and making contraceptive/terminal methods available for desirous couples. It also needs to be observed that the measures through the health system alone do not and cannot assure success in either ensuring reproductive and child health or in controlling population. These objectives are determined concurrently by the following:

1. Policy support expressed publicly by opinion leaders in different sectors of the national system and by the community at large. Without this kind of support, the receptivity of the people to make use of even available services cannot be ensured;

2. Adequate resources for making available Reproductive and Child Health services to all rural and urban communities in the country;

3. Accountability for performance among the health workers and efficiency of the health system. Without such efficiency the quality of services to citizens or even effective access to health services cannot be ensured; and

4. Literacy among women and educational status of families and similarly improvement in economic status of families. The educated and economically well-off families can more rationally assess the options before them and acquire capability/willingness to assess consequences of their present actions for future. Therefore, the effort of the Department of Family Welfare is to collaborate with the related Departments and Non-Governmental Organisations for seeking support of their programmes for the Family Welfare Programmes. This in turn will similarly improve the outcome of related programmes of those departments as well.

The RCH programme for the 9th Plan is a very ambitious programme which aims to effectively bring all the reproductive and child health services within easy reach of the community. Almost all of the large outlay of Rs. 5112.23 crore for the programmes will be for improving facilities and services and the traditional items for creation of posts and construction of buildings will be only nominal. Therefore, the programme will require much greater management skill including a much more professional advanced management information System.

The RCH programme will make reproductive and child health services available at lower level of hospitals like specialist facilities for obstetric care will be available at Sub-divisional hospital level, medical termination of pregnancy services will be available at PHCs and general obstetric care facilities will be strengthened in PHCs. Simultaneously, the RCH programme will make available some new RCH services e.g., Specialist facility for Sexually Transmitted Diseases (STD) and Reproductive Tract Infections (RTI) (which have a high incidence) will be available in all district hospitals and in a fair number at sub-divisional hospitals. At another plane, the RCH programme will seek to broaden ownership of the community in the programme so that it does not remain a purely government programme which, unfortunately has been the situation so far. The non-government medical system will be prominently involved in providing many RCH facilities and Indian Systems of Medicine which are known to be efficacious, will be utilised in a substantial manner in providing RCH services. Certain prominent segments of population which have prominent RCH needs but which have not been adequately addressed in the past like the urban slum population, tribal population and the adolescents will be addressed through specially designed additional programmes. The Panchayati Raj functionaries at village, development block and district level will be involved in sensitisation and training along with health workers and workers of related Government Departments. The Panchayati Raj functionaries will have a central role in determining the need of the local population, for RCH services generally and for contraceptives particularly under the target free (Community Needs Assessment) approach. The Panchayat will also be the agency for implementing the programme and for extending financial and transport support to women from indigent families for taking them to specialist at Sub- divisional hospitals for deliveries.

The RCH programme incorporates the components relating to child survival and safe motherhood and includes two additional components, one relating to sexually transmitted diseases and other relating to reproductive tract infections. The main highlights of the RCH programme are:

1. The programme integrates all interventions of fertility regulation, maternal and child health with reproductive health of both men and women;
2. The services to be provided will be client centred, demand driven, of high quality and based on the needs of the community arrived at through decentralised participatory planning and the target free approach;
3. The programme envisages upgradation of the level of facilities of for providing various interventions and quality of care. The First Referral Units (FRUs), being set up at sub-district level will provide comprehensive emergency obstetric and new born care. Similarly RCH facilities in PHCs will be substantially upgraded;
4. It is proposed to improve facilities for obstetric care. MTP and IUD insertion in the PHCs, also for IUD, insertion in sub-centres;
5. The Programme aims at improving the outreach of services primarily for the vulnerable groups of population who have till now been effectively left out of the planning process e.g.:
   - Special Programme will be taken up for urban slums, tribal population and adolescents;
   - NGOs and Voluntary Organisations will be involved in a much larger way to improve outreach and make it the people's programme;

- Practitioners of Indian Systems of Medicine will be trained and research and development in Indian Systems of Medicine will be supported to improve the range of RCH services.;
- Panchayat Raj System will have a greater role in planning, implementation and assessment of client satisfaction.

Intervention Programmes to Combat Malnutrition

(a) Integrated Child Development Services

The Government of India is making concerted efforts to reduce the prevalence of malnutrition in the country. In consonance with this, the scheme of Integrated Child Development Services (ICDS) was launched in 1975. This programme is implemented by the Nodal Department i.e., the Department of Women and Child Development. Starting with 33 experimental projects in 1975-76, the ICDS programme has been expanded to 2765 projects upto December 1992. This package of services provided to the beneficiaries of the programme are Supplementary Nutrition, Immunisation, Health check-up, Referral Services, Non-formal Pre-school Education and Nutrition and Health Education. Supplementary nutrition is one of the major components of the programmes.

The strategy adopted in ICDS is one of the Integrated delivery of early childhood services so that their synergistic effect will fulfill the objective of the programme. The beneficiaries of the programme are children below 6 years, pregnant and lactating mothers and women in the age group 15-44 years. This programme supplements the health, nutrition and family welfare activities with appropriate co-operation and co-ordination between functionaries of the Health Department and nodal department.

The other programmes in this direction are the Special Nutrition Programme, Balwadi Nutrition Programme, Wheat Based Supplementary Nutrition Programme, Tamil Nadu Integrated Nutrition Programme, Mid Day Meals Programme for school children and other intervention programmes for combating specific nutritional deficiency diseases such as Nutritional Anaemia Prophylaxis Programme, Goitre Control Programme and programme for prevention of Nutritional Blindness due to Vitamin A deficiency.

(b) Special Nutrition Programme

The Special Nutrition Programme (SNP) was launched in the country in 1970-71. It provides supplementary feeding to the extent of about 300 calories and 10 gm. of proteins to pre-school children and about 500 calories and 20 gm. of protein to expectant and nursing mothers for 300 days a year. At present SNP is operated, as a part of the Minimum Needs Programme in the various states. The nutrition component of the ICDS programme is funded by States and Union Territories from the SNP budget. At present about 21.5 million beneficiaries are covered under this programme.

(c) Balwadi Nutrition Programme

The Balwadi Nutrition Programme (BNP) is being implemented since 1970-71 through five national level voluntary organisations. The Central grant is given for supplementary feeding of children. It consists of 300 calories and 12.5 gm of protein every day per child in the age group 3-5 years. At present there are around 5641 Balwadis throughout the country benefiting 2.25 lakh children.

(d) Applied Nutrition Programme

Applied Nutrition Programme (1959): This is an educational Programme at the village and family level which aims to bring about changes in the choice of food and feeding practices that involve little or no extra expense for the family. This programme directly concentrates on the feeding of the young child, both through the education of the mother and by channelling a part of the food produced under various schemes of the programme in the diet of the child.

(e) Wheat Based Supplementary Nutrition Programme

A centrally sponsored scheme called Wheat-based Supplementary Nutrition Programme (WNP) was introduced in 1986. This programme follows the norms of SNP or of the nutrition component of the ICDS. Central assistance for the programme consists of supply of free wheat and supportive costs for other ingredients, cooking, transport etc. At present around 3 million children and expectant and nursing mothers are covered under this programme. This scheme is now being transferred to the State sector.

(f) Tamil Nadu Integrated Nutrition Programme

Tamil Nadu Integrated Nutrition Programme (TINP) is being implemented in the State of Tamil Nadu since 1981. Under this project nutritional surveillance and supplementary nutrition is being provided to children below six years and expectant and nursing mothers. The project is assisted by World Bank. The total outlay for the project is Rs.321 crores.

(g) Mid Day Meal Programme

In 1956 the erstwhile Madras State launched the mid-day meal programme of providing free meal to the elementary school children with a view to: (a) enrolling poor children who generally remain outside the school due to poverty; and (b) giving one meal to the children attending the school. The MDM operates as a centrally sponsored scheme from 1962-63 in all the states. The objectives were (a) to improve nutritional status of the school children; and (b) to attract children to enroll themselves into school and to encourage regular attendance by providing supplementary nutrition.

(h) Nutritional Anaemia Prophylaxis Programme

Taking cognizance of this problem, the Government of India launched a Prophylaxis programme in 1970 to prevent nutritional anaemia in mothers and children. Under the programme, the expectant and nursing mothers as well as women acceptors of family planning are given one tablet of iron and folic acid containing 60 mg elemental iron (180 mg of ferrous sulphate and 0.5 mg of folic acid) and children in the age group 1-5 years are given one tablet of iron containing 20 mg elemental iron (60 mg of ferrous sulphate and 0.1 mg folic acid) daily for a period of 100 days. This programme covered children and pregnant women with haemoglobin level less than 8 gm per cent and 10 gm per cent respectively.

There has been an increase in the number of beneficiaries under this programme from 3.52 million in 1975-76 to 41.20 million in 1988-89. About 30 million women and 50 million children have, however, been identified as eligible beneficiaries for the prophylaxis programme. During 1988-89, the programme envisaged to cover 22 million women and 30 million children.

Fortification of salt with iron, a universally consumed dietary article, has been identified as a measure to control anaemia. Efficacy of fortified salt in both rural and urban communities was assessed by a multicentric study and revealed that iron fortified salt when consumed over a period of 12-18 months reduced prevalence of anaemia significantly. Accordingly, fortification of salt with iron as a public health approach is piloted in Tamil Nadu and Rajasthan.

(i) Prophylaxis Programme Against Blindness, due to Vitamin A Deficiency

The programme was initiated by the Government in 1970. Under this programme children in age group 1-5 years are given an oral dose of 0.2 million I.U of Vitamin A in oil every 6 months. The number of beneficiaries covered under this programme has increased steadily from 4.48 million in 1975-76 to 30.12 million in 1986-87.

An interim evaluation in the States of Kerala and Karnataka after two years of implementation of the programme showed that the coverage was over 75 per cent and there was a 75 per cent reduction in the prevalence of conjunctival signs of Vitamin A deficiency. The evaluation also confirms the administrative feasibility of this approach within the existing health infrastructure.

During 1980, the Department of Food introduced a scheme of Fortification of Milk with Vitamin A to prevent nutritional blindness. At present there are 42 dairies in the country implementing this scheme. During 1988-89, the total quantity of milk fortified with Vitamin A through these dairies was 3.2 million litres per day.

MCH Division of the Ministry of Health and Family Welfare has been implementing the programmes on anaemia prophylaxis and prophylaxis against vitamin 'A' deficiency. These programmes were reviewed by two groups of experts and accordingly certain modifications have been made with concentrated efforts on all pregnant mothers receiving 100 tablets of iron folic acid and universalisation of vitamin 'A' to be provided to all children between 9 months and 3 years of age. The lactating women and those who have accepted certain family planning devices will continue to get the drugs as per earliest schedule. Suitable linkages have also been developed for these programmes with immunisation and arrangements have been made for regular monitoring through the same programme.

(j) Goitre Control Programme

A National Goitre Control Programme was initiated by the Government of India in 1962 to identify goitre endemic regions and to assess the impact of goitre control measures. The availability and production of iodized salt, strengthening of administrative machinery controlling the entry of non- iodized salt in the endemic regions have been recommended as measures to improve the implementation of the programme.

There is an increasing awareness about the broad spectrum of Iodine Deficiency Disorder (IDD) in the country. The Goitre Control Programme has gained momentum in recent years. The Government of India has started a scheme with effect from 1-4-1986 envisaging Universal Iodisation of Edible Salt in a phased manner to cover the whole country by 1992. It has liberalised production of iodized salt under the private sector by issuing licence to 700 salt manufacturers out of which 307 have commenced production. As a result thereof, the production of iodised salt in the country has steadily increased to 25.061akh M.T. in 1990-91 from 7.72 lakh M.T. in 1986-87. Since the inception of this programme in 19 States/Union Territories have so far established Goitre Control Cells in their State Health Directorates for effective implementation and monitoring of the programme.

(k) National Diarrhoeal Diseases Control Programme

The programme was launched in 1981 to reduce the mortality in children below five years due to diarrhoeal diseases through introduction of Oral Rehydration Therapy (ORT). The high priority accorded to the programme is part of the package of services rendered under the MCH programme which was initiated during 1980-85 has now been strengthened extensively. The anganwadi centres of the ICDS Scheme have served as nucleus for the propagation of oral rehydration therapy which has been found to be an effective measure of preventing dehydration caused by diarrhoea.

(l) Education Related Programme

A number of committees and study groups were set-up from time to time suggest ways and means for preschool education families. All these groups emphasised the importance of preschool education but the recommendations remained mostly on paper. The Central Social Welfare Board (CSWB) initiated as a part of its welfare activities in the areas not covered hitherto, the scheme of Welfare Extension Projects. But most of the children education programms are integrated with the health and nutritional programme.

Welfare Extension Projects

This Scheme launched in 1958, provides for a programme of Creches, Balwadis, Craft Education, Social Education for Adult Women, Recreational Activities for Youth, Maternity and Child Welfare Services etc. Each project benefits about 50 families.

Integrated Pre-school Project

This programme provides welfare services like education, health and recreation to the preschool children on an integrated basis. The main object of the programme is to provide all the basic amenities to a child necessary for his growth and mental development. This is particularly necessary in overcrowded areas of low income group localities where there is poverty, lack of space etc.

Other Programmes

The Department of Education, Ministry of Human Resource Development, Government of India, is implementing a number of schemes for the development and welfare of children, namely:

1. Operation black board—It was started as a consequence of the New Education Policy and the purpose is to ensure minimum essential facilities in primary schools;
2. Non-formal Education;
3. Reimbursement - of Tuition Fee charged from girls in higher classes in States/Union Territories;
4. National Scholarships scheme;
5. National Loan Scholarships scheme;
6. Scheme for upgradation of merit of SC/ST students;
7. Scheme of Scholarships at secondary stage for talented children from rural areas;
8. Scholarship scheme for study in approved residential schools;
9. Bal Bhavan society.

The Department of Rural Development runs two programmes which are related to child welfare as the well being and development of children is closely linked with the economic and nutritional status of the family, specially of women.

Integrated Child Development Services

Thus the Indian constitution made primary efforts for the welfare of children well before the declaration of child rights by the United Nations. The Indian government launched several programmes for the welfare of children. Though many of the programmes could not achieve expected results the efforts show the concern of Indian government and policy makers. ICDS is one such ongoing programme which could sustain inspite some shortcomings, ICDS programme caters to the needs of rural, tribal, semi-urban and slum children that is ICDS is one of the largest child welfare programme providing the rightful needs of children in India.

Integrated child development services is India's response to the challenge of meeting the holistic needs of the child. Today, the ICDS is one of the world's largest and most unique programmes for early childhood care and development.

Genesis: On the basis of eight inter-ministerial study teams set up by the Planning Commission, a scheme of ICDS was evolved. It is centrally sponsored scheme, 33 experimental projects were started in different parts of the country on 2, October 1975. During 1978-79, 67 new ICDS projects were started. Along with the ICDS project, adult women are given training in functional literacy which includes skills in childcare, home management, personal and environmental hygiene. Success of the scheme prompted expansion of ICDS to over 1000 blocks by the end of sixth plan (1984-85). During the seventh plan, programme is likely to expand to another 1000 blocks (Goel, S.L., 1980).

ICDS is a multi-sectoral programme and involves several departments, whose services are coordinated at the village, PHC project - district and state levels. The primary responsibility for the implementation of the programme lies with the department of women and child development, Ministry of Human Resource Development at the centre which may be Social Welfare, Rural Development, Tribal Welfare or Health and Family Welfare.

The ICDS beneficiaries are children below 6 years, pregnant and lactating women and women in the age group 15 to 44 years. The beneficiaries are to a large extent identical with those under the MCH and EPI programmes. The infrastructure of ICDS is an additional facility which can be profitably wed to supplement the health, nutrition and family welfare activities with appropriate co-operation and co-ordination between functionaries of the departments viz., health and the nodal departments.

Objectives of ICDS are:

1. To improve the nutritional and health status of children in the age group 0-6 years;
2. To lay the foundations for proper psychological physical and social development of the child;
3. To reduce the incidence of mortality, morbidity, malnutrition and school drop-outs;
4. To achieve effective co-ordination of policy and implementation amongst the various departments to promote child development; and
5. To enhance the capability of the mother to look after the normal health and nutritional needs through nutrition and health education.

Towards achieving these objectives, a package of services is rendered through the anganwadi worker at the village centre called anganwadi. The supportive supervision by the functionaries of the nodal department and health department is essential for the success of the programme. The social welfare functionaries have a primary responsibility of providing supplementary nutrition and non-formal education to the beneficiaries of the programme.

All the ICDS services are provided through the anganwadi in an integrated manner to enhance their impact on childcare. Each anganwadi is run by an anganwadi worker supported by a helper in integrated service delivery, and improved linkages with the health system—thus increasing the capacity of community and women—especially mothers—for childcare, survival and development.

REFERENCES

1. Avindrani, D.N., 1990. *Family and Child Welfare*. Published by Ashish Publishing House, New Delhi.
2. Bakshi, S.R. and Kiranbala, 2000. *Child Welfare and Development*, Published by Deep and Deep Publications, New Delhi, pp. 28-29.
3. Chaturvedi, T.N., 1979. *Administration for Child Welfare*. Published by Indian Institute of Public Administration, New Delhi, pp. 169-176.

4. Devi, L., 1998. *Encyclopaedia of Child and Family Welfare*. Published by Anmol Publications, Vol.5, New Delhi, pp. 111, 366.

5. Dreze and Sen, 2004. *Universalisation with Quality: An Agenda for ICDS*. Report prepared for the National Advisory Council, www.righttofoodindia.org.

6. Dutta, P.K., 1993. *Scope of Health Systems Research in Child Survival and Safe Motherhood Programme*. Indian Journal of Maternal Child Health.

7. Ghosh, S. 1997. *Integrated Child Development Programme*. Published by Indian Paediatrics 34, pp. 911-18.

8. Goel, S.L., 1980. *Health Care Administration Policy making and Planning*. Published by Sterling Publishers, New Delhi, p. 203.

9. Gupta, A., 2003. *Status of Infant and Young Child Feeding: A National Report of Quantitative Study*. Published by Breast Feeding Promotion Network of India.

10. Gupta, S., 1996. *Rights of the Child Workers*. Published by Ministry of Social Justice and Empowerment, Vol. XXXVIII (124), New Delhi, pp. 1-3.

11. Joshi, S., 1996. *Child Survival Health and Social Work Intervention*. Published by Concept Publishing Company, New Delhi, pp. 65-67.

12. Kumar, R., 2002. *Child Development in India: Health Welfare and Management*. Published by Ashish Publishing House, Vol. I, New Delhi, pp. 157-163.

Empirical Studies

7

Reflection of Child Rights in the ICDS Programme

—**Ms. T. Mamatha** and **Prof. D. Sarada**

Introduction

The Rights of the child as enshrined in the convention apply equally to all children irrespective of colour, creed, sex, language, political and other opinions, ethnic and social origins, property conditions and birth status.

The Rights of the child adopted by the United Nations General Assembly on the 20th November 1989 declares that every child has the inherent Right to life (Art.6) and has the Right to a name to acquire nationality and to be cared for by his or her parents (Art.7). The Child's Right to parental care and family life is emphasised. All children shall have the Right to freedom of expression, freedom of thought, conscience and religion and freedom of association (Art. 13, 14 and 15) more importantly, the child has the Right to express the opinion and views in all matters concerning him/her (Art.12). The child has the Right to access to all information from various sources (Art.17). The convention guarantees the Right of the child to health and enjoyment.

The Article 28 and 29 deal with the child's Right to education. Article 28 recognises the Right to education and to achieve the Right progressively on the basis of equal opportunity. It makes primary education compulsory and free to all and encourages the development of different forms of secondary education, including general and vocational education. It makes educational and vocational information and guidance available and accessible to all children. It also enjoins that all states promote and encourage international cooperation in matters relating to education, in particular with a view to contributing to the elimination of ignorance and illiteracy throughout the world. In this regard, particular account shall be taken of the needs of the developing countries.

Education was recognised as an inalienable right of the human and early childhood education (Pre-school Education) was given the highest priority in spite of rising malnutrition and deterioration of health services in many parts of the world. Pre-school education was realised as a pre-condition to success of the project "Education for all" and an imperative for effective education.

The integrated Child Development Services (ICDS) is currently the biggest programme of early childhood development. This over the years has demonstrated that even a modest investment in child development goes a long way in developing human resources. It needs to be fully integrated with the universal immunisation programme started with effect from 19th November, 1985. ICDS aims at providing basic needs to the children of India. Basic needs of children have been included in the UN declaration of child Rights as Rights of children. So the needs of children have become the Rights of children, fulfillment of which is a responsibility of families, societies and the state. Hence it has become necessary to assess the child welfare programmes in view of child Rights and their coverage. As ICDS is the largest and chief child development programmes in India, the reflection of child Rights in ICDS programme was studied.

Methodology

A study on the Reflection of Child Rights in ICDS programme was carried out in Tirupati Urban Mandal of Chittoor district, Andhra Pradesh. The study was an attempt to know the extent of coverage of Child Rights in the training programmes of Anganwadi workers and to assess the knowledge. Attitudes and Practice of Child Rights by the Anganwadi workers in their work in the Anganwadi centres. The ICDS programme is the largest child development programme covering a major section of child population in the urban slums, rural and tribal areas in India. Hence, it is important to know the coverage of Child Rights in the training programmes of the field level functionaries of ICDS. The Anganwadi workers' knowledge, attitudes and practice of Child Rights were assessed in order to form a basis for education programme in the area of Child Rights.

Locale of the Study

The Tirupati rural mandal is one of the important municipalities in Andhra Pradesh. Being a reputed pilgrim centre has largest floating population. The population of the town are heterogeneous with good number of settlers from neighbouring states and districts.

The Tirupati urban mandal was covered by ICDS programme consisting of 110 Anganwadi Centres. The programme is run by a reputed Non-Governmental Organisation – Rastriya Seva Samithi (RASS). For the present study the sample was selected from these Anganwadi Centres.

Sample Selection

All the Anganwadi workers working at the time of the conduct of study in Anganwadi Centres run by Rastriya Seva Samithi (RASS) were selected. Although 110 Anganwadi workers were selected for the study, 10 of them were excluded as they were substitutes for the regular Anganwadi workers who were on leave.

Research Design

A research design was developed to facilitate smooth conduct of the study and also to have a clear understanding of the research process. The research design developed for the study is presented as follows: (*See flow chart I on next page*)

Selection of Variables

After the review of relevant literature, the following variables were chosen for inclusion in the present study.

Independent variables: As the study focusses on Anganwadi workers who are women the variables such as age, educational status, duration of service, marital status, training received were included.

Dependent Variables

The knowledge, attitudes and practice of Child rights and coverage of Child rights in the training programme of Anganwadi workers were included as dependent variables in the present study. (*See flow chart II on page 132*)

Tools for Data Collection

In order to measure the variables selected the following tools were employed.

1. General Information Schedule

A schedule was developed to collect the general profile of the sample under study. The schedule consisted of questions which covers the personal profile or Anganwadi worker and the professional experience, training inputs and working conditions of the Anganwadi workers.

2. Child Rights Knowledge Scale

A scale consisting of 26 statements was constructed to assess the knowledge of Anganwadi workers. The responses were rated on Yes/No type of answers. For the response 'Yes' a score of '1' was assigned and for the response 'No' a score of '0' was assigned.

FLOW CHART – I

Research Design

REFLECTION OF CHILD RIGHTS IN THE I.C.D.S. PROGRAMME

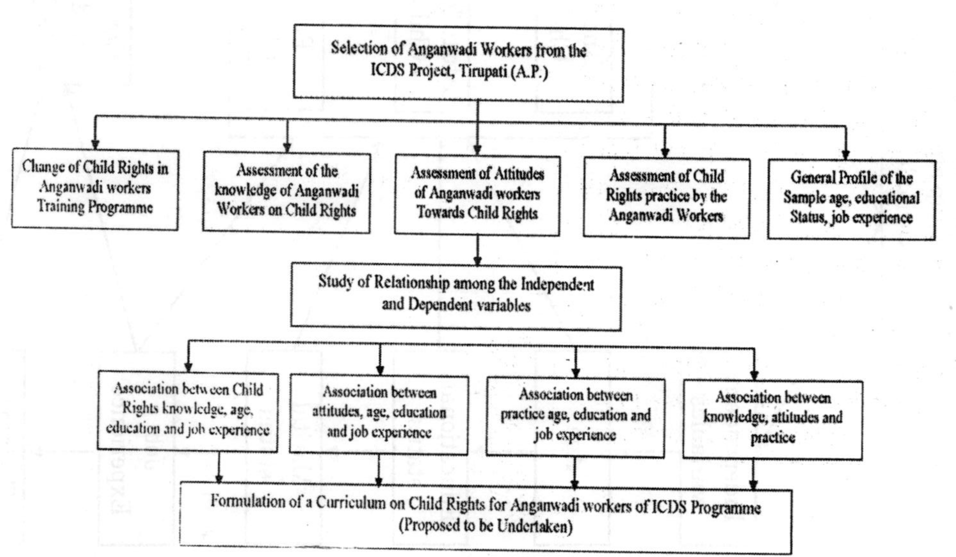

The relationship among the independent and dependent variables were presented as follows:

FLOW CHART – II

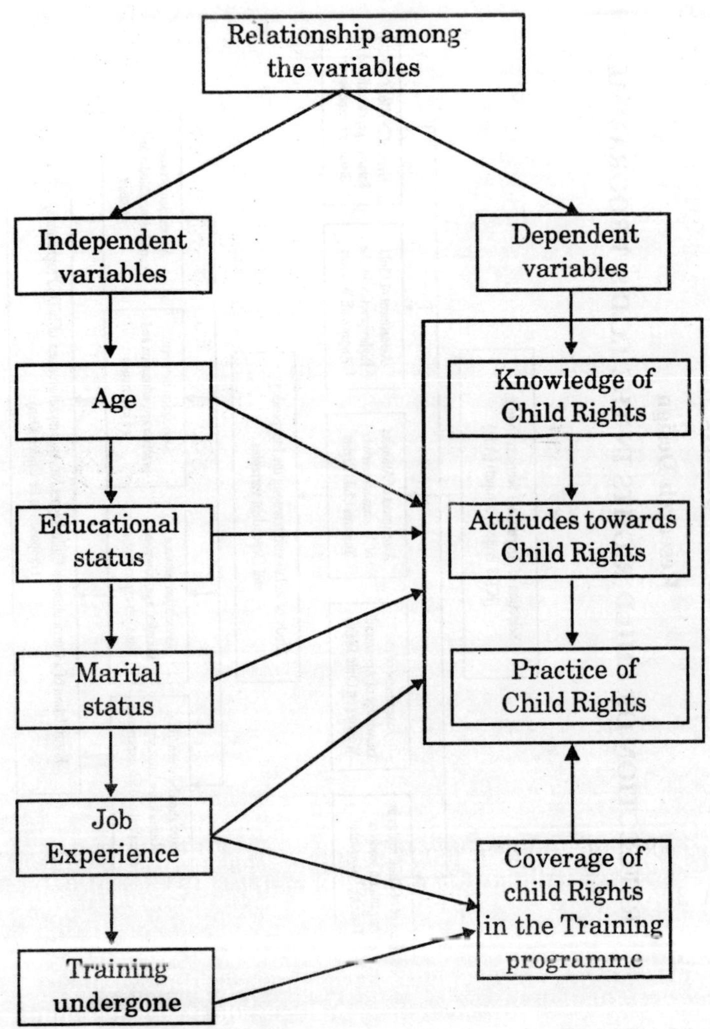

3. Attitudinal Scale on Child Rights

An attitudinal scale consisting of 17 statements was constructed. The sample responses were rated on a 3 point scale that is strongly agree/agree/ disagree. The responses were scored by giving '2' for 'strongly agree', '1' for 'agree' and '0' for 'disagree'. The total score for each respondent was calculated and the respondents were classified as 'high' and 'low' depending on their total score.

4. Practice of Child Rights Scale

In order to assess the levels of practice of Child Rights by the Anganwadi workers (in the Anganwadi centre) a scale was developed. The scale consisted of 4 areas such as Health and Nutritional Rights, Educational Rights, Psycho-social Rights and Family Rights. Under each area few statements were included with Yes/No type and multiple choice type of responses. The responses were scored, totalled and the respondents were classified on the basis of total scores as 'high' and 'low'.

Data Collection

With the help of aforesaid scales the data was gathered from the Anganwadi workers using interview method. The data was pooled, tabulated and analysed.

RESULTS AND DISCUSSION

The results of the study were discussed as under:

Age

The chronological age of the sample in completed years was recorded from their SSC certificates and service registers, the age of the sample ranged from 18 to 51 years. Majority of the sample (52 per cent) belonged to an age group of 31-40 years. A 33 per cent of the sample were in the age group of 41-51 years. Around 41 per cent of the sample belonged to an age group of 21-30 years. Only 1 per cent of the sample were aged between 18-20 years.

Educational Status

The formal education received by the sample was recorded. The educational status of the sample ranged from 10th Class to

Degree level. Most of the Anganwadi workers (75 per cent) were educated upto 10th class. Around 19 per cent have had intermediate education and only 6 per cent of the sample were educated upto degree level.

Job Experience

The number of years of service put in as Anganwadi worker was considered as job experience. The experience at work situation always helps in learning and also contributes to knowledge. The job experience of the sample ranged from 1 to 15 years. Around 38 per cent of the sample had a job experience of 1-5 years. A 25 per cent of them were in service for 5-10 years. Around 37 per cent of the sample had a experience of 10-15 years.

Training Status

Anganwadi workers training encompasses knowledge and skills related to child development, childcare, Early childhood Education etc., which may have an influence on the child rights knowledge, attitude and practices of Anganwadi workers. Hence training status was also included in the study. The training status of the sample that is untrained, trained and refresher trained were recorded, which showed that 32 per cent of the sample were untrained, 68 per cent of the sample were trained. Around 40 per cent of the sample underwent a training and a refresher course also. This shows that a good percentage of the sample were untrained, due to which their performance as Anganwadi workers may not conform to the expected standards.

Marital Status

The marital status of the sample was also included in the study as a variable. The data on marital status showed that 13 per cent of the sample were unmarried, 72 per cent of the sample were married and 15 per cent of the subjects were widowed/separated. This shows that a major per cent of the sample were married followed by widowed/separated and unmarried.

Child Rights Knowledge of Anganwadi Workers

Knowledge is the information/content known to an individual on a given topic. Knowledge helps in understanding day to day experiences in life and taking appropriate decisions at the right time. Information on child Rights may be known from various sources such as mass media (print and electronic), peer group, family members, work situation, schools/academic institutions. Individual's knowledge on Child Rights may vary depending one's exposure on various sources information.

In the present study the Anganwadi workers knowledge on Child Rights was assessed with the help of a scale developed. Each respondent's knowledge score was calculated, the lowest score was 25 and the highest was 26. The mean score of Child Rights knowledge was 25.89 and the standard deviation was 0.31.

Child Rights Knowledge and the Age of the Sample

The sample was distributed according to their age into two groups i.e., 18-30 years and 31-51 years. The mean knowledge scores of these two age groups were 25.80 and 25.90 respectively. The standard deviation values of these two age groups' knowledge scores were 0.63 and 0.60 respectively, which shows that both the age groups of Anganwadi workers did not vary in their knowledge on Child Rights irrespective of their age.

Table 7.1

Child Rights Knowledge Scores and the Age of the Sample

S. No.	*Age of the Anganwadi workers (years)*	*Mean Child Rights knowledge scores*	*SD*	*Z values*		*Significant Difference at 5% level*
				Zo value	*Ze value*	
1.	18-30	25.80	0.63	0.45	1.96	@
2.	31-51	25.90	0.60			

Note: @ No significant difference at 5% level.

The Zo values (0.45) further confirm that there is no significant difference between the two age groups with regard to their child Rights knowledge as the calculated value is much lower than the table value (Ze=1.96).

Child Rights Knowledge and the Educational Status of the Sample

The sample was classified into two groups as per their formal educational level, that is upto 10th class and Intermediate to degree level. The mean knowledge scores of these two groups were 25.89 and 25.88 respectively. The standard deviation values of these two groups were 0.44 and 0.77 respectively, which indicates that the two groups of the sample did not vary much in their Child Rights knowledge irrespective of their levels of education.

Table 7.2

Child Rights Knowledge and Educational Status of the Sample

S. No.	*Educational status of the sample*	*Child Rights knowledge scores*	*SD*	*Z values*		*Significant Difference at 5% level*
				Zo value	*Ze value*	
1.	Upto 10th class	25.89	0.44	0.055	1.96	@
2.	Intermediate to Degree level	25.88	0.77			

Note: @ No significant difference at 5% level.

The Zo values was 0.055 which is much lower than the calculated value (Ze=1.96) which indicates that statistically there is no significant difference between the two groups with regard to Child Rights knowledge.

The Child Rights Knowledge and the Job Experience of the Sample

The number of years of service put in by the Anganwadi workers was taken as the job experience of the sample. The sample was classified into two groups based on their date of joining and total number of years of service as shown in Table 7.3.

Table 7.3
Child Rights Knowledge and the Job Experience of the Sample

S. No.	*Date of joining*	*Years of service*	*Mean child rights knowledge score*	*SD*	*Z values*		*Significant difference at 5% level*
					Zo value	*Ze value*	
1.	1984-'90	15	25.9	0.66	0.450	1.96	@
2.	1991-'99	10	25.8	2.23			

Note: @ No significant difference at 5% level.

The mean knowledge scores of the two groups were 25.9 and 25.8 respectively. The standard deviation values of the two groups of the sample were 0.66 and 2.23 respectively. These values show that the two groups did not vary much in their child Rights knowledge.

The Z values Zo = 0.450, Ze 1.96 further confirm that the two groups of the sample did not differ significantly in their Child Rights knowledge irrespective of their job experience.

Attitude of the Anganwadi Workers Towards Child Rights

Attitudes are formed over a period of time. The individuals past experience, knowledge, culture values, norms present in the family and society influences the attitudes of the individuals. Attitudes of individuals affects the acceptance of a knowledge and its practice. Hence it is important to study the attitudes of sample towards child rights.

The attitudes of Anganwadi workers was assessed. The samples' scores for attitudes ranged from 29 (highest) to 20 (lowest). The mean attitudinal score was 25.36 and the standard deviation was 2.03. The sample varied in their attitude towards Child Rights, though not significantly.

Age of the Sample and Attitudes Towards Child Rights

The mean attitudinal scores of Anganwadi workers of 18-30 years age group was 25.26 and 31-51 years age group was

25.37. The standard deviation value of Anganwadi teachers of 18-30 years age group was 1.35 and 31-51 years age group was 2.06. These values indicate that the Anganwadi workers of 18-30 years age group did not vary much in their attitudinal scores. The Anganwadi workers of 31-51 years age group varied in their attitudinal scores.

Table 7.4

Age of the Sample and Attitudes towards Child Rights

S. No.	*Age of the Anganwadi workers (years)*	*Mean Child Rights attitude scores*	*SD value*	*Z values*		*Significant difference at 5% level*
				Zo value	*Ze value*	
1.	18-30	25.26	1.35	0.33	1.96	@
2.	31-51	25.37	2.06			

Note: @ No significant difference at 5% level.

The Z values calculated (Zo = 0.33) was less than the table value (Ze-1.96) at 5 per cent level which indicates that there is no significant difference between the two age groups with regard to their Child Rights knowledge.

Educational Status and Attitudes Towards Child Rights

The sample was divided into two groups based on their educational status, as those who have studied upto 10th class and those who had intermediate to degree education. The mean attitudinal scores of these two groups were 25.17 and 25.85 respectively. The standard deviation values of the two groups were 2.06 and 2.01 respectively. These values indicate that the two groups deviated mildly in their attitudinal scores.

The Zo value (2.194) is greater than the table value Ze=1.96) at 5 per cent level of significance. This shows that the two groups of Anganwadi workers (based on their education) differed significantly in their attitudes towards Child Rights.

Table 7.5

Educational Status and Attitudes towards Child Rights

S. No.	*Educational status of the sample*	*Child Rights Attitude mean scores*	*SD*	*Z values*		*Significant Difference at 5% level*
				Zo value	*Ze value*	
1.	Upto 10th class	25.17	2.06	2.194	1.96	*
2.	Intermediate to Degree level	25.85	2.01			

Note: * Indicates significant difference at 5% level.

Job Experience of Anganwadi Workers and their Attitudes Towards Child Rights

Based on the job experience, the Anganwadi workers were divided into two groups i.e. those with 15 years and those with 10 years of service, their mean attitudinal scores were 23.83 and 25.45 respectively. The standard deviation values of these two groups were 8.35 and 2.0 respectively. This shows that the sample with less than 10 years of job experience varied in their attitudinal scores.

Table 7.6

Job Experience of Anganwadi Workers and Their Attitudes Toward Child Rights

S. No.	*Date of joining*	*No. of years of service*	*Mean child rights attitude score*	*SD*	*Z values*		*Significant difference at 5% level*
					Zo value	*Ze value*	
1.	1984-'90	15	23.83	8.35	3.84	1.96	*
2.	1991-'99	10	25.45	2.0			

Note: * Indicate significant difference at 5% level.

The Zo value (3.84) is greater than the table value (Ze = 1.96) at 5 per cent level of significance, which indicates that there is a significant difference between the two groups with regard to their attitudes towards child rights.

Practice of Child Rights by the Anganwadi Workers

Practice means application of knowledge in day to day life/ work. Practice of knowledge is the ultimate objective of learning. Practice helps in sustenance of knowledge and skills that are learnt. The practice of child rights by the Anganwadi workers was assessed using a scale developed for this purpose. The mean scores of Anganwadi workers for practice of Child Rights is 36, the lowest score was 32 and the highest score was 41.

Child Rights Practice by Anganwadi Workers and Their Age

The Child Rights practice of Anganwadi workers of different age groups was assessed and the mean scores of two groups were 38.0 and 36.83 respectively. The standard deviation values of the two groups were 1.74 and 2.15 respectively, which shows that the second age group (31-51 years) varied in their Child Rights practice score than the first age group (18-30 years).

Table 7.7

Child Rights practice by Anganwadi workers and their age

S. No.	*Age of the Anganwadi workers (years)*	*Mean Child Rights practice score*	*SD Value*	*Z values*		*Significant Difference at 5% level*
				Zo value	*Ze value*	
1.	18-30	38	1.74	3.128	1.96	*
2.	31-51	36.83	2.15			

Note. * Indicates significant difference at 5% level.

The Zo value was 3.128 which is greater than the table value (Ze=1.96) at 5 per cent level of significance, which indicates that the two age groups differed in their practice of child rights significantly.

Educational Status and the Practice of Child Rights by the Anganwadi Workers

The mean Child Rights practice scores of the two educational status groups were 37.04 and 36.92 respectively. The standard deviation values of these two groups were 1.625 and 2.0 respectively which implies that the second group varied to the first group.

Table 7.8

Educational status and the practice of Child Rights by the Anganwadi workers

S. No.	*Educational status of the sample*	*Child Rights Practice mean scores*	*SD*	*Z values*		*Significant Difference at 5% level*
				Zo value	*Ze value*	
1.	Upto 10th class	37.04	1.625	0.39	1.96	@
2.	Intermediate to Degree level	36.92	2.0			

Note: @ Indicates no significant difference at 5% level.

The Zo value was 0.39 which is much less than the table value Ze=1.96, at 5 per cent level of significance. This means that there is no significant difference between the two groups with regard to their child rights practice.

The Job Experience of Anganwadi Workers and the Child Rights Practice

The mean child rights practice scores of Anganwadi workers of two service groups were 36.67 and 37.26 respectively. The standard deviation values of these two groups were 2.09 and 3.0 respectively.

Table 7.9

The Job Experience of Anganwadi workers and the Child Rights Practice

S. No.	*Year of joining*	*No. of years of service*	*Mean child rights practice*	*SD Value*	*Zo Value*	*Ze Value*	*Significant Difference at 5% level*
1.	1984-1990	15	36.67	2.09	1.88	1.96	@
2.	1991-1999	10	37.26	3.085			

Note: @ Indicates no significant difference at 5% level.

The Zo value was 1.88, which is less than the table value (Ze = 1.96) at 5 per cent level of significance. This indicates that the Anganwadi workers did not differ significantly in their Child Rights practice as per their job experience.

Association of Child Rights Knowledge with the Independent Variables of Anganwadi Workers

Using χ^2 test, the association between the Child Rights knowledge and the job experience of Anganwadi workers was studied. The association between the other independent variables viz. age, educational status could not be studied as their expected frequency was less than five.

The calculated χ^2 values ($\chi^2_o = 0.21$) is less than the table value ($\chi^2_e = 3.84$) which indicates that there is no association between the job experience and Child Rights knowledge. This may be because the sample may not have studied about the topic Child Rights either in the school or in their training programmes.

Association of Child Rights Attitude with the Independent Variables

The relationship between the independent variables viz., Age, educational status and job experience of the sample and their Child Rights attitudes was assessed using χ^2 test.

Table 7.10

Association of Child Rights Attitudes with the Independent Variables

S. No.	*Independent variables*	*χ^2 Calculated values*	*χ^2 table value level*	*Significance*
1.	Age	0.07	3.86	@
2.	Educational Status	0.07	3.86	@
3.	Job experience	8.33	3.86	*

Note: @ Indicates no significant association at 5 per cent level.

* Indicates significant association at 5% level.

From the above table it is clear that there is no association between the Child Rights attitudes of Anganwadi workers and their age and educational status, but association was found between the job experience and Child Rights attitudes, though the Anganwadi workers' knowledge was not found to be associated with their job experience. This reflects that they had a positive attitude towards Child Rights. This may be due to their work association with Children.

Association of Child Rights Practice with the Independent Variables

Practice is application of skills. The behaviour and acts of an Anganwadi worker in her work situation reflects her practice of Child Rights. One may possess knowledge and favourable attitude towards Children and their Rights, but in practice they may not act so. The practice of Child Rights may be associated with other factors such as age, educational status, job experience, which was studied using a level χ^2 test.

From the Table 7.11 it is evident that the age and job experience found to have an association with the practice of Child Rights by the sample. The educational status was found to be not associated with the practice of child rights. The results when compared with the Table 7.1 show that though age was not associated with the attitudes, it is found to be associated with the practice. This implies that the age of the Anganwadi worker had influence on the practice.

Table 7.11
Association of Child Rights practice with Independent Variables

S. No.	*Independent variables*	*χ^2 Calculated values*	*χ^2 table value*	*Significance*
1.	Age	6.33	3.86	*
2.	Educational Status	1.28	3.86	@
3.	Job experience	5.09	3.86	*

Note: @ Indicates no significant association at 5 per cent level.

* Indicates significant association at 5% level.

Conclusion

The present study allows to conclude that the Anganwadi workers training programme did not cover child rights component. Inspite of it, the Anganwadi workers knowledge on child rights was fairly good and they also possessed positive attitude towards child rights. The child rights practice by the Anganwadi workers is not adequate. The independent variable: job experience found to have an association with the child rights attitudes and practice but not with child rights knowledge which implies that working with children might have contributed to their positive disposition towards child rights. The study further affirms that there is a great need to educate the Anganwadi workers on child rights by including this topic in their training programmes. For such inclusion it is necessary to assess their child rights knowledge, attitudes and practices in order to make the educational programme a need based one.

REFERENCES

1 Grant, J.P., 1989: *The State of the World's Children*; Oxford University Press Published, New Delhi.

2. Laxmi Devi, 1998: *Policies and Programmes Related to Child Development*; Anmol Publicataions Pvt. Ltd., New Delhi, pp. 384-386.

3. Laxmi Devi, 1998: *Encyclopaedia of Child and Family Welfare, Health, Nutrition and Early Childhood Education*; Vol. 2, Anmol Publications, New Delhi, p. 354.

4. Nayana Tara Usha Ram Kumar, S., 1988: *Integrated Child Development Services—An Evaluation*; Ashish Publishing House, New Delhi, pp. 2-3.

5. Varma, S.K., 1998: *Rights of the Child*; Journal of the Indian Law Institute, Vol. 41(1).

8

Child Rights Education to the Mothers of Children Attending ICDS Programme

—**Ms. K. Mithila Jyothsna** and **Prof. D. Sarada**

Introduction

The Child Rights declared by the United Nations was signed by India and many of the rights contained in the convention draft is already included in the Indian Constitution, well before the declaration of "The Rights of the Child". Though Twelve Fundamental Rights which are enforceable and Six Directive Principles provide Child Rights to children of Indian subcontinent.

Inspite of provision of Rights in Indian Constitution and implementation of welfare programmes reflecting many of these Rights could not satisfy the needs of a major percentage of children on a regular basis in India. The awareness of these Rights by all sections of population in India is said to be low.

As 1995-2004 is declared as "The Decade for Human Rights Education by United Nations", a need was felt to assess the knowledge of mothers of children attending the largest child welfare programme 'ICDS', and impart Child Rights Education to a sample of mothers of children attending ICDS programme.

The ICDS should also undertake a Nation wide programme to assess the Child Rights knowledge of mothers, field level functionaries and children themselves and it should undertake Child Rights Education Programme to its personnel and beneficiaries.

The Government of India has launched several welfare programmes for women and children after the independence. All these programmes are extended to provide basic needs to children irrespective of their religion, caste, creed and race. Majority of these programmes have failed to reach the needy groups. The ICDS a nationwide programme launched in 1975 on October 2nd, has made an appreciable impact on Mothers and children attending the programme. It is meant for the welfare, growth the development of children and their mothers. The programme objectives and package of services covers a part of Child Rights and needs. Efforts are being made to strengthen this nationwide programme through building the capabilities of the trainers in training the mothers in the care of the children. Such a programme should adopt Child Rights component in the training programmes.

In this context and background the investigator made an attempt to assess the knowledge of mothers of children attending Anganwadi Centers (of ICDS programme) and impart Child Rights education to the Mothers and assess their impact through the present study entitled "Child Rights Education to the Mothers of Children attending ICDS programme".

Methodology

The study entitled "Child Rights Education to the Mothers of Children Attending ICDS Programme" was conducted in Tirupati Urban Mandal of Chittoor district (Andhra Pradesh). From the 50 Anganwadi centres of RASS located in the urban mandal. 12 Anganwadi centres were selected from four corners of the Urban mandals i.e. 3 centres from each area East, West, North and South.

The twelve (12) Anganwadi centres selected for the study was visited personally. From the list of children attending

Anganwadi programme ten(10) children were selected from each Anganwadi, thus the sample comprised of 120 children attending Anganwadi programme in 12 centres. The residence address of each child was noted from the records of the Anganwadi centre and the investigator visited all the 120 houses and met the mothers of children and got their willingness to respond to the present study.

The fulfillment Child Rights is associated with the following independent and dependent variables: Age of the Mother, Educational Status, Family Literacy Index (FLI), Occupation, Place of Residence, Family Income, Family Type, Family Size, Knowledge of Child Rights, Attitudes towards Child Rights, Practice of Child Rights.

The following tools were used to measure the variables selected. General information schedule, Child Rights knowledge scale, Child Rights attitudes scale and Child Rights practise scale.

Results and Discussion

The results of the study entitled "Child Rights Education to the Mothers of Children Attending ICDS Programme" are discussed under the following heads:

(a) General profile of the sample;

(b) Knowledge regarding the Child Rights;

(c) Attitude towards the Child Rights;

(d) Practice of Child Rights by the mothers.

The personal and Demographic variables which may have an influence on the knowledge, attitudes and practice of Child Rights were included in the study. The information was gathered on these variables and presented.

The data for the present study was collected by administering the Scales and Schedules (4) developed, on the selected sample. Though the schedules were developed in the local language also, the statements in the scales and schedule were read out to the respondents by the investigator and the responses were recorded. As majority of the respondents are illiterates and ignorant of the topic under study, the scales and schedule was filled in by the respondent by using interview method. The tabulated data was analysed employing the relevant Statistical Techniques such as Percentages, Mean, Standard Deviation, χ^2-Test and F-Test.

The major findings of the study were as follows:

1. That the majority of the sample belonged to an age group of 20-25 years, followed by 35 per cent of mothers belonging to 25-30 years of age group. The lowest percentage (14 per cent) of mothers belonged to 30-35 years of age group;

2. The majority (43 per cent) were illiterates, a 34 per cent of the sample had primary education, a 19 per cent were educated upto secondary school; only 4 per cent were graduates. This shows that the mothers varied quite widely in their educational status;

3. None of the sample belonged to suburban and rural areas. Only 17 per cent belonged to urban area and majority of the sample (83 per cent) belonged to slum area. This may be due to their low economic status and accessibility to Anganwadi Centres which are located usually in slum areas;

4. 70 per cent of mothers were daily wage earners, followed by 17 per cent of business women, 8 per cent of private employed and 5 per cent of government employed. This shows that a major section of the sample are working in unorganised sector, where there is no guarantee of employment and uniform wages;

5. A good percentage (48 per cent) had an annual income of less than 12,000 rupees, which is less than the poverty line. Around 23 per cent of the sample had income between 12,001-18,000 rupees. A 17 per cent of the sample had 18,001-24,000 rupees as their annual income. Only 12 per cent had an income above 24,000 rupees;

6. A major percentage of the sample had bigger family sizes of 4-8 members. Only a 12 per cent of the sample had family sizes less than 4 members, and 5 per cent of the sample had family size of above 8 members;

7. A major percentage of the sample (95 per cent) belonged to nuclear families. Only 5 per cent of the sample had joint families. None belonged to extended family. The type of family determines the autonomy and freedom available for decision making and also the assistance available for the care of children;

8. A major percentage of the sample (84 per cent) had 2-4 children, a 15 per cent of sample had less than 2 children and only 1 per cent had more than 4 children, which shows that a major per cent of the sample had more children in their families;

9. Majority of the sample (58 per cent) possessed a Ration Card Surprisingly; around 42 per cent of the sample did not have ration card. Among the ration cardholders 66 per cent had white-ration card, 23 per cent had yellow-ration card, a 11 per cent had pink-ration card.

10. The data on annual income of the sample did not comply with the date on the colour of the Ration card. This may be due to the discrepancies in the issue of Ration card.

Ration Card for Civil Supplies

The Government of Andhra Pradesh like other State Governments provides basic food materials such as rice, dhal, oil, sugar at subsidized rates to the poor. The poor are identified and given a ration card which makes them entitled to receive the provisions at subsidised rates in the local outlets (shops). This is meant to ensure minimum nutrition to the poor who otherwise cannot purchase food, which affects their family's nutritional status. Provision of food, health and nutrition are the responsibilities of state as per Human Rights declared by the United Nations. Hence, the investigator included the availability of ration card and its colour of the selected sample as a variable in the present study.

Fig. 8.1

Distribution of sample according to their ration card colour and availability

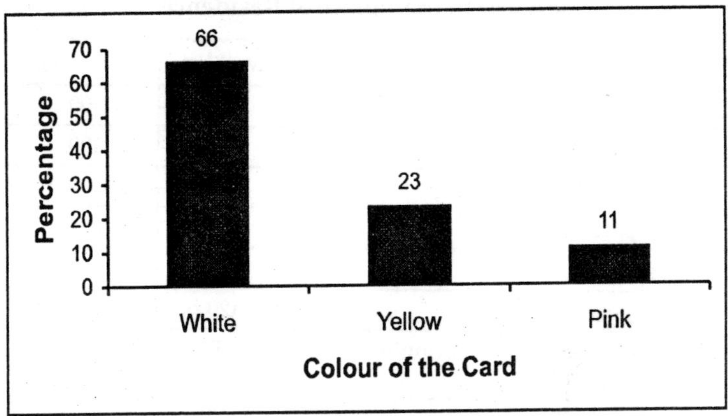

From the above figure, it is clear that majority of the sample (58 per cent) possessed a Ration card. Surprisingly, around 42 per cent of the sample did not have ration card. Among the ration card holders 66 per cent had white-ration card; 23 per cent had yellow-ration card, a 11 per cent had pink-ration card. The white card holders were the poor having less than 12,000 rupees as Annual income. The yellow card holders are the low-middle income group. The pink card holders are middle and high income group.

The data on Annual income of the sample did not comply with the data on the colour of the ration card. This may be due to the discrepancies in the issue of ration card.

Availability of Public Services

The public services are meant for the welfare and development of the families living in a particular area. These are provide by the state through its local governments. The services in the area of health, nutrition, sanitation, education, utilises law and order were included in the Human Rights. The Human Rights are also Child Rights. Hence, availability and accessibility of these services were studied. (see Table 8.1).

Table 8.1

Distribution of the sample according to the availability of services in their place of Residence

Services available	*Number*	*Percentage*
Government Hospital	120	100
Anganwadi services	120	100
Municipal water availability	120	100
Municipal services	81	68
Civil supplies	76	63
Primary school education	120	100
Non-formal education/continuing education centre	Nil	–
Electricity facility	102	85
Law and order (Utilising constitutional legal provision)	25	21

It shows that the health, Anaganwadi, Municipal water and School facilities were available to all the sample. The public sanitation (Municipal Services) and Civil supplies were available to 68 per cent and 63 per cent respectively. The electricity facility was available to 85 per cent and only 21 per cent have stated that they had accessibility to law and order services. None of the sample had access to non-formal and continuing educational facility.

Participation of mothers in ICDS programmes

The ICDS Programme is advocating participatory approach for all its activities. Participation of Mothers in ICDS programmes commits them to its achieves and utilisation of ICDS services will be improved. The package of services delivered through ICDS Programme are meant to fulfill the Rights of the child in the area of Health, Nutrition, Education and General Development. If these services are not availed by the children due to lack of participation of their mothers then, their Rights are not fulfilled. In this context the participation of Mothers in the ICDS Programme was assessed with the help of a schedule developed for the study.

Visit to Anganwadi

The frequency of Mothers visit to the Anganwadi was collected which showed that almost all the mothers visited Anganwadi every week and the frequency of their visit (from Table 8.2) indicate that it ranged from 1 to 8 times a week. Visits to Anganwadi facilitates rapport building between the mothers and the Anganwadi workers.

Table 8.2

Visit to Anganwadi in a week

Participation in a week	*Sample Number*	*Percentage*
1	1	1
2	3	3
3	46	38
4	21	17
5	22	18
6	6	5
7	2	2
8	17	14
More than eight	2	2

Participation in Anganwadi Programmes

It was found that around 66 per cent of mothers participated in the programmes organised by the Anganwadi Centre. Only 34 per cent did not participate in these programmes.

The reasons for non-participation was gathered which include: lack of knowledge (22 per cent), lack of time (32 per cent) and lack of interest of family members (46 per cent).

The frequency of participation in the Anganwadi Programmes by the Mothers during the previous year was recorded which indicated that 50 per cent have participated 2-4 times, around 24 per cent have participated more than 4 times, 16 per cent have participated only 1-2 times. This shows that though the Mothers visit the Anganwadi centre every week, their participation in the Anganwadi Programmes was moderate.

Type of Participation in the ICDS Programme

In order to know the quality and involvement of Mothers in the ICDS Programme the data on type of participation was gathered, which showed that 56 per cent of the sample played the role of an audience, 35 per cent were actively involved in the conduct of the programme, only 9 per cent extended help for the conduct of the Programme. None of the sample played a role in every stage of the programme.

The opinion of the sample regarding their participation in the ICDS programmes was collected. Around 70 per cent stated that their participation is satisfactory. A 7 per cent of the sample felt that they should have put in more effort, around 10 per cent stated that they liked to participate many times and 13 per cent stated that they are not satisfied with their participation.

Whether the participants benefited from the participation was recorded which indicates that a 91 per cent of the sample learnt more facts regarding child rearing practices, a 6 per cent developed awareness on nutritional needs of children and only 3 per cent became more confident through their participation in the ICDS programmes.

Performance of the Anganwadi Worker

The Anganwadi workers performance is crucial to utilisation of Anganwadi services. The Mothers opinion on Anganwadi workers performance was gathered, which showed that 17 per cent of Mothers opined that Anganwadi workers are skilled in everything, 44 per cent perceived the Anganwadi workers as being skilled in some works, a 30 per cent felt that the Anganwadi workers are not skilled and a 9 per cent opined that they have to improve their skills as Anganwadi workers.

Role of Anganwadi in Educating the People About its Services

The Anganwadi staff include a worker and an ayah. It is their responsibility to publicise about the Anganwadi centre services. In may places only few of the ICDS services such as early childhood Education, immunisation and feeding are known to people. The other services related to long term goals such as mother's education, referral services etc, are not being extended in many Anganwadi centres. If these services are made known to the public a demand for these services may come from them.

The samples responses were as follows: A 50 per cent felt that its role is nominal. 1 per cent felt it is known to few people, around 42 per cent felt that the Anganwadi should conduct public meeting to explain all about its services which indicates that there is a need to publicise Anganwadi services. Though the ICDS Programme is in existence from 1975, its services in total are not known to many of the young mothers and are also not explained to the public by the Anganwadi workers.

The Quality of Physical Facilities at the Anganwadi Centre

The Anganwadi centres due to paucity of funds could not be located in good buildings with safety and sanitary conditions. This is very much so in urban slums. The data on this aspect was gathered and presented in Table 8.3.

Table 8.3

Distribution of the sample according to their perception of physical facilities at Anganwadi Centre

S. No.	*Facilities Provided*	*Yes*		*No*	
		Number	*Percentage*	*Number*	*Percentage*
1.	Accessibility to Anganwadi centre	68	57	52	43
2.	Building provided for Anganwadi centre	–	–	120	100
3.	Cleanliness in Anganwadi centre	21	18	99	82
4.	Protection in Anganwadi centre	112	93	8	7
5.	Anganwadi has water facility	73	61	47	39
6.	Toilet facility in Anganwadi centre	17	14	103	86

From the table it is evident that a major percentage felt that the Anganwadi centre is accessible to children and 43 per cent felt it is difficult to access. Almost all the respondents perceived the building housing the Anganwadi centre is poor and not suitable. The cleanliness around Anganwadi centre was perceived to be very poor by 82 per cent of the sample and 18 per cent felt it is good. The protection in Anganwadi centre that is safety was rated as good by 93 per cent of the mothers. The water facility availability in the Anganwadi centres was rated as good by 61 per cent and rated as poor by 39 per cent. Regarding the toilet facilities 86 per cent of the sample stated that there is no toilet facility for children and a 14 per cent stated that there is toilet facility for children.

The above data reflects that physical facilities at the Anganwadi centre are poor and does not fulfill the child Rights.

Participation in the ICDS Programmes and the Independent Variables

The comparison of the variability between the various groups with an independent variable was studied using F-Test. There are a variety of analyses of variance. The most frequently used are the one-way analysis of variance and the two-way analysis of variable. One-way (or one factor) analysis of variance is done with one dependent and one independent variable.

The independent variables such as Age, Educational status and Annual family income of the sample was compared with the levels of participation in the ICDS programme (as shown in Table 8.4).

From the Table 8.4, it is clear that the three age groups of mothers differed significantly at 2 per cent level in their participation. Similarly the mothers belonging to four income groups also showed variation in their participation in the ICDS programme at 3 per cent level of significance. In contrary to the above two independent variables, the mothers belonging to six educational groups showed no difference in their participation at 3 per cent level of significance. This may be because age and family income may have influence on their participation in the ICDS programme.

Table 8.4

Distribution of street boys according to their levels of hygiene

S. No.	*Independent Variables*	*F value*	*F Table value*	*Significance level*
1.	Age of mothers	3.8221	3.07	* (2% level)
2.	Education of mother	.3007	2.68	@ (3%)
3.	Income of the family	3.2104	2.68	* (37%)

Association of Independent Variables with the Levels of Participation of Mothers in the ICDS Programme

In order to know the relationship between the independent variables such as age, educational status and annual income and the participation of mothers in ICDS programme a χ^2-test was conducted. The results are given in Table 8.5.

Table 8.5

Association of independent variables with the levels of participation of Mothers in the ICDS programme

S. No.	*Independent Variables*	*χ^2 value*	*χ^2 table value*	*Significance level*
1.	Age of the mother	3.1916	5.991	* (2%)
2.	Education of the mother	3.7779	7.815	@ (3%)
3.	Income of the family	6.1984	7.815	@ (3%)

The χ^2-values indicate that there is association between the age of the sample and their participation. No association was found between the educational status, annual income of the sample and their participation. Though the F-test results showed that the sample varied among themselves in their levels of participation as per their annual income the χ^2-test results did not comply with this finding.

Child Rights Knowledge of Mothers and the Independent Variables

The variation among the different groups of sample with their Child Rights knowledge was studied using F-test (See Table 8.6).

Table 8.6

Child Rights knowledge of mothers and the independent variables

S. No.	*Independent variables*	*F value*	*F Table value*	*Significance level*
1.	Age of the mothers	2.0329	3.07	@ (2%)
2.	Education of mothers	0.8689	2.68	@ (3%)
3.	Income of the family	2.1599	2.68	@ (3%)

From the above Table it is evident that the mothers of different age groups, education groups, income groups did not differ significantly in their Child Rights knowledge. This may be because the topic Child Rights is of recent origin.

Association of Child Rights Knowledge of Mothers with the Independent Variables

The independent variables relationship with that of Child Rights knowledge of Mothers were studied with the help of χ^2-Test (Table 8.7).

Table 8.7

Association of Child Rights knowledge of Mothers with the independent variables

S. No.	*Independent Variables*	χ^2 *value*	χ^2 *table value*	*Significance level*
1.	Age of the mother	3.1916	5.991	* (2%)
2.	Education of the mother	3.7779	7.815	@ (3%)
3.	Income of the family	6.1984	7.815	@ (3%)

From the above table it is evident that the sample showed no association between the Child Rights knowledge and the independent variables such as age, educational status and annual income. This complies F-test results.

Child Rights Attitudes and the Independent Variables

The difference among the different groups of sample in their Child Rights Attitudes was studied using F-Test (Table 8.8).

Table 8.8

Child Rights Attitudes and the Independent Variables

S. No.	*Independent variables*	*F value*	*F Table value*	*Significance level*
1.	Age of the mothers	0.2450	3.07	@ (2%)
2.	Education of mothers	1.0981	2.68	@ (3%)
3.	Income of the family	3.0543	2.68	* (3%)

The results indicate that the mothers of three age groups, and six educational groups did not differ in their attitudes towards Child Rights significantly at 2 per cent and 3 per cent levels respectively, in contrary, the mothers belonging to four income groups. The attitudes are the opinions of the mothers developed over a period of time depending on their past experiences. Many times it was though that knowledge changes attitudes. In the present study though there was no difference between the knowledge of the sample and different income groups, a difference was found between different income groups and their Child Rights attitudes.

Association of Child Rights Attitudes with Independent Variables

The attitudes are formed and changed with age, experience, education in exposure, income and several other factors. In the present study the association between age, educational status and family income with the Child Rights Attitudes of the mothers was studied which is given in Table 8.9.

From the Table 8.9 it is clear that there is no association formed between Child Rights Attitudes and the age and educational status of the sample. An association was found between the family income and the Child Rights attitudes, which may be due to reasons.

Table 8.9

Association of Child Rights Attitudes with the Independent Variables

S. No.	*Independent Variables*	χ^2 *value*	χ^2 *table value*	*Significance level*
1.	Age of the mothers	8.509	5.991	@ (2%)
2.	Educational status	1.5452	7.815	@ (3%)
3.	Income of the family	10.2136	7.815	* (3%)

Practice of Child Rights by Mothers of Children Attending ICDS Programme

The practice of Child Rights by mothers in four areas such as Health and Nutrition, Education, Psycho-social and Recreation. Family was studied for normal children. Another area was added to know Child Rights Practices in the case of Handicapped Children.

Rights Related to Health and Nutritional Needs

Health and Nutrition of children is still continued to be the important responsibility of mothers especially in India. The awareness, attitudes and practice of health and nutrition related activities by mothers has a direct bearing on the health and nutritional status of children. Hence, these components were assessed in the Present Study.

The data revealed that 92 per cent of mothers were aware of school health clinic services, only 8 per cent of mothers did not know about school health clinic services. Around 87 per cent of mothers utilised the school health clinic services, whereas 13 per cent of mothers did not avail these services. The reason for non-availing these services were lack of time, the place of their residence is far away from the urban school health clinic.

The Primary Health Centres (PHC) were known to 84 per cent of the sample and is not known to 16 per cent of the sample. Around 60 per cent of the sample were utilising the PHC services and 40 per cent were not utilising these services. The reasons for non-utilisation of PHC services were location of PHC (Very far from the place of residence, lack of medicines, time taking process at the PHC and lack of time).

The responses of the sample to a question "Incase of ill-health of your child do you"? was as given in Table 8.10.

Table 8.10

Distribution of the sample according to the type of treatment given

S. No.	*Type of treatment given*	*Number*	*Percentage*
1.	Seek medical attention	20	17
2.	Self medication	26	22
3.	Depend on medical stores person	54	45
4.	Use of folk medicines	20	16

From the above Table it is clear that 17 per cent of the mothers sought medical attention, 22 per cent depended on self medication, 45 per cent depended on medical stores and only 8 per cent of mothers used folk medicines. This shows that only a small percentage of mothers utilised the public health services.

Around 80 per cent of mothers were attending to their children's health and nutritional needs personally and only 20 per cent of mothers did not attend in person to their child's health and nutritional needs.

Around 58 per cent of mothers stated that they were aware of foods needed to their children whereas 42 per cent of mothers were not aware of the foods needed for their children.

Majority of mothers (64 per cent) stated that they are providing foods needed for the child. Only 36 per cent of mothers were unable to provide foods needed for the child though they are aware about them.

The sources which were helpful in training nutrition and health information by mothers were: Doctors (42 per cent),

Dietitian (0 per cent), Media (25 per cent), Anganwadi (33 per cent). This shows that major source of information was Doctors followed by Anganwadi and media.

Around 30 per cent of mothers kept track of their child's growth and 70 per cent of mothers did not keep track of their children's growth. Among those who kept track of their children's growth did so through: observation (39 per cent), periodical check-up (22 per cent), measuring height and weight (39 per cent). This shows that a good percentage of mothers followed up their children's growth in a fairly scientific manner.

Rights Related to Educational Needs

The ICDS Programme offers Early Childhood Education through its Anganwadi Centres. The Early Childhood Education prepares the child to the Primary school and is found to reduce the school dropout rate among rural and urban poor children.

Table 8.11

Rights related to Educational needs

S. No.	*Educational needs*	*Yes*		*No*	
		Number	*Percentage*	*Number*	*Percentage*
1.	Attends Anganwadi Centre regularly	58	48	62	52
2.	Attends Anganwadi Centre in time	34	28	86	72
3.	Child is allowed to practise whatever he learnt at Anganwadi centre	39	33	81	67
4.	Participation in Anganwadi Centre	35	29	85	71

The data (as shown in Table 8.11 reveals that around 48 per cent of children attend Anganwadi regularly and a 52 per cent of children do not attend regularly. Only 28 per cent of children reach Anganwadi centre on time whereas 72 per cent of children do not reach on time. Around 33 per cent of mothers allow their children to practise whatever they learnt at the Anganwadi centre and 67 per cent of mothers do not allow their children to practise whatever they have learnt. Around 29 per cent of mothers participated in programmes organised by Anganwadi centre and 71 per cent of mothers did not participate in any programme of the Anganwadi Centre. This shows that the participation of mothers in Anganwadi activities was low. The reasons for non-participation were family members did not allowed the mothers to participate (41 per cent) and lack of time (59 per cent).

Rights Related to Psychosocial and Recreational Needs

The psycho-social needs such as love, affection, recognition, reward etc. are known to improve child's self-concept and adjustment. The recreation such as play and other self-expressing games and activities help the children in bringing out their talents, emotions and improving themselves. Hence, these two types of needs (Psycho-social and Recreational) were included in the Child Rights.

The data on the time-spent with the Child by father and mother per day in hours was gathered which showed (Figure 8.2) that mothers spent more time than fathers. It is surprising to note that around 4 per cent of fathers and 8 per cent of mothers did not spend any time in a day with the child.

Figure 8.2

Time spent with the child by Mother and Father

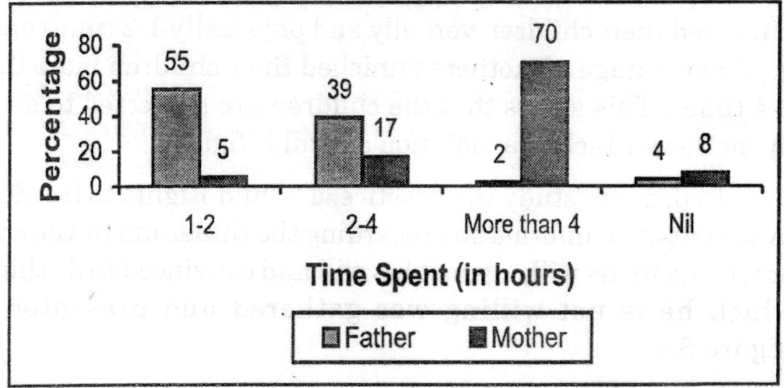

The number of times the child is taken outside to meet the friends and relatives in a week was gathered which showed that around 27 per cent of mothers took their children out 1-2 times, 10 per cent of mothers took their children 2-4 times, only 3 per cent of mothers took their children outside more than 4 times and a major percentage (60 per cent) did not take their children outside to meet friends and relatives.

The punishment given to the children verbally and physically was also studied (Figure 8.3).

Figure 8.3

Distribution of Mothers according to the frequency of punishment given to the children

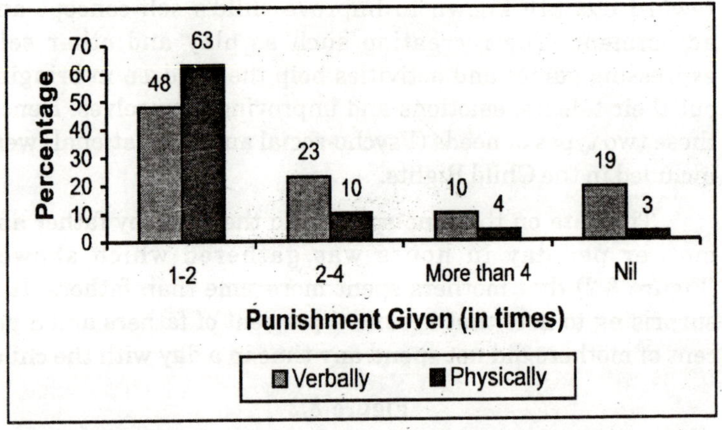

The data reveals that a major percentage of mothers punished their children verbally and physically 1-2 times and a good percentage of mothers punished their children more than 2-4 times. This shows that the children are subjected to abuse by mothers which is a violation of Child Right.

In order to study the practice of "Child Rights to freedom" by parents, the information regarding the things did by the child according to his will, against his will and convinced to do things which he is not willing was gathered and presented in Figure 8.4.

Figure 8.4

Practise of Child Rights to Freedom

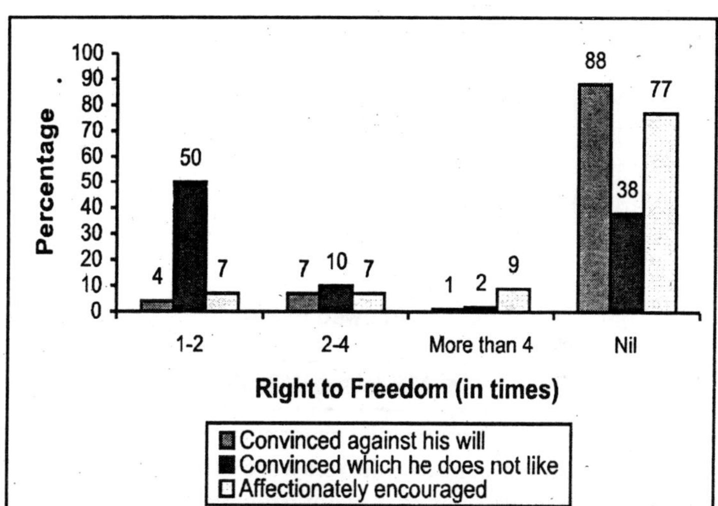

From the above figure, it is clear that a major percentage of mothers did not convince their children to do things against their will, around 38 per cent of mothers did not convince their children to do things which he did not like and 77 per cent of mothers did not affectionately encourage their children to do things which he usually does not like. A small percentage of parents convinced their children more than one time in a day to do things against their will and also encouraged affectionately to do things which the children usually does not like. A major percentage of mothers convinced their children to do things which they did not like. This shows that a major percentage of mothers made their children to do things against their will without convincing them about it.

Play is an important activity of childhood. It's significance in child development is thoroughly researched and conformed. The data on "Child's Right to Play" with friends and play materials was collected (Figure 8.5).

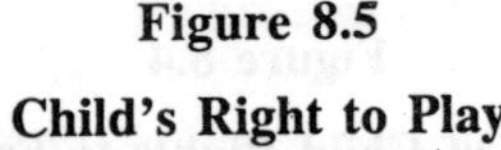

Figure 8.5
Child's Right to Play

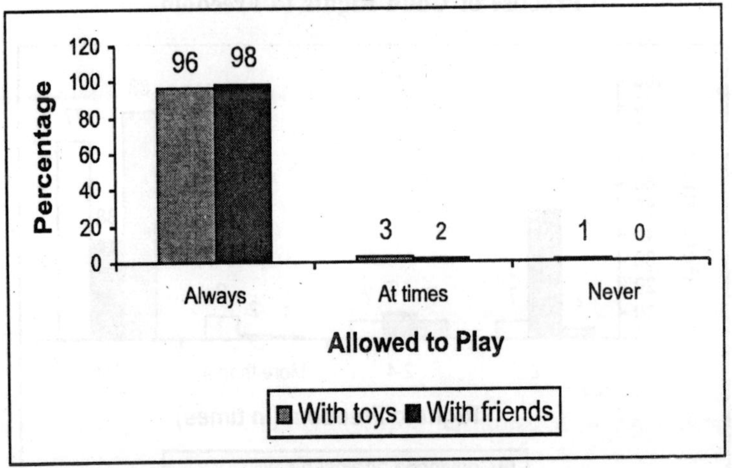

Around 96 per cent of children were allowed to play with friends always, only 3 per cent of children were allowed to play at times and only one per cent of children were never allowed to play. With regard to playing with toys around 98 per cent of mothers allowed their children to play with toys followed by 2 per cent of mothers who allowed their children to play at times with toys.

Almost All Mothers Gave Freedom to Their Children in Choosing Their Friends

With regard to freedom to express their views and self around 83 per cent of children were given freedom to express themselves always, 17 per cent of children were given freedom at times to express themselves.

The children's doubts need to be cleared to avoid confusion and also to gain insight into various natural phenomenon. Around 57 per cent of mothers cleared their children's doubts always and 43 per cent of mothers cleared their children's doubts at times.

The family is the first social institution in which the child receives his inputs for growth and development. Equilibrium in the family lays a good foundation for a sound individual. Hence, United Nations has included "Right to Family" as one of the Child Rights.

The data on the Child Rights related to familial needs is given in Table 8.12.

Table 8.12

Rights related to Familial needs

S. No.	*Familial needs*	*Number*	*Percentage*
1.	Recognised as a member of family	120	100
2.	Allowed to live with his biological parents	120	100
3.	Involved in almost all familial activities	120	100
4.	Scope to learn familial activities	120	100

From the table it is clear that almost all the children were recognised as a member of their family, allowed to live with their biological parents, involved in their familial activities and were given scope to learn familial activities.

The data further reveals that the children's familial needs are met satisfactorily.

Conclusion

The study allows to conclude that the ICDS programme is very much relevant to the needs of children and its total services are not well utilised by the beneficiaries. The reasons being lack of awareness regarding the services such as mothers education, referral services. The quality of physical facilities available in the Anganwadi centres were also found to be poor and makes it difficult for the Anganwadi worker to conduct a quality programme for the children. ICDS being the largest national programme encompassing Child Rights reach to be improved in terms of physical facilities and publicity. The participation of mothers was also found to be inadequate. The mothers knowledge on Child Rights needs to be improved. Though they possess a favourable attitude towards Child Rights, in practice especially with regard to punishment, healthcare and nourishment, they are not implemented. Unless Child Rights are practised, mere knowledge and attitudes are not of any value.

REFERENCES

Arvindrani Desai, N., (1990), "*Family and Child Welare*", Ashish Publishing House, New Delhi.

Barooah, P.P., (1992), "*Handbook on Child*" (*with historical background*), Concept Publishing Company, New Delhi.

Beulah Compton, R., (1980), "*Introduction to Social Welare & Social Work*", Dorsey Press, America.

Basotia, G.R., Sharma, K.K., (1999), "*Research Methodology*", Mangal Deep Publications, Jaipur, pp-125.

British National Corpus, (1998), "*LongMan Ddictionary of English*", New Edition, 3rd (ed.), LongMan Group Limited, England, pp. 25, 71, 441, 782, 1104, 977.

Carol Bellamy, UNICEF, (1997), "*The State of the World's Children*", Published by Oxford University Press, U.K., pp. 9-14.

Deogaohkar, S.G., (1980), "*Administration for Rural Development in India*", Concept Publishing Company, New Delhi.

Dolly Singh, (1995), "*Child Development – Issues, Policies and Programmes*", Volume'3, Kanishka Publishers & Distributors, Printed in India, Delhi, pp. 339-341.

Duvall, E.M. (1977), "*Marriage and Family Development*", J.B. Lippincott, Philadelphia.

Laxmi Devi, (1998), "*Policies and Programmes Related to Child Development*", Anmol Publications Private Limited, New Delhi, pp. 59-60.

Nayana Tara, S & Usha Ramkumar, (1998) "*Integrated Child Development Services – An Evaluation*", Ashish Publishing House, 8/81, Punjabi Bagh, New Delhi – 110000, pp. 2-4.

Tendon, R.K., (1999), "*Organising Childcare Services*", Rajat Publications, New Delhi, pp. 4-7.

9

Affect of Primary School Education Programme on Rural Primary School Children

—**Ms. K. Hymavathi** and **Prof. D. Sarada**

Introduction

Majority of the rural schools are located in main villages or on the outskirts, which are difficult to access especially when school is meant for a cluster of villages, in such cases there is a need for sub-centres in each habitation to impart at least primary education. That is when the school is located far away from the residential area or habitation. The working parents are unable to drop their children in schools personally and are afraid to send them alone. So the children stay at home without attending the school. The physical facilities available are inadequate in many rural schools. That is poor seating arrangement, crowded classrooms, poor ventilation, water and sanitation facilities. These make school less appealing to children.

The rural families in Andhra Pradesh and other backward states are facing the problems with regard to livelihood opportunities due to failure of crops, increased expenditure on agriculture poor returns from Agricultural produce, lack of employment opportunities locally. The families in rural areas are forced to migrate, migration is affecting children's education. As migrants the rural families are unable to support and take care of their children leave alone educating them.

Though the rural families are interested in educating their children, they are not able to afford it, for the reasons:

1. Location and inadequate facilities at school;
2. Parents not in a position to provide educational materials like books, pens and pencils;
3. Age old stringent disciplinary methods followed in schools;
4. The children's assistance at home and is required in absence of the adult members.

The rural primary schools through their location, facilities and methods of teaching and disçiplinary are dissuading the rural children from attending the school.

The teaching and disciplinary methods followed in schools focus more on children with above average intelligence. The academically backward and the less intelligent children are made to cope up through punishments and stringent disciplinary methods. These make the children keep away from school and dropout, these children are automatically placed in work adding to the existing child labour.

The Government's efforts to raise the income levels of rural families through sanction of loans for development works in turn are affecting the primary education programmes. That is the beneficiaries of such programmes are none other than the parents of school children. The parents due to heavy work, using their children in rearing sheep, goat, cattle and other works. Hence it is necessary to see that children should not be used for such works by parents. This component should be considered while sanctioning funds for Income Generation Programmes.

At this stage it is necessary to realise that education is for individuals development but not mere preparation for employment. This clarification implies, there is a need for more than one channel of primary education to suit the needs of intelligent, less intelligent that is fast learners and slow learners. If the objective of education is to make the children literate and more functional, then educational system needs to be changed to offer opportunities of education for all types of children that is able and children with learning difficulties.

Majority of slow learners tend to dropout from school, the parents have no other go except to send such children to work, keeping children idle at home, especially in absence of adult members is leading to problems like mingling with delinquents and anti-social elements living in the neighbourhood. The parents resort to sending school dropout to work in order to protect the child from bad elements.

Studies on street children reveal (Swarupoorani and Sarada, 2000) that academic stress is one of the major reasons for child streetism in Andhra Pradesh. This further endorses the need for alternative systems of primary school education.

The boost which the experience of the last ten years has given rise to the prospects for universal primary education lies not so much in new and cheaper techniques but in the growing realisation that education enhances the investments made in almost every other aspect of the development efforts. There is also an intangible human dimension to those benefits in a world where, increasingly, to be illiterate is to be excluded. If the enhancement of people's capacity to improve their own lives is the main aim and measure of development, then nothing could contribute more directly to its achievement than education and literacy.

The value of this process is beyond purely economic calculation. But over all the World Bank's researches on this subject have led to the conclusion that investment in education yields a return, which is normally higher than the investment in physical capital. "*World-wide experience over the two past decades*" concludes that the education is prudent economic investment, one that consistently earns high rates of return. Research also shows that returns are particularly high for educational investment in the poorest countries.

On any and all of these grounds minimum of four or five years in school for every boy and girl is therefore another obvious priority of real development (UNICEF, 1989).

Methodology

Primary School Education is a constitutional right of every child in India irrespective of their place of residence and other variations. The present study was designed and carried out to examine the "Affect of Primary School Education policy on rural primary school children". Lack of infrastructure, physical facilities in rural schools and involvement of children in family and agricultural works is affecting implementation of Primary Education Programme (PEP) in rural areas.

Locale of the Study

The study was conducted in Tirupati rural mandal of Chittoor District, Andhra Pradesh. Tirupati rural mandal is spread around the famous Temple town "Tirupati". The villages coming under this Mandal are drought prone, the population live on agriculture (dry land) and allied occupations such as poultry, goat and sheep rearing, dairy, sericulture.

Sample Selection

In order to select the sample for the study, the Mandal wise list of villages of Tirupati rural mandal was collected from Mandal office. As all the villages have primary schools, the names of all the villages were arranged in alphabetical order and three villages were selected at random. From each school, children studying third, fourth and fifth classes were selected.

Thus the sample selected consisted of 90 boys and 90 girls of which 30 boys and 30 girls studying third class, another 30 boys and 30 girls studying fourth class and 30 boys and 30 girls studying fifth class.

Variables Selected

In order to study the variables influencing the primary education of rural children the relationship between independent and dependent variables was assumed/arrived after a thorough review of literature, which is as follows.

Physical facilities, teaching and disciplinary methods, Age, Sex, Educational status, Occupation, Annual income, Birth order, Family size, Family type, Family literacy index were the independent variables chosen for the study.

1. **Age:** The chronological age in years as mentioned in school records was taken as age of the child. Age indicates physical and mental maturity of the child.

2. **Sex:** The sex of the child as male or female is noted. Sex discrimination in providing education is prevalent in Indian families, hence it was included as a variable in present study.

3. **Educational Status:** The educational status of parents in terms of number of years of formal education received is considered as a variable.

4. **Occupation:** The type of work done for a livelihood is considered as occupation of parents.

5. **Annual Income:** The money earned by the parents in an Annum was considered as Income of the parents.

6. **Birth order:** The respondents order of birth among his or her living siblings was taken as birth order.

7. **Family size:** The total number of members living permanently in the family was taken as size of the family.

8. **Family type:** The structure of the family in terms of biologically related members, their relationship and decision making powers was classified in a traditional way as Joint, Extended and Nuclear types of Families and included in the present study.

The Dependent Variable for the Present Study is Affect of Primary Education

The child's interest and satisfaction with the schools is assessed and considered as the affect of primary education, that is unless the child is able to cope up with the school environment and has co-operation at home, he/she may not like to continue attending the school.

In order to measure the variables under study a questionnaire was developed. The questionnaire consisted of four parts namely:

1. Address and personal profile of the child;
2. Family profile of the child;
3. School profile of the child;
4. Affect of primary education on primary school child.

Under each of the parts' structured questions were included. The questionnaire was first developed in English and translated into Telugu for use in the rural schools, as they are more familiar with the local language "Telugu".

As the school children are young, the investigator used interview method to gather information using questionnaire and filled in the questionnaire.

Data Collection

In order to measure the independent and dependent variables selected for the study a questionnaire was developed and administered.

Analysis of Data

The data gathered was subjected to statistical analysis using the statistical formulae of Mean, Standard deviation 't' test, Chi square text.

Besides the above statistical tests, qualitative analysis of data was also done to focus on information, which can explain well in words.

Results and Discussion

The data collected was tabulated, analysed, interpreted and discussed in this chapter. The results and discussion is presented under four heads namely:

1. Personal profile of the sample;
2. Family profile of the sample;

3. School profile of the sample;

4. Affect of primary education.

Personal Profile of the Sample

Age and Sex

The sample selected were boys and girls studying third, fourth and fifth classes in rural primary schools of Tirupati. The age of the children were noted from the school registers. The children's age and sex are as follows:

Table 9.1

Distribution of the children according to their Age and Sex

S. No.	*Class of study*	*Age in Years*	*Number of Boys*	*Number of Girls*	*Total*
1.	Third	7-8	30	30	60
2.	Fourth	8-9	30	30	60
3.	Fifth	9-10	30	30	60
	Total		**90**	**90**	**180**

The boys and girls having the required age for their class of study were selected.

Birth Order

Birth order of the child seems to determine the responsibilities shouldered at home and deprivation of school education also. Such cases are more commonly seen in rural poor families, where the first borns are given the responsibility of care of younger children and their assistance is often sought in domestic work and farm work, hence it was included as a variable in the present study.

From the Table 9.2 (*See on next page*) it is evident that most of the boys (47.78 per cent) were second born, followed by 28.89 per cent of first born, 17.78 per cent of third born and 4.44 per cent of fourth born children. With regard to girls, 37.78 per cent of girls are first born, followed by 35.56 per cent of second born, 18.89 per cent of third born and 7.78 per cent of fourth born. This shows that majority of the sample are second and first born and only a small percentage were third and fourth born.

Table 9.2

Distribution of the sample according to their Birth Order

S. No.	*Birth Order*	*Boys*	*Girls*	*Total*
1.	First Born	28.89	37.78	66.67
2.	Second Born	47.78	35.56	83.34
3.	Third Born	17.78	18.89	36.67
4.	Fourth Born	4.44	7.78	12.22
	Total	**100**	**100**	**200**

Family Profile of the Sample

The family inputs and environment influences the education of the child. It is necessary to examine the family inputs of a child. In the present study six family related variables were studied which are as follows.

Educational Status of Fathers and Mothers

The formal education received by the parents was studied separately for fathers and mothers of the sample, which is shown in Table 9.3. (*See on next page*)

From the Table 9.3, it is clear that a good percentage of boys' and girls' fathers (24.44 per cent and 32.22 per cent respectively) were illiterates. Around 26.67 per cent of boys' and 20 per cent of girls' fathers had only primary school education. A small percentage of fathers of boys and girls had college education. Although a good percentage of fathers of boys' and girls' had high school and secondary education, majority of fathers were illiterates and some had elementary education.

With regard to mothers' educational status majority of them were illiterates, followed by primary school education. Only a small percentage of mothers had high school and secondary school education. A negligible percentage (1.11 per cent) of mothers had college education.

Table 9.3

Distribution of the sample according to their Parents' Educational Status

S. No.	*Educational Status of Parents*	*Father*		*Total*	*Mother*		*Total*
		Boys	*Girls*		*Boys*	*Girls*	
1.	Illiterates	24.44	32.22	56.66	38.89	35.56	74.45
2.	Primary School	26.67	20	46.67	35.56	33.33	68.89
3.	High School	16.67	10	26.67	14.44	12.22	26.66
4.	Secondary School	27.78	33.33	61.11	11.11	17.78	28.89
5.	Intermediate	2.22	2.22	4.44	0	0	0
6.	Degree/College	2.22	2.22	4.44	0	1.11	1.11
	Total	**100**	**100**	**200**	**100**	**100**	**200**

Parents education influences children's academic achievement as they may be in a position to assist/help their children in education at home. Children of illiterate and poorly educated parents may either have to seek assistance from others or depend on school teachers, who may or may not be available in rural areas unless they reside in the same village.

Occupation of Fathers' and Mothers'

Occupation of fathers and mothers determine their availability at home and also the amount of leisure time the parents may have. The samples' parents occupation was collected separately which is given in Table 9.4. (*See on next page*)

The Table 9.4 shows that a majority of fathers of boys' (43.33 per cent) and girls' (50 per cent) were daily wage earners. Around 27.78 per cent boys' and girls' fathers are doing business. 23.33 per cent of boys' and 16.67 per cent of girls' fathers are employed in government and private sector. It is interesting to note that 5.56 per cent of boys and girls' fathers do not do any work inspite of being normal.

Table 9.4

Distribution of the sample according to their Fathers' and Mothers' Occupation

S. No.	*Type of Occupation of Parents*	*Father*		*Total*	*Mother*		*Total*
		Boys	*Girls*		*Boys*	*Girls*	
1.	Not working	5.56	5.56	11.12	5.5	45.55	92.2
2.	Daily wage earner/ labourers	43.33	50.00	93.33	50.00	38.89	78.89
3.	Business	27.78	27.78	55.56	27.78	5.56	12.23
4.	Employed (Government/Private	23.33	16.67	40.00	16.67	10.00	16.67
	Total	**100**	**100**	**200**	**100**	**100**	**200**

Among the mothers of children under study, majority of boys (45.55 per cent) and girls (46.67 per cent) were housewives. Around 38.89 per cent of boys' mothers and 40 per cent of girls' mothers' were daily wage earners. Only a small per cent of the mothers of boys and girls were doing business and were in employment.

Annual Income of Parents of the Primary School Children

The money earned by the samples' fathers and mothers in an annum was taken as annual income. This is to see the financial contribution of mothers' to the family. Studies on women Self Help Groups (DWCRA, 1995) have revealed that women's income is directly related to family's development. The annual income of fathers and mothers of the sample was as follows.

The Table 9.5 shows that the majority of the fathers had annual income of 10,001 to 20,001 rupees, followed by families having an annual income of 20,001 rupees and above. Very small percentage of fathers of boys' (5.56 per cent) and girls' (6.67 per cent) had annual income below poverty line. This indicates that majority of fathers had annual income of low middle-income category.

Table 9.5

Distribution of the sample according to their Fathers' and Mothers' Annual Income

S. No.	*Fathers and Mothers Annual Income in Rupees*	*Fathers*		*Total*	*Mothers*		*Total*
		Boys Per cent	*Girls Per cent*		*Boys Per cent*	*Girls Per cent*	
1.	Less than 10,000	5.56	6.67	12.23	45.56	46.67	92.23
2.	10,001-20,000	40.00	43.33	83.33	40.00	36.67	76.67
3.	20,001-30,000	28.89	21.11	50.00	10.00	13.33	23.33
4.	30,001-40,000	13.33	16.67	30.00	3.33	2.22	5.55
5.	40,001-50,000	8.89	8.89	17.78	1.11	1.11	2.22
6.	Above 50,001	3.33	3.33	6.66	0	0	0
	Total	**100**	**100**	**200**	**100**	**100**	**200**

With regards to mothers, majority of them had an annual income below poverty line, that is 45.56 per cent of boys' and 46.67 per cent of girls' mothers. A good per cent of mothers of boys (40 per cent) and girls (36.67 per cent) had an annual income of 10,001 to 20,001 rupees. Only a small per cent of mothers had annual income above 20,001 rupees.

This shows that the parents of the sample are not very poor as majority has incomes above 10,001 to 20,000 per annum.

Family Size

The number of members in a family was considered as the size of the family. The size of the family has a bearing on access to family resources. This is especially so in the case of flow-income groups.

Majority of children (53.33 per cent of boys and 53.33 per cent of girls) belonged to the family sizes of 5 to 6 members and a good per cent of girls belonged to small families. Only a small per cent of boys and girls belonged to families of 7 to 8 members.

Table 9.6

Distribution of the rural primary school children according to their Family Size

S. No.	Family Size	Per cent of Boys	Per cent of Girls	Total
1.	Less than 4 members	40	27.7	67.78
2.	5 to 6 members	53.33	53.33	106.66
3.	7 to 8 members	6.67	12.22	18.89
4.	Above 8 members	0	6.67	6.67
	Total	**100**	**100**	**200**

Family Type

The families of sample were categorized in a traditional manner as nuclear, joint and extended. The pattern of decision making varies depending on the type of family; hence it was included as a variable in the present study.

Table 9.7

Distribution of the sample according to their Family Type

S. No.	Family Type	Boys	Girls	Total
1.	Nuclear	93.33	80.00	173.33
2.	Joint	3.33	13.33	16.66
3.	Extended	3.34	6.67	10.01
	Total	**100**	**100**	**200**

The above table shows that a majority of the sample belonged to nuclear type. Only a small per cent of the sample belonged to joint and extended families.

Family Literacy Index (FLI)

The total number of years of formal education received by the total members of a family is summed up and the mean is taken as of Family Literacy Index of that family. The FLI is useful to know the influence of other members educational level on children in family.

Table 9.8

Distribution of the sample according to their Family Literacy Index

S. No.	*Family Literacy Index*	*Boys*	*Girls*	*Total*
1.	Less than 5	84.44	80	164.44
2.	6 and above	15.56	20	35.56
	Total	**100**	**100**	**200**

From the above table it is evident that a majority of the children belonged to families having a Family Literacy Index of less than five and very few families had a Family Literary Index of above six; this shows that the mean educational level of majority of families were low, that is primary school level.

Workplace of the Parents from the Residence

The parents' workplace from the residence also determines the availability of parents. The parents' working closer to the house have opportunities to attend to their children's needs. In the present study the proximity of parents' workplace from the house is as follows:

Around 49.91 per cent of children's fathers work close to the house, 29.41 per cent worked far away from home and 21.18 per cent work very far away from home. With regard to mothers' workplace 73.19 per cent work close to the house; 11.34 per cent work far away from the house and 15.46 per cent work very far away from house. The accessibility of parents in their workplace to the children, gives them a feeling of security and comfort. In case of need they can approach their parents in their workplace to seek help.

Substitute Availability at Home

The children's responses to a question "Is there anybody else in your house besides your parents", was collected which showed that around 38.33 per cent of children have adult members besides their own parents. Out of which 23.18 per cent were grand parents and 76.81 per cent were uncles and aunts, and all of them found to help in domestic chores/attend to family needs.

Siblings Enrolment in School and Participation in Work

Around 67.23 per cent of children's siblings were attending school and 32.77 per cent of the children's siblings were not attending school, out of which 20.33 per cent were employed (In foot ware units, construction works, private water works), 59.32 per cent were daily wage earners (as labourers) and 20.33 per cent were not doing any work.

Work Profile of Primary School Children

Majority of children (96.11 per cent) under study attend to work after school hours and 3.99 per cent of children do not do any work after school hours. On an average around 53.78 per cent of children work for an hour per day, 36.67 per cent of children work for two hours per day and 10.56 per cent of children work for three hours per day. The nature of work of children varied from domestic work, shopping, errand work and assistance in farm activities.

Parents' Role in Children's School Education

Around 99.44 per cent of children stated that their parents encourage them to study and provide all the material needed for the school. Only 0.56 per cent of children stated that "parents do not encourage them to study and do not provide any material needed for the school". The reason for this is the girls' mother is abroad (in Kuwait) and the money sent for her is not given to her. So he earns money by doing errand work for neighbours and uses for school material.

Around 70 per cent of parents meet school teachers regarding their children's education and 30 per cent of parents do not meet the school teachers. This reflects parents concern for the children's ucation.

Location of the Scnool

The proximity of the school from children's residence is gathered, which showed that around 51.11 per cent stay very near to the school; 4.11 per cent reside far away from school and 7.78 per cent of children stay very far away from school and carry lunch with them.

Among the sample studied 92.22 per cent reach school by walk and 7.78 per cent go to school by bicycle.

School Profile of the Sample

Basic Facilities Available at School

The basic facilities needed to conduct school activities were identified and listed. Information on their availability was gathered using interview and observation methods, which are as follows.

Among the three schools selected for the study, one school had only one among the eight facilities, the second school had only three out of eight facilities and the third school six out of eight facilities. This shows that schools do not have basic facilities, without which it is difficult to conduct the school programme. The children attending schools do not have access to basic amenities like running water, toilets, seating, physical space etc.

Provision of Books and Study Material

All the three schools provide textbooks to school children and do not provide note books and writing materials.

PTA Meetings and Health Check-ups

All the three schools have conducted health checkups with the help of Primary Health Centre staff and none of the three schools conducted Parent Teacher Association meetings. This shows that the school is functioning on its own without involving parents.

Staff Strength of School

The basic staff strength needed to run a school was listed in the questionnaire to know the staff position in rural schools. Around six to seven categories of staff are required to offer a quality primary school education. The study revealed that school one and two had only two teachers for all the five classes and no other staff. School three had three teachers for all the five classes, a sweeper and watchman. None of the schools had supporting staff like clerk, typist and attenders.

The above staff strength reflect poor working situation for teachers working in rural areas. It further indicates that the children of these schools are being used to attend to the works of an attender, sweeper, watchman and clerk as those categories of staff are not available.

Teaching and Disciplinary Methods

Academic achievement of a child mostly depends on teaching methods, regularity of the child to school, disciplinary methods followed at schools, hence information on these aspects of schooling were gathered which are as follows:

Around 27.2 per cent of children found teaching as easy to follow, whereas 59.44 per cent of children stated that the lessons were moderately understood, whereas 13.33 per cent of children felt it difficult to follow lessons taught at school.

Almost all the children under study felt that the disciplinary methods followed by the teachers were rational and reasonable as they were given punishments only when they do not do the work assigned to them. All the children stated that they were given corporal punishment; the frequency of the punishment ranged from twice in a week (48.33 per cent) to once a month (51.67 per cent).

Affect of Primary Education

The primary education programme if effective results in continuation of school education and if not effective results in dropping out of school. Sometimes the children dropout of the school due to the emergencies at home or unfavourable home environment. The children like to re-enroll into the primary school due to change in the situations at home.

In Andhra Pradesh efforts to re-enroll the school dropouts, was launched as a special drive, involving teachers, local administration and bodies. This also has an influence on re enrollment of school dropouts into regular schools.

The present study gathered following data on affect of primary education.

(a) Around 99.9 per cent of children liked going to the school and only 1.1 per cent did not like attending the school and preferred staying at home.

(b) The data on age at which the children join the school was collected which showed that 4.44 per cent had pre-school education, 79.44 per cent have joined directly into primary school at the age of 5 years and 16.11 per cent have joined primary school directly at the age of 6 years.

(c) Among the sample studied 2.78 per cent were school dropouts re-enrolled.

(d) The reasons for dropping out of school earlier were:

- Lack of money, domestic work, migration of parents, health problems, mothers' death, land disputes, alcoholic father.

(e) The reasons for re-enrolment into primary schools were:

- As they are giving rice;
- Change of old/former teacher;
- Changed situation at home.

The study reveals that the school enrollment of the child needs to be improved in order to sustain the children in school and also to make school education interesting, the families of rural children are in need of social supportive systems to help them in lean periods. The existing Poverty Alleviation Programmes need to be coordinated, converged to help rural families so as to maintain minimum quality of life and lay a healthy foundation for their children's life through education.

REFERENCES

1. Digumari Bhaskara Rao, I., 1998: *District Primary Education Programme*; Published by Discovery Publishing House Pvt. Ltd., pp. 60-69.
2. Jagannath Mohanty, 1994: *Education for All*; Deep & Deep Publications, New Delhi, pp. 33-90.
3. Parmar, M., 1998: *Universalisation of Elementary Education, Evolving State will*; Education in IASE Bulletin, New Delhi, pp. 250-290.

10

Affect of Primary School Education Programme on Urban Primary School Children

—Ms. K. Rajitha and Prof. D. Sarada

Introduction

The education policy of the Government of India in the post independence era has promised to provide free and compulsory education to all children at least upto the elementary stage. Recognising the need for a literate population and provision of elementary education as a crucial input for nation building, the governments stand was reiterated in the National Policy on Education (NPE, 1986) and the Programme of Action 1992, to work towards provision of education of a satisfactory quality to all children upto 14 years of age before the commencement of the 21st century.

In pursuance of Constitutional directives, State governments have abolished tuition fees in the Government, local bodies and aided schools upto the upper primary level. Accessibility of schooling facilities is no longer a major problem. 8.26 lakh habitations covering 94 per cent of the country's population have now schooling facilities within one km distance at primary stage. At upper primary stage also 7.26 lakh habitations covering 83.98 per cent of rural population have a school within 3 km distance. Enrolment ratio is 104 for classes I-V and 67 for classes VI-VIII.

While the Gross Enrolment Ratio (GER) at primary stage in the country as a whole and in most of its States exceed 100 per cent, there are quite a few States including Bihar, Haryana, Jammu and Kashmir, Meghalaya, Rajasthan and Uttar Pradesh where the ratio is considerably low. At the upper primary stage, these States and in addition, Andhra Pradesh, Orissa and Sikkim have GERs lower than the national average. Most of these States have literacy rates lower than the national average also. There is thus a strong regional dimension of Universalisation of Elementary Education (UEE).

DPEP Versus the Earlier Efforts

District Primary Education Programme is conceptualised and concretised on the basis of varied experience. The country has acquired and expertise gained in the process of planning and implementing educational programmes in India.

First, our experience of practising decentralized planning has shown that in the present setup the scope for local initiatives in district planning is very limited. This is primarily due to the fact that crucial resource allocation decisions are taken at the national or state level. The districts have virtually very little authority to allocate resources to the programme or activities which they consider to be dear to them. DPEP attempts to alter the pattern of resource decisions to encourage local initiatives at the district level. Under this programme the district plans are assessed and resources are allocated directly to the districts.

Second, the experience of centrally sponsored programmes show that it increases bureaucratisation of planning process and reduces the role of local level units implementation agencies. Normally, these schemes are planned at the central level and executed at the local level. Under the DPEP only guidelines are prepared at the national level. The plans are to be prepared at the local level. Local initiatives and educational innovations are almost impossible in a departmental mode of planning. Therefore DPEP, unlike other centrally sponsored schemes envisages to go beyond the departmental concerns to plan education through involvement of local bodies and community at large.

Third, planning in India continues to be largely sectoral. Sectoral planning helps to exercise bureaucratic controls and establish vertical linkages. DPEP attempts to provide an area approach to planning emphasising on the horizontal linkages in place of vertical linkages. The ideas of convergences of services, inter-departmental co-ordination and public participation in planning are supposed to promote area approach to planning.

Fourth, the Total Literacy Campaigns (TLCs) are initiated and completed in many districts in India. TLCs are major effort in successfully mobilising local initiatives to prepare comprehensive plans at the district level. The successful completion of TLC projects have shown that planning competencies, if needed, can be developed at the local level. The DPEP attempts to build on this experience gained by the districts and the preference given to TLC districts in DPEP funding helps to strengthen this experience further.

However, there is a basic difference in the approach to and process of planning adopted under TLC and DPEP. The Adult Education Departments have played very marginal role in TLCs. It is largely planned and implemented through different committees not necessarily connected directly to the education departments. Primary education is a continuing programme and is implemented through the existing institutions and control mechanism. Therefore, unlike, TLCs, DPEP envisages a stronger role for the education department both in facilitating planning and implementing programmes. Therefore DPEP is envisaged to be more departmentalised and bureaucratised than TLCs.

Fifth, primary education in India has reached a stage where the focus needs to be shifted from increasing access to improving achievement level. Therefore, emphasis in DPEP planning is increasingly shifted from creation of new institutions to improving effectiveness of the existing institutions. Perhaps, planning and management of existing institutions and the teaching-learning process therein forms the focus of DPEP planning exercise.

Sixth, India has some experience in planning and managing externally funded projects. But most of these projects are small scale projects focusing on selected aspects of primary education. Although project planning is a part and parcel of these exercises, comprehensive, area specific plans keeping district as the unit was never attempted under the externally funded projects in India.

The DPEP builds on the experiences gained from these project planning exercises. Bihar education project funded by the UNICEF, Lok Jumbish Project and Shiksha Karmi Project funded by SIDA, Andhra Pradesh District Primary Education Project funded by ODA, Mahila Samakhya project funded by the Dutch and Uttar Pradesh Primary Education. Project funded by ODA are some of the externally funded projects operating in India. DPEP expands the scope of educational planning from project planning to district planning. In fact DPEP an exercise in decentralised planning in a project mode.

Lastly, DPEP attempts to professionalise educational planning. As noted earlier, planning competencies are virtually non-existent at the district level. The Indian experience shows that percolation of competencies from national to state level and further to lower levels is difficult, if impossible. DPEP is an experiment to alter this process of competency building exercise by starting from local level to the state level.

The primary schools in urban areas in general are better organised than in rural areas for three reasons:

1. There is more possibility for district officials to visit the schools due to easy accessibility in terms of their location in urban areas. The possibility of official visits seems reduce frequency of teachers absence to school duties;

2. The parents of urban children realise the importance of education as a basis for better livelihood opportunities and encourage their children to attend school;
3. Regularly, usually both the parents of urban children may go out to work, especially in the lower economic strata, who do not want their children to be left idle at home for the fear of their association with the antisocial elements and delinquents.

Thus majority of the parents are for the primary school education inspite of economic problems and other basic problems at home the parents are willing to send their children to primary schools, where again the facilities are inadequate and the educational programme is not very attractive for the children which in most cases dissuading the children from attending school and dissuading parental efforts to keep the children in school for their own reasons.

METHODOLOGY

The primary education policy is being implemented through District Primary Education Programme (DPEP) in Andhra Pradesh. The affect of this programme on primary school age children is studied by using interview and observation methods on urban primary school children. The study was conducted in Tirupati town located in Chittoor District. Tirupati is an internationally known pilgrim centre having a floating population of around one lakh per day.

Selection of Sample

A list of registered schools in Tirupati was obtained from District Educational Office, Chittoor (A.P.), there were sixty six registered schools as per the list. The names of the schools were arranged in alphabetical order and every twenty second school was selected for the study, thus three schools were selected. The sample was drawn from third, fourth and fifth classes of each school.

Variables Selection

Primary education of children (urban) is found to be dependent on several variables. Unless these variables are included in the study, the affect of primary education cannot be studied holistically. In the present study the following independent and dependent variables were included.

Independent Variables

1. **Age:** The chronological age in years as mentioned in school records was taken as age of the child. Age indicates physical and mental maturity of the child.
2. **Sex:** The sex of the child as male or female is noted. Sex discrimination in providing education is prevalent in India, hence it was included as a variable in present study.
3. **Educational status:** The educational status of parents in terms of number of years of formal education received is considered as a variable.
4. **Occupation:** The type of work done for a livelihood or earn a living is considered as occupation of parents.
5. **Income:** The money earned by the parents in an Annum was considered as Income of the parents.
6. **Birth order:** The respondents' order of Birth among his or her living siblings was taken as birth order.
7. **Family size:** The total number of members living in a family was taken as size of the family.
8. **Family type:** Basing on the structure of family in terms of biologically related members, their relationship and decision making powers was classified in a traditional way as joint, extended and nuclear types of families and included in the present study.
9. **Family Literacy Index:** The number of years formal education received by each family member was taken and the sum total was divided by the number of family members the resultant mean is considered as Family Literacy Index.

Dependent Variables

Affect of Primary Education: The influence of independent variables on primary education of children is the dependent variable.

For Measurement of Variables Understanding

A questionnaire developed, which is a structured one and consisted of four parts:

1. The first part is about name and address of the child;
2. The second part consisted of questions related to family profile of the child;
3. The third is intended to gather information on school profile of the child;
4. The last part of the questionnaire is meant to collect data on Affect of Primary Education on urban school children.

Data Collection

To measure the variables selected for the study a questionnaire was developed and administered. For the collection of data, interview and observation methods were used. The investigator asked the questions from the questionnaire and the responses were recorded.

Analysis of Data

The data collected is tabulated and subjected to statistical analysis. The tests used their formula are as follows:

1. Mean $\bar{x} = \frac{\sum x}{N}$ for boys

Mean $\bar{y} = \frac{\sum y}{n}$

2. Standard Deviation $= c = +\sqrt{\frac{\sum x^2}{n} - \left(\bar{x}\right)^2}$ for boys

$c = +\sqrt{\frac{\sum y^2}{n} - \left(\bar{y}\right)^2}$ for girls

3. 't' $= \frac{-\bar{x}_1 - \bar{x}_2}{\sqrt{S^2\left(\frac{1}{n_1} + \frac{1}{n_2}\right)}}$ where $o^2 = \frac{n_1 s_1^2 + n_2 S_2^2}{n_1 + n_2 + 2}$

4. Chi-Square text $= X_0^2 = \frac{\Sigma O^2}{E_t} - N$

In addition to statistical analysis qualitative interpretation of data is also done in order to focus on the details, which cannot be brought to light through numbers.

RESULTS AND DISCUSSION

The data collected on the Topic "Affect of Primary Education Policy on Urban Primary School Children" is tabulated, analysed, interpreted and discussed as follows.

Personal Profile of the Sample

Age and sex: The children (boys and girls) studying third, fourth and fifth were taken for the study. The third class children aged between 7 to 8 years, the fourth-class children aged between 8 to 9 years and fifth class children aged between 9 to 10 years were selected purposively for the study because those are the right ages for the classes they are studying.

Birth order: The studies on primary education and school dropouts have indicated that the first born girls and boys are mostly used at home to attend to younger siblings, domestic chores, care of livestock and other works. Hence it was included as a variable in the present study.

Table 10.1

Distribution of the sample according to their Birth order

S. No.	*Birth order*	*Percentage of Boys*	*Percentage of Girls*	*Total*
1.	1st born	47.75	53.62	101.37
2.	2nd born	38.74	40.58	79.32
3.	3rd born	11.71	5.79	17.5
4.	4 & above	1.80	0	1.80
	Total	**100**	**100**	**200**

From the above table it is evident that most of the (47.75 per cent of boys and 53.62 per cent of girls) children were first born. Around 38.74 per cent of boys, 40.58 per cent of girls were second born. Only a small per cent of sample were third and fourth born. The finding of the present study with regard to birth order and primary education is in contrary to the general trend. This may be because of the place of residence that is Urban where small family norm is in vogue.

Family Profile of the Sample

Educational Status

The formal educational levels of mothers and fathers of primary school children was recorded, which is as follows:

Table 10.2

Distribution of the sample according to their mothers and fathers Educational Status

S. No.	*Levels of Education of Parents*	*Mothers*		*Total*	*Fathers*		*Total*
		Boys Per cent	*Girls Per cent*		*Boys Per cent*	*Girls Per cent*	
1.	Uneducated	0.91	0.00	0.91	0.90	0.00	0.90
2.	Primary	3.60	5.79	9.39	1.80	5.59	7.39
3.	High School	11.71	13.04	24.75	2.70	8.70	11.4
4.	Secondary	34.23	37.68	71.91	23.42	21.74	45.16
5.	Inter	23.42	23.18	46.6	18.02	26.09	44.11
6.	B.Sc.	22.52	18.84	41.36	45.95	27.55	73.5
7.	M.Sc.	2.70	1.44	4.14	7.21	10.14	17.35
	Total	**100**	**100**	**200**	**100**	**100**	**200**

From the above table it is clear that a good per cent of mothers had education above the high school and college level. Similarly majority of fathers had college education and a good per cent had education above high school level. The educational level of mothers and fathers could be a reason for enrolment of children in primary schools.

Occupation of Mothers and Fathers

Occupation is the determinant of Income continuity and also the social status. Nature of work also determines the amount of free time available for the parents to spend with their children. Hence it was included in the present study as a variable.

Table 10.3

Distribution of the Sample According to their Mothers and Fathers Occupation

S. No.	*Occupation of Parents*	*Mothers*		*Total*	*Fathers*		*Total*
		Boys Per cent	*Girls Per cent*		*Boys Per cent*	*Girls Per cent*	
1.	Housewife	82.88	82.60	165.48	–	–	–
2.	Labourers/ Daily wage earners	0.91	0	0.91	0.90	0.00	0.90
3.	Business	2.70	4.35	7.05	52.25	44.93	97.18
4.	Employed (Private & Government)	13.51	13.04	26.55	46.85	55.07	101.92
	Total	**100**	**100**	**200**	**100**	**100**	**200**

The Table 10.3 shows that majority of mothers of boys and girls (82.88 per cent and 82.6 per cent respectively) are housewives, and small per cent were employed and doing business.

With regard to fathers occupation, majority of fathers of boys (52.25 per cent) were engaged in business. Majority of girl's fathers (55.07 per cent) were employed. Further it may be noted that except for 0.9 per cent of boy's fathers, all others are in business and employed.

Annual Income of Mothers and Fathers

The income levels of a family influences its purchasing power and quality of life. The annual income earned by mothers and fathers was collected separately in rupees, which is as under:

Table 10.4

Distribution of the sample according to their mothers and fathers Annual Income

S. No.	*Annual Income in rupees*	*Mother*		*Total*	*Father*		*Total*
		Boys	*Girls*		*Boys*	*Girls*	
1.	No income	82.88	82.60	165.48	–	–	–
2.	10,000-30,000	5.41	11.59	17	9.01	13.04	22.05
3.	30,000-50,000	7.21	5.79	13	31.53	33.33	64.86
4.	50,000-80,000	4.50	-	4.50	49.55	49.28	98.83
5.	80,000 and above	–	–	–	8.11	4.35	12.46
6.	1,00,000 and above	–	–	–	1.80	–	1.80
	Total	**100**	**100**	**200**	**100**	**100**	**200**

From the above table it may be known that a large per cent of mothers of boys (82.88 per cent) and girls (82.6 per cent) have no income as they are housewives without any economic activity. Only a small percentage of women have income above 50,000 per annum.

With regard to fathers' income only a small percentage have income between 12,000 to 30,000 rupees. Majority of fathers of both boys and girls have income between 50,000 to 80,000 rupees per annum followed by a 1.8 per cent of boys' fathers having income above 1,00,000 rupees. This shows that none of the boys' and girls' families belonged to below poverty line.

Family Type

The decision-making powers and pattern of communication tend to be influenced by the Type of family, which also influences children's education; hence it was included as a variable in the present study.

Table 10.5

Distribution of the sample according to their Family Type

S. No.	*Family type*	*Boys Per cent*	*Girls Per cent*	*Total*
1.	Nuclear	96.40	92.75	189.15
2.	Joint	2.70	2.90	5.6
3.	Extended	0.90	4.35	5.25
	Total	**100**	**100**	**200**

Majority of the families were nuclear and only a small percentage of the sample had joint and extended families. This may be due to urbanization.

Size of the Family

The size of the family determines the distribution of family resources and communication. The size of the family of sample is given in Table 10.6.

Table 10.6

Distribution of the sample according to their Family Sizes

S. No.	*Family size*	*Per cent of Boys*	*Per cent of Girls*	*Total*
1.	Less than 4 members	62.16	79.71	141.87
2.	5-6 members	35.14	18.84	53.98
3.	7-8 members	2.70	1.44	4.14
	Total	**100**	**100**	**200**

It shows that a major per cent of boys (62.16) and girls (79.71) had family sizes less than four, followed by 35.14 per cent of boys and 18.84 per cent of girls having family sizes between 5 to 6. Only a small per cent had family sizes between 7 to 8. This reflects urban trend of small families.

Family Literacy Index (FLI)

The total number of years of formal education received by the family members is totalled and the mean is calculated which is considered as Family Literacy Index of that family.

Table 10.7

Distribution of the sample according to their Family Literacy Index (FLI)

S. No.	*Family Literacy Index in years*	*Boys Per cent*	*Girls Per cent*	*Total*
1.	Less than 5	5.40	5.80	11.2
2.	6 - 10	84.68	86.96	171.64
3.	11 and above	9.91	7.25	17.16
	Total	**100**	**100**	**200**

The above table indicates that a majority of boys and girls have come from families with FLI of 6 to 10, followed by FLI of 11 and above. Only a small per cent 5.4 per cent of boys and 5.8 per cent of girls) come from families with less than 5 as FLI. This shows that educational levels of family members of children under study are above average. This is a contributing factor to children's education.

Proximity of Parents' Work Place

The parental attention to children is more when they are available nearer to the house that is work place is close by. The responses of the children to questions on proximity of parent's workplace are as follows:

- Among the working mothers 64 per cent work close to their house and 36 per cent have their work place far away from home.
- Majority of the fathers (75.56 per cent) have their work place far away from home. Around 21.11 per cent work close to their house. Only 3.33 per cent work very far away from home.

- Around twenty per cent of children have somebody at home besides their parents, out of which 86.11 per cent are grand parents and 13.89 per cent are uncles and Aunts. These additional members of family attend to family needs and assist in domestic chores.
- The siblings enrolment in school was found to be around 95.55 per cent. Among the remaining 4.45 per cent, 62.5 per cent are below the school age and 37.5 per cent are only children not having siblings. This shows that almost all their children have the siblings attending school.
- A large section of children that is 96.11 per cent do work after school hours. The work hours ranged from one hour to three hours. The nature of work is mostly shopping, fetching water and errand work.
- Almost all children's parents encourage them to study and provide necessary school material and meet school teachers about their children's education.
- The accessibility to school is as follows: 65 per cent live near the school and 35 per cent stay far away from school and carry lunch with them to school. With regard to reaching the school, 52.22 per cent go by walk, 9.44 percentage by bicycle, 11.67 per cent by bus and 26.67 per cent have other modes of transport.

School Profile of the Sample

- The quality of school environment depends on the basic facilities available to the children. The data collected in this regard reveal that out of eight families listed in the questionnaire two schools have all the eight and one school has only seven facilities that is, it doesn't have running water facility.
- None of the schools provide textbooks, Note books and writing material on free of cost to the children. This is because they are private schools. All the three schools conduct health checkup and Parent Teacher Association meetings every year.

- With regard to staff strength two of the schools have all categories of staff, where as one school does not have typist, attender and watchman.
- The teaching and disciplinary methods followed in the school are perceived by children as under.
    - ➢ All the children have stated that they are happy to go to school.
    - ➢ The classroom teaching is easily understood by 71 per cent, moderately understood by 23.8 per cent and 5.2 per cent of children find it difficult to follow. This shows that majority of children were able to understand the lessons taught in the class.

Almost all children felt that the disciplinary methods followed in the school are reasonable and rational. It was found that corporeal punishment is given in the school. With regard to frequency of punishment, around 25 per cent of the children are given corporeal punishment twice in a week and 75 per cent are given punishment once or twice in a month.

Affect of Primary Education

The quality of primary education influences school enrolment and retention. The positive perceptions of children about school itself indicates the effectiveness of primary education. The data collected on this aspect is as follows:

- All the children under study stated that they liked going to the school everyday;
- Almost all the children had preschool education prior to joining primary school;
- None of the children were school dropouts re-enrolled in schools;

This shows that children are satisfied with the primary education.

The study reveals that the Primary Education has a positive effect on Urban Primary School children, despite of the limitations in the facilities provided in the school and also the home environment, which is a contributing factor for the promotion of Primary Education.

REFERENCES

1. Agrawal, S.P. (1999): *Development of Education in India*; Concept Publishing Company, New Delhi, Vol. V, pp. 39-42.
2. Digumari Bhaskara Rao, I., 1998: *District Primary Education Programme*; Published by Discovery Publishing House Pvt. Ltd., pp. 60-69.
3. Jagannath Mohanty, 1994: Education for All; Deep and Deep Publications, New Delhi, pp. 33-90.

11

Affect of Primary School Education Programme of Tribal Children

—Ms. N. Venkatalakshmi Sowjanya and Prof. D. Sarada

Introduction

The schedule tribe population in India in 1991 was recorded as 67.7 million. This accounts for about eight per cent of the population of the country. They are concentrated in various zones, particularly in Central India and the North-East. They are divided into nearly 400 communities, each with a distinctive culture. They differ in the levels of their socio-economic development, language, religion, ecology and means of subsistence. As compared to other population, their technology is poor and they inhabit areas of difficult access. These societies are tradition bound. By and large, they are in the grip of object poverty and their quality of life is poor.

The education of Scheduled tribes suffer from a number of constraints emanating from their location in hills and forests, in deserts and perpetually snow bound areas. Some tribal groups are nomadic. Small and scattered population in difficult climate regions demand relaxation of norms regarding opening of schools.

Education development has been deemed central to strengthening human resources for which primary education is the necessary foundation. Low educational achievement among certain population sections, particularly among the poor scheduled tribes, scheduled castes and women is a major constraint to their social and economic development. Scheduled castes and tribes have remained socially, educationally and economically disadvantaged and have infact been subjected to exploitation despite various constitutional provisions, legislation, policies and programmes intended to assure them social justice. This situation can be partially attributed to their social and geographic isolation from the majority population and also to the apathetic attitude towards them. Women in India experience a similar situation.

In their case, however, their social status and attitudes of others towards them are largely responsible for the discrimination and social injustice they face. Thus the general improvement in the standards of primary education depends largely on the augmented participation of those social sections/ groups, which had been difficult to reach or had eluded reach for some reasons. It would be appropriate to state the policy perspectives in this context.

The National Policy on Education (NPE), 1986 (as modified in 1992) makes particular mention of education for equality. It emphasises the removal of disparities and equalisation of educational opportunity by attending to the specific needs of those who have been denied equality so far.

The NPE details the policy approach to women, scheduled castes, scheduled tribes, other educationally backward sections, minorities and the handicapped. It also spells out the approach to Adult Education, Early Childhood Care and Education (ECCE) and Non-Formal Education (NFE) as necessary support for attaining the larger objectives of Universalisation of Elementary Education (UEE).

The Education of Scheduled Tribes: Measures such as the following are envisaged to bring Scheduled Tribes on par with others:

- Opening primary schools in tribal areas;
- Development of curricula and devising instructional materials in tribal languages at the initial stages, with arrangements for switching over to the regional language;
- Encouraging educated and promising ST youth to take up teaching in tribal areas after the training;
- Providing large-scale establishment of residential schools, including Ashram schools;
- Introduction of incentives/scholarships among STs;
- Opening Anganwadis, Non-formal and Adult Education Centres on a priority basis in areas predominantly inhabited by STs;
- Designing curriculum at all stages of education to create an awareness of the rich cultural identity of the tribal people as also of their enormous creative talent.

In the field of tribal education, the results achieved are not commensurate with the concern expressed by the society and the financial inputs made. The progress is slow due to low participation, high dropout rate and wastage, the urban, based content and curriculum, and ineffective pedagogy combined with teachers lack of commitment. The socialisation pattern at home and the education in the school are generally in conflict. Students show low interest in school activity and do not reach the expected levels of performance. The tribal child who is used to freedom at home has to face rigid norms in the school resulting in resistance and conflict. While tribal societies encourage group competition, the school puts a premium on individual achievement. Thus, there is no compatibility between the culture and the school system. The formal system of education thus needs intensive adoption to suit the culture needs and characteristics of tribal communities.

Education is necessary for tribal children as it is for rural and urban children like several cultural groups in the past which have transitional to join mainstream due to the industrialisation and urbanisation. Tribal children need to be assisted in achieving educational status by providing need based and relevant curriculum and primary school system.

In this context it becomes necessary to study the affect of primary education policy on tribal primary school children. The Present study "Affect of Primary School Education Policy on Tribal Children" attempts to study the tribal children attending primary school in Chintoor Mandal of Khammam District a densely populated tribal area.

Statement of the Problem

Affect of primary education policy on tribal children.

Objectives

1. To study the personal and family background of the tribal primary school children;
2. To study school environment of the tribal primary school children;
3. To study the affect of primary school education and tribal children with special reference to "Konda Reddy" community.

Hypotheses

1. The personal independent variables such as age and sex of tribal school children may have an influence on primary education;
2. The independent variables related to family background (Educational status, Occupation, Annual income, Family type, Family size and Family Literacy Index) may have an influence on primary school education of tribal children;
3. The school environment may have an influence on primary school education of tribal children;
4. A change in school and family environment may influence primary school education of tribal primary school children.

Sample Selection

The Tribal Community predominant in Khammam district is "Konda Reddy". These tribals live on agriculture and forest produce. A small percentage of them are engaged in carpentry and sheep rearing. The "Konda Reddy" are a backward tribal community on whom very few studies were conducted. The tribal children attending primary school in Chintoor Mandal of Khammam district are selected for the study.

The information on the primary school having these tribal was collected officially from mandal education officer, Chintoor Mandal, Khammam district (A.P.). The mandal upper primary school in Chintoor and Mothugudam of Chintoor mandal were recommended and permitted for the present study by the Mandal Development Officer, Chintoor.

The sample was selected from two schools, Chittoor and Mothugudam upper primary schools. The sample comprised of 60 boys and 60 girls that is 30 boys and 30 girls were selected from each school.

Selection of Variables

Several variables influence primary education of tribal children. They may be related to personal background, family background and school background. They may be independent and dependent with regard to the problem under study. It is necessary to understand the cause and effect relationship that exists among these variables to study them.

The variables selected for the present study are:

1. **Age:** The physical maturity of children is studied through chronological age in years. The age of the children as recorded in the school register is taken as it is.
2. **Sex:** The sex of the child is included in the study in order to know the discrimination in educational opportunities for tribal boys and girls.
3. **Birth order:** The order of birth of sample among siblings is recorded in order to study the birth order in relation to educational opportunities.
4. **Educational status:** The formal education received by mothers, fathers are taken as educational status of parents.
5. **Occupation:** The main work done by the mothers and fathers to earn a livelihood is considered as their occupation.

6. **Annual Income:** The money earned in rupees during one year by mother and father is considered as the annual income of mothers' and fathers'.

7. **Family type:** On the basis of the structure of the family in relation to the number and their biological/legal relationship is classified as joint/ extended nuclear type of families.

8. **Family Size:** The number of members living together in a family is considered as size of the family.

9. **Family Literacy Index:** The number of years of formal education had by all the family members is added and divided by number of family members. The resultant mean is considered as Family Literacy Index.

Affect of Primary Education Policy on Tribal Children

Influence of primary education on tribal children is the dependent variable studied in terms of children's satisfaction with their studies.

Questionnaire

The questionnaire for data collection was prepared both in English and Telugu. The questions were framed in easy and understandable manner. Majority of the questions were of **Yes/ No** and multiple-choice type. Very few questions are open-ended, meant to gather reasons and opinions.

Data Collection

In order to collect the data on the topic under research a questionnaire was developed to collect data on family profile, school profile and affect of primary education on tribal children. The data was collected using interview method and the questionnaire was filled in by the investigator.

Analysis of Data

The data collected was tabulated, subjected to statistical analysis. The tests employed were Mean, standard deviation, 't' test, χ^2 test.

The results were interpreted and presented as follows:

1. Personal profile of the sample;
2. Family profile of the sample;
3. School profile of the sample;
4. Affect of primary education policy.

Personal Profile of the Sample

The personal information of the sample was gathered using a questionnaire in order to understand the background of the sample.

Age and Sex

The tribal children studying third class, fourth class and fifth class in each school were selected that is 20 boys and 20 girls studying third class aged between 7-8 years, around 20 boys and 20 girls studying fourth class and aged between 8-9 years, and fifth class boys (20) and girls (20) aged between 9-10 years were selected purposively for the study.

Table 11.1

Distribution of the sample according to their Age and Sex

S. No.	*Age and Sex*	*Boys*	*Girls*	*Total*
1.	7-8 Years – 3rd class	20	20	40
2.	8-9 Years – 4th class	20	20	40
3.	9-10 Years – 5th class	20	20	40
	Total	**60**	**60**	**120**

Birth Order

The birth order of a child and the number of children in a family seem to influence the educational opportunities of children. Hence the birth order was included as a variable in the present study.

Table 11.2

Distribution of sample according to their birth order

S. No.	*Birth Order*	*Boys*	*Per cent*	*Girls*	*Per cent*
1.	I Born	17	28.3	19	31.7
2.	II Born	23	38.3	23	36.3
3.	III Born	10	16.7	11	18.3
4.	IV Born	8	13.3	4	6.7
5.	V and above	2	3.4	3	5.0
	Total	**60**	**100**	**60**	**100**

The above table shows that the majority of boys (38.3 per cent) and girls (38.3 per cent) were second born, around 28.3 per cent of boys and 31.7 per cent of girls were first born and only small per cent of sample were third and fourth born. The boys and girls did not vary much in their birth orders.

Family Profile of the Sample

The responses of the children to the questions on family environment was gathered and presented as under.

Family Size

The number of people living in family is considered as the family size. In small families the resources available will have to be distributed among fewer members. In large families resources have to be shared among more number of people. As lack of resources is identified as one of the reasons for school dropout and poor enrolment, Family size was included as a variable in the present study.

The sample is distributed according to the family size as shown in the Table 11.3 which indicates that majority of boys (50 per cent) and girls (46 per cent) had families of 5-6 members, followed by boys (30 per cent) and girls (35 per cent) having family sizes of less than 4 and only small per cent of sample have family sizes above 8 members.

Table 11.3

Distribution of sample according to their family size

S. No.	Family Size	Boys	Per cent	Girls	Per cent
1.	Less than 4 members	18	30.0	21	35.0
2.	5-6 members	30	50.0	28	46.7
3.	7-8 members	9	15.0	9	15.0
4.	> 8 members	3	5.0	2	3.3
	Total	60	100.0	60	100.0

Family Type

Several studies have indicated that the decision-making power and pattern depends upon the family type. Children's education also depends upon the decision-making power of the mother. It was observed that in nuclear families the mother seen to exercise such decision-making power, hence included as a variable in the present study.

Table 11.4

Distribution of sample according to their family type

S. No.	Type of Family	Boys	Per cent	Girls	Per cent
1.	Nuclear	50	83.3	49	81.7
2.	Joint	8	13.3	9	15.0
3.	Extended	2	3.3	2	3.3
	Total	60	100.0	60	100.0

The Table 11.4 shows that the majority of boys (83.3 per cent) and girls (81.7 per cent) of sample belonged to nuclear families; Boys (13.3 per cent) and girls (15 per cent) had joint families and boys (3.3 per cent) and girls (3.3 per cent) of sample had extended families. This shows that majority belonged to nuclear type of families.

Family Literacy Index (FLI)

The number of years of education had by each family member was collected and added and sum total of years was divided by the size of the family, which is considered as Family Literacy Index. In a family the family members education and knowledge directly or indirectly influences the children that is children's interest in education also depends on educational status of family members. Hence Family Literacy Index was also studied in the present study.

Table 11.5

Distribution of sample according to their Family Literacy Index

S. No.	*FLI*	*Boys*	*Per cent*	*Girls*	*Per cent*
1.	Below 5	49	81.7	48	80.0
2.	Above 5	11	18.3	12	20.0
	Total	**60**	**100.0**	**60**	**100.0**

From the Table 11.5 it is clear that majority of boys (81.7 per cent) and girls (80 per cent) had a Family Literacy Index of less than 5 and boys (18.3 per cent) and girls (20 per cent) of sample had Family Literacy Index of above 5. This shows that majority had family members with low educational status.

Educational Status of Fathers and Mothers

In order to know the educational status of father and mother separately the data regarding their educational levels is gathered, which is as under.

Table 11.6

Distribution of the sample according to their fathers' educational status

S. No.	*Educational Status*	*Girls*	*Per cent*	*Boys*	*Per cent*
1.	Primary	15	25.0	21	25.0
2.	Upper Primary	18	30.0	17	28.3
3.	High School	8	13.3	7	11.7
4.	Intermediate	15	25.0	9	15.0
5.	Degree	4	6.6	6	10.0
	Total	**60**	**100.0**	**60**	**100.0**

The Table 11.6 indicates that the education of fathers of girls and boys separately which shows that there is not much difference in the educational levels of fathers of boys and girls. Although slightly greater number of boys fathers were less educated.

Table 11.7

Distribution of sample according to their mothers educational status

S. No.	*Educational Status*	*Girls*	*Per cent*	*Boys*	*Per cent*
1.	Primary	38	63.3	31	51.7
2.	Upper Primary	9	15.0	12	20.0
3.	High School	5	8.3	15	25.0
4.	Intermediate	7	11.7	2	3.3
5.	Degree	1	1.7	0	0
	Total	60	100.0	60	100.0

The above table shows the educational status of mothers of boys and girls. Majority of mothers had education below primary level and mothers of boys and girls did not differ much in their educational status.

Occupation of Fathers and Mothers

Occupation is the livelihood of people; this can be any work done to make a living. In tribal areas the livelihood opportunities are limited. Hence more than one occupation is taken up in a year to earn a living. The occupation of parents influences the education of children. In families where livestock is source of income, children are also used to grazing and feeding of livestock. Hence occupation of fathers and mothers are included in the present study as under.

The Table 11.8 shows that majority of fathers were daily wage earners, labourers, a sample per cent were employed in private sector, followed by 15 to 20 per cent doing petty business. It is interesting to know that 5 per cent of boys and 3.3 per cent of girls fathers do no work in spite of being normal and healthy. The fathers of boys and girls did not vary much with regard to their occupation.

Table 11.8

Distribution of sample according to their fathers occupation

S. No.	*Type of occupation*	*Father of Boys*	*Per cent*	*Father of Girls*	*Per cent*
1.	Not working	3	5.0	2	3.3
2.	Labourers	32	53.3	31	51.7
3.	Petty Business	9	15.0	12	20.0
4.	Employed in Private Sector	16	20.7	15	25.0
	Total	**60**	**100**	**60**	**100**

Table 11.9

Distribution of sample according to their mothers occupation

S. No.	*Type of occupation*	*Boys*	*Per cent*	*Girls*	*Per cent*
1.	Domestic work and seasonal work	41	63.3	29	48.3
2.	Labourers	15	25.0	16	26.7
3.	Petty Business	3	5.0	8	11.7
4.	Employed in Private Sector	1	1.7	7	11.7
	Total	**60**	**100**	**60**	**100**

From the Table 11.9 it is clear that mothers of boys (63.3 per cent) and mothers of girls (48.3 per cent) attend to domestic work and seasonally outside the home, around 25 per cent of boys' mothers and 26.7 per cent of girls mothers were working as labourers, 5 per cent of boys and 13.3 per cent of girls mothers were engaged in petty business. A small per cent of mothers were employed in private sector.

Annual Income of Fathers and Mothers

Income determines the economic status and purchasing power of a family. Many a times Fathers income is not contributed to the family. This may be due to addiction to alcohol and other habits. Hence it is difficult to collect information on actual income used by the family in a year. In the present study the annual income of fathers and mothers was collected separately with the assumption that income is used for the family.

Table 11.10

Distribution of sample according to their fathers income

S. No.	*Annual Income in Rs.*	*Boys*	*Per cent*	*Girls*	*Per cent*
1.	< 11 thousands	3	5.0	3	5.0
2.	12-20 thousands	1	1.7	4	6.7
3.	21-30 thousands	15	25.0	10	26.7
4.	31-40 thousands	2	36.7	2	36.7
5.	51-50 thousands	8	13.3	6	9.9
6.	50 thousands above	8	13.3	6	9.9
	Total	**57**	**95.0**	**58**	**96.0**

The Table 11.10 shows that the majority of the fathers of boys and girls had annual Incomes above 11,000. Only a small per cent of fathers of boys and girls had Income below 11,000.

Table 11.11

Distribution of sample according to their mothers Income

S. No.	*Annual Income in Rs.*	*Boys*	*Per cent*	*Girls*	*Per cent*
1.	Less than 10 thousands	43	71.6	3.0	50.0
2.	11-20 thousands	13	21.7	15	25.0
3.	21-30 thousands	3	5.0	8	13.3
4.	31-40 thousands	1	1.7	7	11.7
	Total	**60**	**100.0**	**60**	**100**

The Table 11.11 shows that majority of members had income below 10,000 per annum. Around 21.7 per cent of boys and 25.0 per cent of girls mothers had an annual income between 11000-20000. A small per cent of girls and boys mothers had income above 21,000.

Parents Work Place

The sample studied showed that 71.7 per cent of children's parents worked close to their houses. A 21.7 percentage had their workplace far away from home and 5.8 per cent were working very far away from home and 0.8 per cent has migrated for work. The distance of work place from home is an influencing factor on education of children. Absence of parents deprives children of parental care, timely feeding and surety. It further burdens children with adult responsibilities.

It was found that 5 per cent of children had grand fathers, 6.6 per cent had grand mothers, and 0.8 per cent had other adult members to attend to family chores in the absence of their parents.

The Siblings Education

The information on samples siblings (brothers and sisters) education and occupation was gathered which is as follows.

Around 80.84 per cent of children, siblings attend school and 19.16 per cent do not attend school. It was found among the siblings of the sample 1.6 per cent were doing jobs, 2.5 per cent were working as labourers and 5 per cent attend to household work.

Children and Work

It was found that 58.3 per cent of Children were working after school hours. Out of which 11.6 per cent were working at home and 30 per cent were working outside the home. The nature of work of these children are varied such as

1. Assistance in kitchen;
2. Fetching water;
3. Firewood collection;

4. Assistance in parents occupation;
5. Errand work outside the home.

This shows that the children are engaged in the work both at home and outside the home, which may have a negative influence on children's education, especially academic performance.

Parental Support in School Education

The parents' participation in Children's education and their support were studied.

The study revealed:

(a) Around 90 per cent of parents found to encourage their children to study at home and a 10 per cent do not encourage their children to study at home;

(b) Around 90 per cent of parents provide necessary school materials to their children and a 10 per cent do not provide any school material;

(c) Around 69.1 per cent of children live close to the school, 25 per cent live faraway from school;

(d) Around 3.3 per cent of children carry lunch with them and 96.7 per cent do not carry lunch with them;

(e) 95.84 per cent reach the school by walk, 4.16 per cent by bicycle;

(f) Only 80.84 per cent of parents meet the schoolteachers during the academic year and 19.16 per cent of parents do not meet the School Teachers.

School Profile of the Sample

The information from the school environment in terms of it, services for students was collected, which is as follows.

Facilities Available at School

Around 8 to 9 facilities generally needed in a school were listed. Their availability and utilisation was observed and gathered from children. In Mothugudem Upper Primary School, seven out of eight facilities were available. That is except toilet other facilities were available. In Chintoor Upper Primary School, six out of eight facilities were available, that is seating arrangement and toilet facilities are not available. Though a first aid kit is present it is not being used in any of the schools.

Provision of Study Material

It was found that the school provides textbooks to all tribal children, does not provide notebooks and pencils.

School Health Services

Both the schools under study conduct Health Check-ups by Primary Health Center doctors and also Parent Teacher Association meetings annually.

Staff Strength

Both the schools have sufficient staff that is teachers for every class, one clerk, two attenders, one ayah and one sweeper.

Teaching Technology Followed

Almost all the children indicated that they feel happy to go to school. Around 18.3 per cent of children expressed that the lessons taught were easily understood and 45 per cent stated that the lessons taught in the class were moderately understood.

Disciplinary Methods Followed

The children's opinion on the disciplinary methods followed in the school was gathered which showed that a 91.6 per cent of children felt that the disciplinary methods followed were good, and 8.3 per cent felt that the disciplinary methods were rational. It was found that corporeal punishment is given to Children in the School. The frequency of such punishments found to be everyday (33.3 per cent), twice a week (59.2 per cent) and once or twice in a month (5 per cent). The Children felt that the corporal punishment was reasonable as it is given only when children do not do their work. This also indicates that the children were unaware of the rules against corporal punishment and the teachers can make the children attend to their academic work without punishing them physically.

Affect of Primary Education

Almost all the children joined the School at 5-6 years of age. It was found that nine children were school dropouts re-enrolled in schools. The reasons for dropping out and re-enrolment is as given in Table 11.12.

Table 11.12

Reasons for Dropping out and Re-enrolment in Primary School

S. No.	*Reasons for Dropping out*	*No. of Children*	*Reasons for re-enrolment*	*No. of Children*
1.	Due to lack of interest	2	They had interest in studies	2
2.	Discontinued studies due to the death of father	1	Teachers convinced the parents	4
3.	Due to financial problems	2	They controlled their health problems after they came back to the school	3
4.	Due to absence of people to do work at home	1	–	–
5.	Due to health problem	3		
		9 (Nine)		9 (Nine)

The Table 11.12 indicates that the health problems, domestic help, financial problems, death of a parent, lack of interest were the reasons for dropping out. The reasons for re-enrolment were teachers effort in convincing parents, recovery from health problems and renewed interest in studies.

Difference Between Boys and Girls

The difference between boys and girls with regard to their family profiles, school profile and affect of primary school education was studied with the help of the total scores calculated for each area for boys and girls using 't' test.

Table 11.13

Difference between boys and girls with regard to family school and affect of primary education

Area	*GEN*	*N*	*MEAN*	*SD*	*T-VAL*	*DF*	*P-VAL*	*Significance*
FSTOT	BOYS	60	10.500	2.135	1.106758	118	0.27065	NS
	GIRLS	60	10.900	1.811	–	–	–	
STOT	BOYS	60	21.483	1.172	0	118	1	NS
	GIRLS	60	21.483	1.228	–	–	–	
EDTOT	BOYS	60	7.133	0.536	0.593497	118	0.553984	NS
	GIRLS	60	7.067	0.686	–	–	–	
GTOT	BOYS	60	39.117	2.505	0.766755	118	0.444759	NS
	GIRLS	60	39.450	2.251	–	–	–	

The Table 11.13 shows that boys and girls did not differ significantly in any of the three areas studied.

Conclusions

The primary schools run under the District Primary Education Programme in Chintoor Mandal of Khammam District is fairly successful as children's and parents participation were fairly good, in spite of the shortcomings in provision of basic amenities like toilet facilities and seating arrangements. For better results more facilities should be provided in the schools to promote children's participation and interest in education.

REFERENCES

1. Agrawal, S.P. (1999): *Development of Education in India—Selected Documentation 1995-1997*; Volume-5, Concept Publishing Company, New Delhi-59.

2. Ambaasht, N.K. (1993): *Education of Tribal Communities in Pandyal and Sharmods* (eds), Contemporary Indian Society; Anmol Publication, New Delhi.

3. NCERT (1979): *Comprehensive Access to Primary Education* (CAPE), New Delhi.

4. Varghese, N.V. (1996): *In Strict Primary Education Programme. The Logic and Logistic*. Journal of Education Planning and Administration 8 (iv) October.

12

Knowledge, Attitudes and Practice of Child Rights by Mothers of Rural Pre-school Children

—Ms. M. Deepa and Prof. D. Sarada

Introduction

Early childhood education is provided with the assumption that the rate of child's growth – physical, mental, emotional and social is most rapid in the early years of development. Therefore, if a child is provided stimulating experiences early in life it will pave the way for his optimum growth and development. Blank (1970) and Sigel (1973) have provided the following rationale for early 'psycho educational' experiences to the children:

1. Children are, by nature, malleable and their growth and development can be modified extensively in a variety of directions;
2. The earlier one can effect a plausible intervention, the better;
3. The manipulation of early experience will influence psychological functioning;

4. The provision of qualitatively sound experience can modify or compensate for basic lacks in children's environment. Such lacks define the basis on which experiences can be built;

5. Since a well-developed cognitive ability is one of man's greater assets, children who fail to fulfill their potential and actualise their capacities are causing both a personal and national loss.

The current literature on child development and education reveal the importance of early childhood years on later functioning and behaviour development. It has also drawn the attention of professionals in the field of Home Science interested in early childhood care, education and development. Over the years, child psychologists have also proved that there is continuity between infancy, early childhood and late childhood. While discussing various aspects of growth and development certain age, specific changes have been observed which have been related to the performance of these children in the pre-school years as well as in later school years. The recent literature reveals considerable agreement as to the significance of early childhood and the importance of providing education for young children. During past few decades there has been an accumulation of scientific evidences that has strengthened the conviction that the first few years in the child's life are crucial time for learning. The developmental approach stresses the importance of learning that is continuous and is result of a meaningful integrated early childhood education programme.

Private and Government bodies organise the pre-schools in India. The private schools offering early childhood education in the form of pre-school programme mostly focus on learning; language, mathematics and science concepts, with very limited scope for play and creativity. It is more so, with the schools located in crowded pockets of urban and semi-urban areas. The quality of physical facilities provided in these pre-schools are also very poor. The Government pre-school education programmes are mostly offered as a welfare component of child development programmes, such as Balwadi and Anganwadi centres. These programmes also have the problem of physical facilities. Thus both the private and Government pre-school education programmes fail to provide necessary physical set up due to paucity of funds. In other words they are not able to provide qualitative pre-school education programme to the children in India.

A large percentage of parents of pre-school children in India are unable to provide good home environment needed for proper growth and development of children due to their low purchasing power, ignorance and illiteracy. This situation of poor school and home environment deprives the pre-schooler/pre-school age children of their rightful needs. Deprivation of needs further manifests into psychological problems whose cost is too much to pay.

Provision of child's needs is a responsibility of parents and the family. If the family and the parents are not capable of fulfilling the basic needs of the child, then the responsibility falls on the State. The State should extend support to such families through social support systems. With the declaration of child rights by United Nations every child is entitled to fulfillment of his/her needs as a Right.

Therefore, it is important that parents, teachers and the members of the society should know the rights of the child, develop favourable attitudes towards child rights and put them into practice so as to provide a healthy and encouraging environment to achieve their fullest potential. An attempt to study the knowledge, attitudes and practice of child rights among the parents of pre-school children in rural areas of Tirupati.

METHODOLOGY

A study on knowledge, attitudes and practice of Child Rights by mothers of rural pre-school children was undertaken with an assumption that mothers continue to play the pivotal role in the childcare and education in majority of the households in India, though the fathers involvement in childcare has also increased to an extent. In the present study only the mothers of Pre-school Children were included as the respondents.

Sample Selection

The list of villages and the registered pre-schools in Tirupati rural mandal was obtained from the Mandal Development Office (M.D.O.). The list of villages were arranged in alphabetical order and four villages were selected. That is, from the 29 villages the First, Tenth, Twentieth and Twenty ninth village were selected. From each village one school was selected and from each school thirty children were selected. Thus the sample consisted of 120 children aged between 3-6 years. The sample was drawn from four villages, four schools of Tirupati Rural Mandal.

Variables Selected

The independent variables, which have an influence on the knowledge, attitudes and practice of Child Rights of mothers of pre-school children, were included in the present study. They are: Age, Birth order, Type of family, Family size, Family income, Family Literacy Index, Occupation. The independent variables usually have direct or indirect influence on dependent variables and also on other independent variables.

Measurement of Variables

The variables selected, were studied using the following tools, which were developed specifically to measure the variables selected.

General Information Schedule

A schedule was developed to gather information such as personal profile of the sample and demographic details. The schedule was prepared in English and Telugu and administered to the mothers of rural pre-school children. As some of the mothers were illiterates, interview method was used to fill in the schedules.

Child Rights Knowledge Scale

In order to assess the knowledge of mothers on child rights a scale was developed, which consisted of thirty-eight questions and responses in the form of Yes/No. The respondents response were scored by assigning "1" for "Yes" response and "0" for "No" response. Thus the total scores obtained by each respondent for Child Rights Knowledge Scale was considered as the knowledge of that respondent.

Attitudinal Scale

An attitudinal Scale to measure the attitudes of the respondents towards the Child Rights was developed and administered. The scale consisted of thirty statements covering Child Rights. Each statement was rated on a three point scale "Strongly Agree, Agree, Disagre". The scores assigned were as follows: for Strongly Agree – 2, for Agree – 1, for Disagree – 0. Thus the total score of each respondent was computed depending on their rating on three point scale. Later the respondents responses were classified as high, medium, low attitudes.

Practice of Child Rights

A scale was developed to know the levels of Practice of Child rights by the mothers of pre-school children. The scale consisted of questions stated under five heads that is, Health and Nutritional needs, Educational needs, Psycho-social needs, Familial needs and needs of Disabled. The responses to these statements were given in the form of multiple choice and Yes/ No type. Scores were assigned to the responses in order to quantify the responses. The total scores of each respondent indicated the respondents practice of Child Rights.

Data Collection

The tools developed for measuring the variables selected were used for data collection. The investigator used Interview method for data collection. The data was later pooled, tabulated and computed.

Statistical Analysis

Selected statistical techniques, which are relevant to the topic under study, were used for Analysis of Data.

RESULTS AND DISCUSSION

General Profile of the Sample

Age: None of the fathers belonged to 18-20 years of age group, while 6.67 per cent of mothers belonged to this age group. Around 19.16 per cent of fathers and 18.7 per cent of mothers were aged between 21-30 years. Around 80.84 per cent of fathers and 5.83 per cent of mothers belonged to 31-34 years of age. None of the parents were above 41 years of age.

Educational Status: Education promotes thinking and widens one's horizons, hence it was included as a variable in the present study. Majority of the fathers (49.16 per cent) were educated upto high school, 32.5 per cent of fathers had college education and only 18.34 per cent of fathers had primary education. Majority of the mothers (51.66 per cent) had primary education, 25 per cent of mothers were educated upto high school, 18.34 per cent of mothers had college education and 5 per cent of mothers were illiterates. This shows that the educational status of mothers were comparatively lower than their male counterparts.

Occupation: Occupation is the nature of work done to earn our income. The occupation of an individual usually depends on one level of education. A good per cent of fathers (38.34 per cent) were daily wage earners, 25 per cent were employed in Government and Private sectors, 15 per cent were doing business, 11.66 per cent were self employed and only 10 per cent were engaged in agriculture and allied occupation. In the case of mothers 50.84 per cent were engaged in agriculture and allied work, 40 per cent were daily wage earners and only 9.16 per cent were employed in private and Government sectors.

Annual Income: A good percentage (35 per cent) of fathers had an annual income less than 12000 rupees. Around 37.5 per cent of fathers had an annual income between 12001-24000 rupees, 17.5 per cent of fathers had an annual income of 24001-36000 rupees and only 10 per cent of fathers had an annual income between 36001-48000 rupees. In case of mothers it can be noted that 25 per cent had annual income of less than 12000 rupees, which is below poverty line. Only 2.5 per cent of mothers had an annual income between 12001-24000 rupees and 24001-36000 rupees respectively. Studies on Development of women and children in Rural Areas (DWCRA) have revealed that money earned by women was contributed towards their family development, which is not so in case of men in rural areas.

Place of residence: All the sample belonged to rural area located 10 kms. away from Tirupati town. The place of where one resides its proximity to urban area and other infrastructural facilities influences one's knowledge and awareness.

Type of Family: Majority of the families (66.67 per cent) were of nuclear type followed by extended (25 per cent), joint (5 per cent) and single parent families (33.3 per cent). This shows that majority of the families have greater scope to practice child rights as they are nuclear in nature. In the joint and extended families even if the mother has child rights knowledge she may have to convince the other elderly members to get their co-operation in practising child rights.

Size of the family: Around 64.16 per cent of the sample had small families of less than five members and 35.84 per cent had family sizes of 5-10 members. The larger the family size the limited will be scope for interaction and also time available for childcare. In small families the opportunities for interaction will be more.

Family Literacy Index: In the present study it was found that almost all the sample had the Family Literacy Index of less than five which is very low.

Birth Order: The birth order was included as a variable with an assumption that it has an influence on knowledge of mothers with regard to childcare. Around 48.34 per cent were first born, 44.16 per cent were second born only 7.5 per cent were third born and none had a birth order above three. This shows that majority of the sample were first born.

Type of House: The housing facility is one of the basic needs of every human being. It provides privacy, security and a place to live with one's family. The type of house determines the scope for various familial activities. Hence it was included in the present study. The type of house was classified into single room, two room and three room houses. It was found that 69.16 per cent of the sample had two room houses and 30.84 per cent had three room houses. This shows that the housing facilities were not adequate and is not congenial for children to grow up as there is no place of their own to play, to share, to study and to keep their things.

Toilet Facility

The availability of toilet facility within the premises of house was gathered. It was found that 63.34 per cent of the sample had toilet facility, whereas 36.66 per cent had no toilet facility. This shows that the children were deprived of toilet facility which is a minimum need.

Ventilation

Majority of the houses constructed in rural areas in and around Tirupati do not have proper ventilation. Moreover the cooking and other domestic activities affects the ventilation available. It was found that 10.83 per cent of the sample had poor ventilation in their houses, 62.5 per cent had moderate ventilation in their houses and only 26.6 per cent had good ventilation.

Child Rights Knowledge, Attitudes and Practice by the Sample

The mean scores obtained by the mothers for Child Rights Knowledge, Attitudes and Practice were 37.15, 53.20, 38.15 respectively. The Child Rights Knowledge of the sample ranged from 37 to 38 and the maximum being 38. Similarly the Child Rights Attitudinal scores of the mothers ranged from 50 to 57 and the maximum being 57. Similarly the Child Rights Practice scores of the mothers ranged from 38 to 42 and the maximum being 44. These values indicate that the mothers of rural pre-school children had good knowledge on Child Rights, positive attitudes and practice of Child Rights. Child Rights are based on the needs of the child. Though the mothers were not aware of Child Rights declared by the U.N. they are sensitive to child's needs and aware of them. This could be a reason for their high knowledge, favourable attitudes and practice of Child Rights.

F Test

In order to compare the variability between the various groups with the sum of variability found within the groups, analysis of variance is done that is, one way analysis of variance is done with one dependent and one independent variable using F Test.

Child Rights Knowledge and Independent Variables

Table 12.1

'F' Values for Child Rights Knowledge and Independent Variables

S. No.	*Independent variables*	*F Table value*	*F Calculated value*	*Significance at 5% level*
1.	Age	3.07	1.0133	@
2.	Birth Order	3.07	2.8122	@
3.	Fathers Education	3.07	0.5428	@
4.	Mothers Education	3.07	0.0598	@
5.	Fathers Occupation	3.07	1.1292	@
6.	Mothers Occupation	3.07	0.6648	@
7.	Fathers Income	3.07	1.1383	@
8.	Mothers Income	3.07	0.9720	@
9.	Type of Family	3.07	0.3474	@
10.	Size of Family	3.07	0.7783	@

Note: @ Indicates no significance at 5 per cent level.

From the above table it is evident that there is variation among the different groups of each variable and the dependent variable Child Rights Knowledge.

Child Rights Attitudes and Independent Variables

Similarly the Child Rights attitudes of the sample and the variation among the different groups of each independent variables was analysed using F Test as shown in Table 12.2.

Table 12.2

'F' Values for Child Rights attitudes and independent variables

S. No.	*Independent variables*	*F Table value*	*F Calculated value*	*Significance at 5% level*
1.	Age	3.07	18.9316	*
2.	Birth Order	3.07	2.8122	@
3.	Fathers Education	3.07	0.9824	@
4.	Mothers Education	3.07	0.5763	@
5.	Fathers Occupation	3.07	0.5951	@
6.	Mothers Occupation	3.07	0.7504	@
7.	Fathers Income	3.07	1.9243	@
8.	Mothers Income	3.07	0.3982	@
9.	Type of Family	3.07	0.3179	@
10.	Size of Family	3.07	0.8725	@

Note: * Indicate significance at 5 per cent level.

@ Indicates no significance at 5 per cent level.

Which shows that the sample did not vary in their Child Rights Attitudes and as per their differences in their general background (Independent variables), except with regard to their age, for which significant variation was found among different age groups and Child Rights Attitudes at 5 per cent level of significance.

Child Rights Practice and Independent Variables

The Child rights practice by mothers and variation among different groups within each independent variable was assessed and it was found that the sample did not vary for any of the independent variables at 5 per cent level of significance. (See Table 12.3).

Table 12.3

'F' Values for Child Rights Practice and Independent Variables

S. No.	*Independent variables*	*F Table value*	*F Calculated value*	*Significance at 5% level*
1.	Age	3.07	1.8694	@
2.	Birth Order	3.07	2.4291	@
3.	Fathers Education	3.07	0.1921	@
4.	Mothers Education	3.07	1.5128	@
5.	Fathers Occupation	3.07	1.1010	@
6.	Mothers Occupation	3.07	0.8741	@
7.	Fathers Income	3.07	1.9852	@
8.	Mothers Income	3.07	1.3407	@
9.	Type of Family	3.07	0.6315	@
10.	Size of Family	3.07	1.6508	@

Note: @ indicates no significance at 5 per cent level.

Chi-square Test

Chi-square (χ^2) test is a measure of association and is widely used in testing the agreement between a given hypothesis and the observed data. The Chi-square test is used when the data are expressed in terms of frequencies. It applied only to discrete data. However, any continuous data which may be divided into several categories, the frequencies under these categories may be put to Chi-square test.

Association Between the Independent Variables and Child Rights Knowledge

In the present study the association between the Independent Variables and Child Rights Knowledge of the Sample was calculated using Chi-square test (See Table 12.4). There was no association found between the Child Rights Knowledge and Age of fathers and mothers, fathers educational status, mothers educational status, mothers occupation, fathers income, mothers income, type of family, and size of family. An association was found between Child Rights Knowledge of the Sample and Birth order of children and fathers Occupation at 5 per cent level of significance. This shows that the birth order and fathers Occupation had an association with the Child Rights Knowledge of the Sample.

Table 12.4

Association between the Independent Variables and Child Rights Knowledge of the Sample

S. No.	*Independent variables*	χ^2 *Value*	χ^2 *Calculated Value*	*Significance at 5% level*
1.	Age	3.86	3.0223	@
2.	Birth Order	3.86	4.6142	*
3.	Fathers Education	3.86	1.1765	@
4.	Mothers Education	3.86	0.1713	@
5.	Fathers Occupation	3.86	4.6109	*
6.	Mothers Occupation	3.86	1.4948	@
7.	Fathers Income	3.86	3.5170	@
8.	Mothers Income	3.86	2.0627	@
9.	Type of Family	3.86	0.1120	@
10.	Size of Family	3.86	0.5977	@

Note: * Indicates significance at 5 per cent level.

@ Indicates no significance at 5 per cent level.

There was no association found between the Child Rights Knowledge and the Independent variables: age, fathers' educational status, mothers' educational status, mothers' occupation, fathers' income, mothers' income, type of family and size of family. An association was found between Child Rights Knowledge of the sample and birth order of children and fathers occupation at 5 per cent level of significance. This shows that the birth order and fathers occupation had an association with the Child Rights Knowledge of the Sample.

Association Between the Child Rights Attitudes and Independent Variables

Attitudes are formed over a period of time due to the exposure to real life experiences, sometimes due to the experiences of family members and peers. Hence attitudes are an outcome of a number of variables. The association between the attitudes of the sample towards child rights and the independent variables was studied using Chi-Square test. (See Table 12.5)

Table 12.5

Association between the child rights Attitudes and Independent variables

S. No.	*Independent variables*	χ^2 *Value*	χ^2 *Calculated Value*	*Significance at 5% level*
1.	Age	3.86	38.5229	*
2.	Birth Order	3.86	7.5720	*
3.	Fathers Education	3.86	4.3095	*
4.	Mothers Education	3.86	3.6588	@
5.	Fathers Occupation	3.86	3.7292	@
6.	Mothers Occupation	3.86	4.3073	*
7.	Fathers Income	3.86	5.0854	*
8.	Mothers Income	3.86	2.2617	@
9.	Type of Family	3.86	4.7506	*
10.	Size of Family	3.86	0.6748	@

Note: * indicate significant at 5 per cent level.

@ indicates no significance at 5 per cent level.

In contrary to the findings for Child rights knowledge, the Child rights attitudes of the sample was found to be associated with the independent variables such as age of the fathers and mothers, birth order of children, fathers educational status, mothers occupation, fathers income and the type family. It was also found that the variables such as fathers occupation, mothers educational status, mothers income, and size of the family did not have an association with the child rights attitudes of the same.

Association Between the Child Rights Practice and the Independent Variables

Practice is an application of knowledge in day-to-day activities. The KAP model of Community education, which emphasises acquisition of knowledge is followed by change in attitudes and leads to change in practice, is not always found to happen in the same order in several community education research studies.

From the Table 12.6 it is evident that there is an association found between the child rights practice by the sample and the independent variables such as age, mothers education, fathers occupation and mothers income. The association was found between the child rights practice of mothers of rural pre-school children and the independent variables, birth order of children, fathers education, mothers education, fathers income, type of family and size of family.

Table 12.6

Association between the child rights Practice and the Independent variables

S. No.	*Independent variables*	χ^2 *Value*	χ^2 *Calculated Value*	*Significance at 5% level*
1.	Age	3.86	4.0506	*
2.	Birth Order	3.86	1.8899	@
3.	Fathers Education	3.86	0.9756	@
4.	Mothers Education	3.86	4.1744	*
5.	Fathers Occupation	3.86	5.2631	*
6.	Mothers Occupation	3.86	1.56335	@
7.	Fathers Income	3.86	1.6445	@
8.	Mothers Income	3.86	4.9331	*
9.	Type of Family	3.86	1.1672	@
10.	Size of Family	3.86	3.1364	@

Note: * indicate significant at 5 per cent level.

@ indicates no significance at 5 per cent level.

Step-wise Multiple Regression Test

In the present study an attempt was made to apply Step-wise Multiple Regression analysis to study the relationship and variation between the dependent and Independent variables.

Step-wise regression is a variation of multiple regression which provides a means of choosing independent variables that yield the best prediction possible with the fewest independent variables. It permits the user to solve a sequence of one or more multiple linear regression problems by step-wise application of the least square method. At each step in the analysis, a variable is added or removed which results in the greatest reduction in the error to sum of squares (Burroughs Corporation, 1975).

Multiple Regression Analysis of Child Rights Knowledge and Independent Variables

As shown in the Table 12.7 (*See on next page*) the Independent variables age, birth order, fathers occupation and fathers income had a variance of 2.16, 3.71, 2.333, 2.81 percentage respectively, which is not significant. The 't' values indicate that the sample differed among themselves with regard to their birth order and fathers income in their child rights knowledge. Because the 't' values for these two Independent variables is greater than the table value (t_e = 1.96, t_0 = 2.12 and 2.03 respectively).

Multiple Regression Analysis of Child Rights Attitudes and Independent Variables

The multiple regression analysis results indicate that (*See Table 12.8 on page 237*) the Independent variables: age of the child, age of the mothers, mothers occupations, fathers income and size of the family had a percentage of variance of 37.02, 1.98, 0.75, 3.82, 0.62 respectively. This shows that the age of the child has contributed much to the attitudes of the mothers when compared to the other variables.

The t-values indicate that the sample differed in their attitudes towards Child Rights as per their Age, Children's age and Fathers Income as their t-values were greater than the table value (1.96).

Table 12.7

Multiple Regression analysis: dependent variable Knowledge: Independent Variables Age, Birth Order, Fathers Occupation and Fathers Income

S. No.	*Variables*	R^2	*Partial regression co-efficient*	*Beta co-efficient*	*Standard error*	*'t' value*	*% of Variance*	*F Ratio*
1.	Age	0.110045	0.0533	0.1367	0.03444	1.547078	2.16	3.555003
2.	Birth Order		0.0976	0.1896	0.04613	2.120567	3.71	
3.	Fathers Occupation		0.0392	0.1415	0.02448	1.599534	2.33	
4.	Fathers Income		0.0666	0.1794	0.03290	2.025387	2.81	

Table 12.8

Multiple Regression analysis: Dependent Variable Attitude: Independent Variables Age, Mothers Age, Mothers Occupation, Fathers Income and Size of Family

S. No.	*Variables*	R^2	*Partial regression co-efficient*	*Beta co-efficient*	*Standard error*	*'t' value*	*% of Variance*	*F Ratio*
1.	Age of the child	0.402299	1.3334	0.7005	0.16606	8.029397	37.02	15.34617
2.	Mothers age		2.0052	0.2867	0.61409	3.265262	1.98	
3.	Mothers Occupation		0.2808	0.1053	0.19592	1.433221	0.75	
4.	Fathers Income		0.3519	0.1939	0.13391	2.628024	3.82	
5.	Size of Family		0.4163	0.1144	0.26618	1.563848	0.62	

Table 12.9

Multiple Regression analysis of Child Rights Practice and Mothers' Age, Fathers' Income

S. No.	*Variables*	*R^2*	*Partial regression co-efficient*	*Beta co-efficient*	*Standard error*	*'t' value*	*% of Variance*	*F Ratio*
1.	Mothers age	4.661177 E-02	0.588	0.1461	0.34639	1.613257	1.94	2.860103
2.	Fathers income		0.1693	0.1706	0.08987	1.883831	2.72	

The findings through multiple regression analysis (Table 12.9) showed that the sample did not have a significant strength of relationship between Child rights practice and their mothers age and fathers income. Further it can be noted that they did not differ in their Child Rights Practice with regard to mothers age and fathers income as the t-values were less than the table value (1.96).

Conclusion

The findings of the study allows to conclude that the child rights are based on the needs of the child. Though the mothers were not aware of child rights declared by the United Nations as they are sensitive to child's needs as they were aware child rights which were formulated based on the needs of the child. This could be the reason for their knowledge, favourable attitudes and practice of child rights.

REFERENCES

1. Alfred, L.B., 1949. Cited by Laxmi Devi; Health, Nutrition and Early Childhood Education. The Effect of Home Environment on Nursery School Behaviour; *Child Development*, pp. 20, 49-62.
2. Garrett, J.N. and Kelly, M.F., 2000: Early Childhood Special Education; *Journal of Childhood Education.*
3. Gesell, A., 1954: Cited by Laxmi Devi; Health, Nutrition and Early Childhood Education. The first five years of life London; Mithven & Co. Ltd, New Delhi.
4. Smith, A.F., 2000: Reflective Portfolios: Pre-school possibilities. *Journal of Childhood Education*, Vol. 76(4), pp. 204-208.
5. Sonawat, R. and Porichha, T., 2000: Scale to Measure the Quality of Early Childhood Care and Education Programmes in the City of Mumbai. *Journal of Perspectives in Social Work*, Vol. XV(2), pp.10-16.

13

Knowledge, Attitudes and Practice of Child Rights by Mothers of Primary School Children

—Ms. P. Bharathi and Prof. D. Sarada

INTRODUCTION

The convention on child rights provides the legal basis for initiating action to ensure the right of children in society. The convention is desired from a core set of human values and ethical premises that recognise the inherent dignity and the equal and inalienable rights of all members of the human family as the foundation of freedom, justice and peace in the world. Accordingly, the convention states that the rights shall be extended to all children without discrimination of any kind, irrespective of the child's or his or her parent's or legal guardian's race, nationality, colour, sex, language, religion, political or other opinion, national/social origin, property, disability, birth or other status. The convention also draws particular attention to the fact that in all countries in the world, there are children living in exceptionally difficult circumstances, and that such children need special consideration. It advocates measures for the protection and harmonious development of the child that are consistent with the traditions and cultural values of different people. By providing safeguards against economic and other policies that have a negative effect on the well-being of children, the convention reaffirms a commitment to promote social progress that will ensure a better quality of life and greater freedom for people in general, and children in particular. It also under scores the importance and potential of international co-operation for promoting and improving the living conditions of children in every country.

The U.N. convention on Child Rights proclaims that all the needs of the child are the rights of a child. Fulfillment of which are the responsibilities of the parents, family and the state. U.N. has also declared the period between 1995 to 2004 as decade for Human Rights Education. All the countries signatory to the convention on Child Rights and Human Rights have undertaken programmes to popularise the Human Rights messages and education.

It is from the primary schools that a major percentage of children dropout and turn to child labour and streetism. The levels of Knowledge, Attitudes and Practise of Child Rights also reflects the responsibility of the parents towards their children. The free and compulsory education of all children in the age group 6-14 should have been brought to school by 1960. But this constitutional commitment made over 40 years ago has not been achieved and the goal of universation of elementary education has not been realised so far completely.

There are also several inequalities in the system that need to be corrected. For instance, fewer girls enroll in primary school and more girls than boys drop-out before completing Grade V. Also, school drop-out rates among children belonging to scheduled castes and schedules tribes continues to be significantly higher than among children belonging to the rest of the population.

Methodology

The study was conducted in Tirupati Urban Mandal of Andhra Pradesh. An education programme in order to be relevant must be based on Knowledge, Attitudes and Practices (KAP) of learners. Similarly for child rights education programme also it is necessary to assess the knowledge, attitudes and practise of learners and develop a need based curriculum. In the present study KAP of the mothers of urban primary school children was assessed with this assumption of study on knowledge attitudes and practise of child rights by mothers of primary school children was undertaken.

Child Rights in one way means adult responsibilities. Any attempt to help children to utilise Rights requires education of adults on Child Rights. Adults include parents, teacher, elders and all those who are involved in development of children with families and without families.

Selection of the Sample

The list of primary schools run by government, private and Tirumala-Tirupati Devasthanam was collected. The names of the schools were arranged in alphabetical order from which three schools were selected at random. Thus two government, private schools and one private primary school were selected for the present study. From each primary school forty (40) children were selected randomly. Thus the sample selected comprised of 120 children for all the three schools. The addresses of all these children was also recorded from school records in order to make home visit for data collection.

Selection of Variables

The variables related to personal and family profile of the sample such as age, type of family, family size, Family Literature Index (FLI), occupation were included as independent variables. The dependent variables such as child rights knowledge, attitudes and practise were studied in relation to the independent variables.

The relationship among the independent and dependent variables were analysed as follows.

Measurement of Variables

The following tools were developed and employed to gather data for the present study.

Questionnaire

A questionnaire was framed to collect personal and family profile of the respondent. The questionnaire was developed both in English and Telugu.

Knowledge Scale on Child Rights

To assess the respondents Knowledge on Child Rights a scale consisting of 38 questions were framed with Yes/No type of responses. For the response 'yes' a score '1' was assigned and for the response 'no' a score of '0' was assigned. The Knowledge scale was also developed in English and Telugu. The knowledge scale covers almost all the Child Rights declared by the United Nations.

Attitudinal Scale on Child Rights

To assess Attitudes of the respondents towards Child Rights a scale was developed, which consisted of 30 statements, which were rated on a three point scale such as strongly agree, agree, disagree. The responses were scored by giving '2' for strongly agree, '1' for agree and '0' for disagree. This scale was also developed in English and Telugu and administered to the sample.

Practices Scale on Child Rights

A scale was developed to assess the practices of mothers with regard to Child Rights. The scale consisted of 34 statements grouped under four areas such as:

1. Rights related to Health and Nutritional needs;
2. Rights related to Educational Needs;
3. Rights related to psycho-social and recreational needs.
4. Rights related to familial needs.

Under each area few statements were included with Yes/No type and multiple choice type of responses. The practises scale was developed both in English and Telugu and the responses were rated on Multiple choice type and Yes/No type of answers.

Data Collection

The investigator visited the houses of all the 120 children and interviewed the mothers and filled in the scales as a good number of mothers were illiterates and majority were not conversant with the topic under study. The data thus gathered was tabulated and subjected to relevant statistical analysis.

Statistical Analysis

The following statistical tests were employed to analyse the data gathered.

Mean Deviation

$$\bar{x} = \frac{\sum x}{N}$$

Standard Deviation

$$S_1^2 = \sqrt{\frac{X^2}{n_1} - (\bar{X})^2}$$

$$S_2^2 = \sqrt{\frac{\sum y^2}{n^2} - (\bar{y})^2}$$

X^2-test chi-square test

This is to find the association between the variables.

$$x^2 = \sum\left(O^2/E\right) - N$$

t-test

$$\frac{\bar{x} - \bar{y}}{\sqrt{2/1/n_1 + 1/n^2}}$$

$$\text{Where } \delta 2 \frac{n^1 S_1^2 - n^2 S_2^2}{N_1 + n_2 - 2}$$

'F' test

Results and Discussion

The data gathered on "Child Rights Knowledge, Attitudes and Practise by Mothers of primary school children" was tabulated, analysed and discussed as under.

Personal and Family Profile of the Respondents

Age: The chronological age of the subjects (primary school children) in completed years was taken from the school records.

The age of the children ranged from 5-12 years; around 5.85 per cent of the children were aged between 5-6 years, 14.61 per cent of the children were of 6-7 years of age and 15 per cent of the children were of 7-8 years of age, 18.3 per cent of the children were aged between 8-9 years and around 13.3 per cent were of 9-10 years of age and around 15.83 per cent had 10-11 years and 17.5 per cent of the children were ranged between 11-12 years.

Sex: Universally all individuals were divided into two permanent classes that is male and female. In the present study the girls constituted 48.33 per cent and boys 51.66 per cent of the sample.

Birth order: Children's birth order is an important variable in the study to know about the knowledge, attitude and practice of mothers. Among the sample studied around 43.33 per cent were first born, 35.84 per cent of were second born and 20.83 per cent were third born children.

Type of School

The sample for the study were drawn from private and Government schools. Their percentage were 33.3 per cent and 66.7 per cent respectively. That is a major percentage of the children were from Government schools.

Mothers Age

The chronological age of the subjects in completed years is taken as age. Age is a steadily changing condition; individuals are strongly influenced by the age norms. Among the sample selected 66.6 per cent belonged to an age group of 21 to 30 years and 33.33 per cent of mothers belonged to an age group of 31 to 40 years.

Mothers Educational Status

Education is essential for every person. It develops the mental faculties of a person acquaints him/her with the world around them and satisfies the need of intellectual development. Levels of one's knowledge may be influenced by one's educational status. Among the sample studied 41.66 per cent of mothers were educated upto primary school; around 32.5 per cent had school education and 25.84 per cent were illiterates.

Occupation

Is the nature of work done to earn money/income. It depends on a person's education, training, personal capabilities and interests. The occupation of mothers and fathers were as follows.

Mothers occupation also indicates the amount of leisure time available to spend with her children. Around 36.6 per cent of the mothers were housewives, and 8.33 per cent of the mothers were employed in government and private sector, 19.66 per cent of the mothers were self employed and 35.34 per cent of the mothers were labourers and daily wage earners.

Fathers Occupation

The fathers occupation also indicates the amount of time available to spend with the family. Around 12.5 per cent of the fathers were government employees, 20 per cent of the fathers were private employed, around 27.5 per cent of the fathers were doing business and 31.67 per cent of the fathers were labourers and daily wage earners and 8.33 per cent of the fathers were agricultural workers. This shows that a major percentage of the fathers of children under study were employed in unorganised sector where job security is low.

Annual Income of the Family

The total income earned by the family in a year is considered as the family's annual income. The total amount of money received by the family in a year and which is utilised for meeting family expenses in that year was considered as family income.

Around 44.17 per cent families had income of less than 12000 rupees per annum which is below the poverty line. A 46.66 per cent of sample had annual income between 12001 to 24000 rupees and 9.17 per cent had income above 24000 rupees per annum. The data shows that almost all the subjects belonged to low and middle income families.

Family size: The number of members in a family determines the size of the family. The mother in a family may have an opportunity to interact with all the members of the family. Hence family size has been included as a variable in the present study. Around 40 per cent of the mothers belonged to the families of less than 5 members, whereas 60 per cent had families of 5-8 size.

Family type: The type of family determines the amount of leisure time available and the level of interaction among the family members. Hence this was chosen for inclusion in the present study. A major percentage of the sample (64.16 per cent) had nuclear families and 35.84 per cent had joint families.

Family Literacy Index (FLI)

The Family Literacy Index is the mean total number of years of education received by the family members. The number of years of education had by the family members may have an influence on their Knowledge, Attitudes and Practice of Child Rights. Hence Family Literacy Index is included as a variable in the present study.

A major percentage (66.66 per cent) of mothers were from families with less than five Family Literacy Index value, 33.34 per cent mothers had a Family Literacy Index value between 5-10 which indicates a low educational status of families.

Child Rights Knowledge, Attitudes and Practice of Mothers

The mean scores of mothers for child rights knowledge was 36.0 for attitude 54.4 and for practices was 39.34. This shows that the mothers Knowledge, Attitudes and Practices with regard to Child Rights were well- above average, which indicates that the mothers possessed Child Rights Knowledge, favourable Attitudes and Practiced Child Rights to some extent without realising about the declaration of Child Rights by United Nations.

Difference Within the Different Groups of Independent Variables with Regard to Child Rights Knowledge, Attitudes and Practice

The Independent variables such as sex, type of school, mothers age, family size, family type, Family Literacy Index were studied by classifying the sample into different groups as per each variable. The difference among the different groups of sample with regard to Child Rights Knowledge, Attitudes and Practice were studied with the help of 't' test.

Independent Variables and Child Rights Knowledge

The difference within the different groups of independent variables with regard to Child Rights Knowledge is presented in Table 13.1.

Table 13.1

Independent Variables and Child Rights Knowledge

S. No.	*Variables*	*'t' Table value*	*'t' Calculated value*	*Significance at 5% level*
1.	Sex	1.96	0.6354	@
2.	Type of School	1.96	3.0451	**
3.	Mothers age	1.96	2.1307	*
4.	Family size	1.96	2.2216	*
5.	Family type	1.96	0.9697	@
6.	Family Literacy Index	1.96	1.0436	@

Note: @: Indicates no significant difference at 5% level.

*: Indicates significant difference at 5% level.

**: Indicates significant difference at 0.01% level.

The Table 13.1 shows that the sample differed significantly in their Child Rights Knowledge among themselves to the variables; type of school, mothers age and family size. The sample did not show significant difference between Child Rights Knowledge and sex, family type and Family Literacy Index. This indicates that the variables type of school, mothers age and family size had influence on Child Rights Knowledge of the sample.

Independent Variables and Child Rights Attitude

The difference within the different groups of independent variables with regard to Child Rights Attitudes of mothers is shown in Table 13.2.

Table 13.2

Independent variables and Child Rights Attitude

S. No.	*Variables*	*'t' Table value*	*'t' Calculated value*	*Significance at 5% level*
1.	Sex	1.96	0.0899	@
2.	Type of School	1.96	0.6622	@
3.	Mothers Age	1.96	1.0221	@
4.	Family Size	1.96	1.6321	@
5.	Family Type	1.96	0.1799	@
6.	Family Literacy Index	1.96	0.9250	@

Note: @ Indicates no significant difference at 5% level.

From the Table 13.2 it is evident that the sample did not differ among themselves with regard to the Child Rights Attitude and any of the independent variables.

Independent Variables and Child Rights Practice

The difference within the different groups of independent variables with regard to Child Rights practice is given in Table 13.3.

Table 13.3

Independent variables and Child Rights Practice

S. No.	*Variables*	*'t' Table value*	*'t' Calculated value*	*Significance at 5% level*
1.	Sex	1.96	0.000	@
2.	Type of School	1.96	2.709	*
3.	Mothers Age	1.96	0.7989	@
4.	Family Size	1.96	0.2220	@
5.	Family Type	1.96	0.1072	@
6.	Family Literacy Index	1.96	1.1583	@

Note: @: Indicates no significant difference at 5% level

*: Indicates significant difference at 5% level.

The sample did not show significant difference between Child Rights practice and the independent variables such as sex, mothers age, family size, family type, Family Literacy Index. But significant difference was found between the two groups of the sample as per the type of school and Child Rights practice by mothers.

The 't' test values of Child Rights Knowledge, Attitudes, Practice and different groups of Independent variables indicate that the sample differed among themselves for three variables. That is type of school, mothers age and family size with regard to Child Rights knowledge. They differed among themselves for type of school and Child Rights Attitude only. In contrary, they did not differ for any of the independent variables and Child Rights practice. This implies that only Child Rights Knowledge and Practice were influenced by one and three variables. But the Child Rights Attitudes of mothers were not influenced by any of the independent variables.

Variation Among the Sample for Child Rights KAP and Independent Variables

Analysis of variance was done with one independent variable and one dependent variable. Analysis of variance is the technique of partitioning the total variation among a number of individual variate belonging to two or more classes or sets into various components such as variation due to different sets or treatments or between treatments and variation due to all other undistinguishing causes including sampling.

The variation among different groups of independent variables with regard to Child Rights Knowledge, Attitudes and Practice was tested using 'F' test.

'F' Values of Child Rights Knowledge and Independent Variables

The variation among the sample for Child Rights Knowledge and independent variables is given in Table 13.4.

Table 13.4

'F' Values for Child Rights Knowledge and Independent Variables

S. No.	*Variables*	*'t' Table value*	*'t' Calculated value*	*Significance at 5% level*
1.	Children's Age	2.17	1.5140	@
2.	Birth Order	3.07	0.8744	@
3.	Mothers Educational Status	3.07	2.1921	@
4.	Mothers Occupation	2.29	1.0276	@
5.	Mothers Income	2.68	1.2755	@
6.	Family Income	3.07	2.4076	@

Note: @ Indicates no significant difference at 5% level.

From Table 13.4 it is evident that the sample did not show significant variation for any of the independent variables and Child Rights Knowledge.

'F' Values for Child Rights Attitude and Independent Variable

The attitudes are formed over a period of time subject to one's experiences in life. Hence it was always thought that individual, family and social factors influence formation of Attitudes. In the present study the variation among the sample with regard to Child Rights Attitudes and independent variable were studied.

Table 13.5

'F' Values for Child Rights Attitude and Independent Variables

S. No.	*Variables*	*'t' Table value*	*'t' Calculated value*	*Significance at 5% level*
1.	Children's Age	2.17	1.1016	@
2.	Birth Order	3.07	5.1634	*
3.	Mothers Educational Status	3.07	0.5506	@
4.	Mothers Occupation	2.29	2.3509	*
5.	Mothers Income	2.68	0.7926	@
6.	Family Income	3.07	0.6775	@

Note: @: Indicates no significant difference at 5% level.

*: Indicates significant difference at 5% level.

The Table 13.5 indicates that the sample varied significantly for two variables – Birth order and mothers occupation. But they did not show significant variation for the variables – children's age, mothers educational status, mothers income, family income, Child Rights Attitudes of the mothers.

'F' Values for Child Rights Practice and Independent Variables

Practice is application of Knowledge in day to day life unless the Knowledge acquired is practised it has no value. For practice of Knowledge there may be some problems which the individual has to overcome. The variation among the sample with regard to Child Rights practice was assessed using 'F' test which is given in Table 13.6. (*See on next page*)

From the Table 13.6 it is clear that the sample did not vary significantly among themselves for the independent variables children's age, birth order, mothers educational status, mothers occupation, family income and Child Rights practice. The sample varied among themselves for mothers' income and Child Rights practice.

Table 13.6

'F' Values for Child Rights Practice and Independent Variables

S. No.	*Variables*	*'t' Table value*	*'t' Calculated value*	*Significance at 5% level*
1.	Children's age	2.17	1.2750	@
2.	Birth order	3.07	2.9282	@
3.	Mothers Educational Status	3.07	0.5604	@
4.	Mothers Occupation	2.29	1.8691	@
5.	Mothers Income	2.68	3.1173	*
6.	Family Income	3.07	1.1495	@

Note: @: Indicates no significant difference at 5% level

*: Indicates significant difference at 5% level.

Association Between Independent Variables and Child Rights Knowledge, Attitudes and Practice

Chi-square Test

Chi-square (χ^2) test is a measure of association and is widely used in testing the agreement between a given hypothesis and the observed data. The chi-square test is used when the data are expressed in terms of frequencies. It applies only to discrete data. However, any continuous data which may be divided into several categories, the frequencies under these categories may be put to (χ^2) test. Using (χ^2) test the association between variables under study was assessed as under.

Association Between Independent Variables and Child Rights Knowledge

From the Table 13.7 it is evident that there is no association between mothers educational status and Child Rights Knowledge. But there is an association between family income and Child Rights Knowledge of the mother which implies a relationship between family income and Child Rights Knowledge of mothers.

Association Between Independent Variables and Child Rights Attitudes

Table 13.7

Association between Independent Variables and Child Rights Knowledge

S. No.	*Variables*	*χ^2 table value*	*χ^2 calculated value*	*Significance at 5% level*
1.	Mothers Educational status	3.86	3.7837	@
2.	Family Income	3.86	10.75	*

Note: @: Indicates no significant difference at 5% level.

*: Indicates significant difference at 5% level.

The Table 13.7 indicates that the Child Rights attitudes of the mothers is not associated with mothers education and family income.

Association Between Independent Variables and Child Rights Practice

Table 13.8

Association between Independent Variables and Child Rights Attitudes

S. No.	*Variables*	*χ^2 table value*	*χ^2 calculated value*	*Significance at 5% level*
1.	Mothers Educational status	3.86	3.3551	@
2.	Family Income	3.86	3.5005	@

Note: @ Indicates no significant difference at 5% level.

The Table 13.8 indicates that there is no association between the Child Rights practice by the mothers, mothers education and family income.

Association Between Child Rights Knowledge, Attitudes and Practices by the Mothers

The Knowledge, Attitudes and Practice are interrelated. The Educationist through various studies proved that

Knowledge changes Attitude and leads to practice. This KAP model is well researched in the area of the community education also. The Child Rights education is also a concern of the community and government. Assessment of KAP should precede any educational programme in order to be successful.

The Association between Child Rights Knowledge, Attitudes and Practice was studied using χ^2 test as shown in Table 13.9.

Table 13.9

Association between Independent Variables and Child Rights Practice

S. No.	*Variables*	*χ^2 table value*	*χ^2 calculated value*	*Significance at 5% level*
1.	Mothers Educational Status	3.86	1.0347	@
2.	Family Income	3.86	1.9612	@

Note: @ Indicates no significant difference at 5% level.

Association Among Child Rights Knowledge, Attitudes and Practice by Mothers of Primary School Children

Table 13.10

Association among Child Rights Knowledge, Attitudes and Practice by Mothers of Primary School Children

S. No.	*Variables*	*χ^2 table value*	*χ^2 calculated value*	*Significance at 5% level*
1.	Knowledge Vs Attitude	3.86	3.8768	*
2.	Knowledge Vs Practice	3.86	3.9771	*
3.	Attitude Vs Practice	3.86	6.9967	*

Note: *: Indicates significant difference at 5% level.

From the Table 13.10 it is evident that Knowledge is associated with Attitudes and practice significantly at 5 per cent level. Child Rights Attitudes is also associated significantly with Child Rights practice. This indicates that the Child Rights Knowledge, Attitude and Practice are significantly associated with each other and they are interrelated.

The mothers possessed Child Rights Knowledge, favourable Attitudes and Practiced Child Rights to some extent without realising about the declaration of Child Rights by United Nations.

REFERENCES

1. Abdulrahim, P., Vijapur and Kumar Suresh, 1999: *Perspectives on Human Rights. The Universal Declaration of Human Rights. A corner stone of modern Human Rights Regime*; Published by Mank Publications (P) Ltd., pp. 12-27.
2. Bani Borgohain, 1999: *Human Rights Social Justice and Political Challenge*; Kanishka Publishers, New Delhi, pp. 68-73.
3. Chit Kara, M.G., 1996: *Human Rights, Commitment and Betrayal*, Published by S.B. Nangia for A.P. Publishing Corporation, pp. 161-173.
4. Khanna, S.K., 1999: *Children and the Human Rights*; Commonwealth Publishers, pp. 339-381.
5. Subramanian Dr. S., 1997: "*Human Rights International Challenges*"; Manas Publication, New Delhi, pp. 115-143.

14

Child Rights Knowledge of School Teachers and Their Role in Promotion of Child Rights

—**Ms. N.C. Krishnaveni** and **Prof. D. Sarada**

INTRODUCTION

The international approach to children has changed dramatically, the idea that children have special needs has given way to the conviction that children have Rights, the same full spectrum of Rights as adults—civil and political, social, cultural and economic.

This conviction, expressed as the convention on the Rights of the child, entered into international law on 2 September 1990, nine months after the convention's adoption by the United Nations General Assembly. Since then, the convention has been ratified (as of mid-September 1996) by all countries except the cook Islands, Oman, Somalia, Switzerland, the United Arab Emirates and the United States, making it the most widely ratified Human Rights treaty in history.

The convention has produced a profound change that is already beginning to have substantive effects on the world's attitude towards its children. Once a country ratifies, it is obliged in law to undertake all appropriate measures to assist parents and other responsible stake holders in fulfilling their obligations to children under the convention. Now, 96 per cent of the world's children live in states that are legally obligated to protect children's Rights.

The convention recognises that not all governments have the resources necessary to ensure all economics, social and cultural Rights immediately. But it commits them to make those Rights a priority and to ensure them to the maximum extent of available resources.

Fulfilling their obligations sometimes requires states to make fundamental changes in national laws, institutions, plans, policies and practices to bring them into line with the principles of the convention.

The first priority must be to generate the political will to do this. As the drafters of the convention recognised, real change in the lives of children will come about only when social attitudes and which progressively change to conform with laws and principles. And when as actors, in the process, children themselves know enough about their Rights to claim them.

Around the world, teachers, lawyers, police officials, judges and care givers are being trained in the principles and the application of the convention.

In a positive initiative to involve the media in educating children about their Rights, the Asian summit on child Rights and the media, held in Manila in July 1996, included a wide range of participants in four days of discussions on how to educate, inform and entertain children while also taking into account their best interests.

The convention, by expressing and protecting all the Rights of children, expands the scope of action required for children and throws a clear shaft of light on paths that extend beyond the year 2000.

The convention requires families, societies, governments and the international community to take action designed to fulfill the Rights of all children in a sustainable, participatory and non discriminatory manner.

The school as one of the basic institutions for child development, next to families should be used for increasing awareness on child Rights. Children spend their time in school and home; the parents and teachers are the shapers of children's behaviour and influence children's views and concepts. Hence, the parents and teachers' knowledge, attitudes and behaviour with regard to child needs and Rights has great influence on child's future. The teachers can play a greater role in providing necessary inputs for the children's development. A child's liking for studies depends on his/her teachers role at school. With this background the investigator made an attempt to study the teacher's knowledge on child Rights and their role in promotion of child Rights.

METHODOLOGY

A study on "Child Rights Knowledge of School Teachers and Their Role in Promotion of Child Rights" was carried out in Tirupati urban mandal of Chittoor District, Andhra Pradesh.

Locale of the Study

Tirupati being a popular temple town has several schools managed by Tirumala Tirupati Devasthanams (TTD), the Tirupati municipality and the private educational institutions (registered). The Tirumala Tirupati Devasthanams has a separate department of education, headed by an education officer of D.E.O. cadre, who is incharge of selection, recruitment and training of teachers of T.T.D. educational institutions within and outside the state.

Similarly the Tirupati municipality also has a separate administration setup for their schools. The private schools though registered do not have teachers with long standing service that is they are changed frequently. For the present study the training inputs received by the teachers during their service is being considered. Hence, the private schools are not included in the present study. Only the TTD and Municipal schools are considered.

Sample Selection

A list of TTD and Municipal schools is prepared from which two Boys High Schools and two Girls High Schools were selected for the study. All the teachers in all four schools are met during their meetings in TTD and Municipality offices. Around thirty teachers from TTD schools and thirty teachers from Municipality were selected for the study (See figure-1). The teachers who are willing to respond only considered.

Figure – 14.1

Sample Selection

(School Teachers)

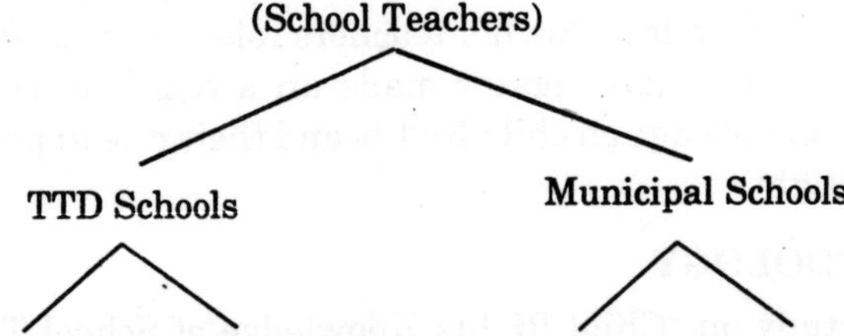

Boys High School Girls High School Boys High School Girls High School

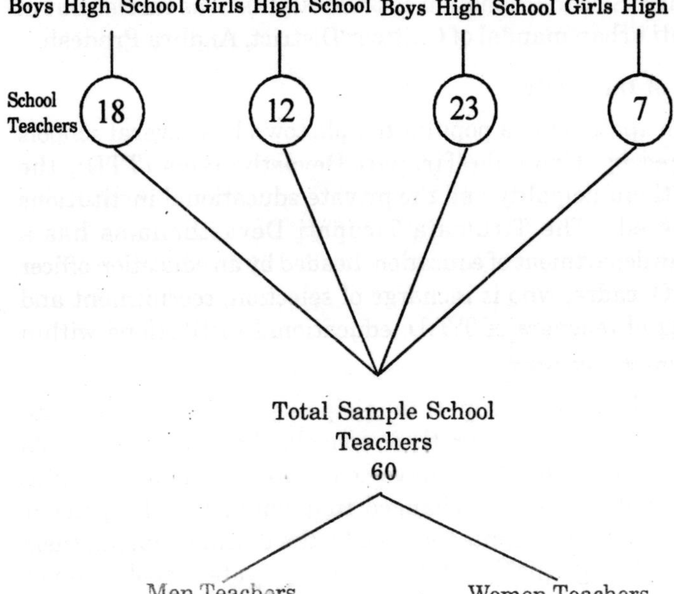

Selection of Variables

The teachers knowledge and role in promotion of child rights may be influenced by several variables both at personal and working level. Hence, the following independent and dependent variables are chosen for in the study.

The independent variables are: Age, Sex, Educational status, Length of service, Orientation/Trainings received. The dependent variables are Child Rights knowledge of teachers and the Role of teachers in promotion of child rights.

Relationship Between the Independent and Dependent Variables Under Study

In order to understand the relationship between independent variables and dependent variables a flow chart was drawn as shown in Figure 14.2.

Fig. 14.2

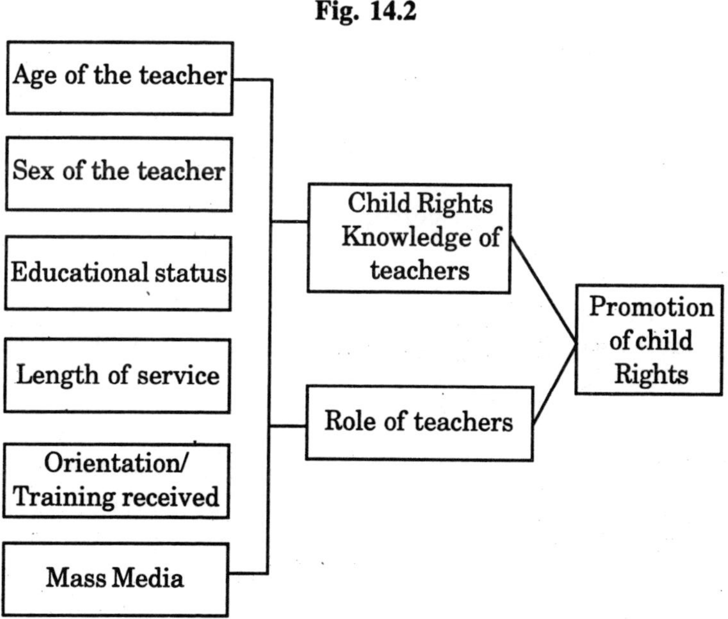

Measurement of Variables

In order to measure the independent and dependent variables a General Information Schedule and a Child Rights Knowledge's Scale was used.

General Information Schedule

The schedule consisted of questions pertaining to personal and professional profile of teachers and also in the sources of knowing child Rights information. The schedule consisted of sixteen questions with Yes/No, multiple choice responses and open ended questions.

Rights Knowledge Scale

The scale consisted of thirty eight statements based on child rights declared by the United Nations. The responses of teachers are rated on Yes/No type.

Data Collection

The teachers are met personally and given schedules. The filled in schedules were collected by the investigator.

Statistical Analysis

The data is pooled, tabulated and analysed using 't' test and chi-square test.

RESULTS AND DISCUSSION

General Profile of the Sample

The personal and professional information relevant to the study is gathered to understand their influence on the dependent variables.

Age and Sex

The data on school teachers age and sex is gathered and the sample is classified into two groups, that is those coming under 20 to 40 years age group and those coming under 41-60 years age group. The data shows that around 30 per cent of men and 46.7 per cent of women teachers belonged to 20-40 years age group. Around 70 per cent of men and 53.3 per cent of women teachers belonged to 41-60 years age group.

Educational Status of the Sample

The actual formal education received by the teachers is gathered. The distribution of the teachers according to their educational status is given in Table 14.1.

Table 14.1

Distribution of School Teachers according to their educational status

S. No.	*Formal Education received*	*TTD*		*Municipal*		*Total*
		Men	*Women*	*Men*	*Women*	
1.	High School Education	5 (33.3)	5 (33.3)	4 (26.4)	3 (20)	17 (28.4)
2.	College Education	10 (66.7)	10 (66.7)	11 (72.6)	12 (80)	43 (71.6)
	Total	**15 (100)**	**15 (100)**	**15 (100)**	**15 (100)**	**60 (100)**

Note: The numbers in parenthesis are percentages.

From the above table it is evident that majority of the school teachers had college education, whereas only 33.3 per cent of TTD and 26.4 per cent of municipal school teachers had only high school education.

Length of Service of the Sample

The number of years of professional experience is considered as the length of service. The experience of teachers in teaching and handling children equips them with better knowledge and understanding of children. Hence it is included as a variable in the present study.

The teachers under study are classified into three groups as shown in Table 14.2.

From the Table 14.2 it is evident that majority of the teachers had less than 10 years of service followed by teachers with more than 15 years of service. A small percentage of teachers had 10-15 years of service.

Table 14.2

Distribution of sample according to their length of service (years)

S. No.	*Length of Service in years*	*TTD*		*Municipal*		*Total*
		Men	*Women*	*Men*	*Women*	
1.	< 10	7 (46.7)	9 (60)	10 (66.7)	12 (80)	38 (63.3)
2.	10-15	2 (13.3)	2 (13.3)	3 (20)	2 (13.3)	9 (15)
3.	> 15	6 (40)	4 (26)	2 (13.3)	1 (6.7)	13 (21.7)
	Total	**15 (100)**	**15 (100)**	**15 (100)**	**15 (100)**	**60 (100)**

Note: The numbers in parenthesis are percentages.

Training/Orientation received by the Teachers

The school administration organises training and orientation courses for teachers to provide current information and also to equip the teachers with necessary skills in teaching and handling children. There is every chance for including child Rights in anyone of the programmes recently organized for teachers. Hence it is included as a variable in the present study. Depending upon number and type of programmes attended, the teachers were classified as shown in Table 14.3. (*See on next page)*

From the Table 14.3 it is evident that almost all the teachers have attended at least one programme during their service. It was also found that none of the teachers are exposed to child Rights information through official sources.

Table 14.3

Distribution of sample according to Training/Orientation received

S. No.	Type of Programme	TTD Schools		Municipal Schools		Total
		Men	Women	Men	Women	
1.	Training programme	5 (33.3)	5 (33.3)	8 (53.4)	8 (53.4)	26 (43.3)
2.	Orientation sessions	5 (33.3)	10 (66.7)	5 (33.3)	4 (26.6)	24 (40)
3.	Any other	5 (33.3)	–	2 (13.3)	3 (20.0)	10 (16.7)
	Total	**15 (100)**	**15 (100)**	**15 (100)**	**15 (100)**	**60 (100)**

Note: The numbers in parenthesis are percentages.

Levels of Awareness About Child Rights Among the Sample

The teachers responses to a question "Are you aware of child Rights declared by United Nations" showed that around 96.7 per cent of the sample are aware of child Rights and only 3.3 per cent are not aware of child Rights. When the teachers were asked to indicate their levels of awareness of child Rights the responses were as follows.

From the Table 14.4 it is evident that 46.7 per cent of teachers knew only about few Rights; 28.3 per cent of teachers know completely about all Rights, followed by a 18.3 per cent of teachers who know vaguely about all Rights. Only 6.7 per cent of the teachers know the gist of child Rights. This indicates that the teachers have a good awareness on child Rights.

Table 14.4

Levels of awareness of teachers about child Rights

S. No.	*Levels of awareness*	*TTD Schools*		*Municipal Schools*		*Total*
		Men	*Women*	*Men*	*Women*	
1.	Know completely about all Rights	2 (13.3)	7 (46.7)	5 (33.3)	3 (20)	17 (28.3)
2.	Know vaguely about all Rights	4 (26.7)	1 (6.7)	3 (20)	3 (20)	11 (18.3)
3.	Know only about few Rights	8 (53.3)	5 (33.3)	6 (40)	9 (60.0)	28 (46.7)
4.	Know the gist of it	1 (6.7)	2 (13.3)	1 (6.7)	–	4 (6.7)
	Total	**15 (100)**	**15 (100)**	**15 (100)**	**15 (100)**	**60 (100)**

Note: The numbers in parenthesis are percentages.

The Sources of Knowing Child Rights by the Sample

The teachers' knowledge on child Rights may be influenced by their exposure to child Rights information dissemination through training programmes of teachers, special programmes organised by Government for teachers, special programmes organised by Non-governmental organisations (NGO) for teachers, mass media and family members/neighbours/friends. Hence data on the above is gathered and presented in Table 14.5.

From the Table 14.5 it is evident that 66.6 per cent of the sample indicated mass media as their source of knowing child Rights information followed by training programmes, others, family members/neighbours/friends and special programmes organised by the Government. The data also reveals that the non government organisations have not contributed to the teachers knowledge on child Rights.

Table 14.5

Sources of knowing Child Rights information by the sample

S. No.	*Sources of child Rights information*	*TTD Schools*		*Municipal Schools*		*Total*
		Men	*Women*	*Men*	*Women*	
1.	Teacher training programmes	3 (20)	–	3 (20)	1 (6.7)	7 (11.7)
2.	Special programmes organized by Government	1 (6.7)	–	2 (13.3)	1 (6.7)	4 (6.7)
3.	Special programmes organized by NGOs	–	–	–	–	–
4.	Mass Media	7 (46.7)	12 (80.0)	9 (60)	12 (80)	40 (66.6)
5.	Family member/ Neighbours/Friends	2 (13.3)		–	–	3 (5)
6.	Others	2 (13.3)	2 (13.3)	1 (6.7)	1 (6.7)	6 (10)
	Total	**15 (100)**	**15 (100)**	**15 (100)**	**15 (100)**	**60 (100)**

Note: The numbers in parenthesis are percentages.

Child Rights Education to Teachers

Majority (96.7 per cent) of teachers felt the need for training in child Rights to school teacher; only 3.3 per cent of the teachers did not feel the need for child Rights education. The samples preference for ways of impacting child Rights Education, Information was sought, which is as given in Table 14.6.

From the Table 14.6 it is evident that 70 per cent of the teachers preferred to have a manual on child Rights for reference and reading. A 13.3 per cent of teachers felt the need for including child Rights as a topic in orientation programmes of newly recruited teachers. Around 15 per cent of teachers felt the need for inclusion of child Rights in the curriculum of teacher education. Only 1.7 per cent felt the need for special programmes on child Rights for school teachers. This indicates that there is a need to prepare and publish a manual on Child Rights for school teachers.

Table 14.6

Distribution of the sample according to their methods of Child Rights education

S. No.	Methods of child Rights Education	TTD Schools		Municipal Schools		Total
		Men	Women	Men	Women	
1.	As part of Teachers Education curriculum	3 (20)	2 (13.3)	2 (13.3)	2 (13.3)	9 (15)
2.	As part of orientation programme of newly recruited teachers	2 (13.3)	2 (13.3)	3 (20)	1 (6.7)	8 (13.3)
3.	In the form of a manual for all teachers	9 (60)	11 (73.4)	10 (66.7)	12 (80)	42 (70)
4.	Any other	1 (6.7)	–	–	–	1 (1.7)
	Total	**15 (100)**	**15 (100)**	**15 (100)**	**15 (100)**	**60 (100)**

Note: The numbers in parenthesis are percentages.

School Administrative Set-up and Facilities

Around 93.3 per cent of the school teachers felt that the school administrative set up and facilities are favorable for promotion of child Rights. Only 6.7 per cent of school teachers felt in contrary to that. When the 6.7 per cent of teachers are asked to indicate the kind of administrative set-up and facilities at school, they envisage for promotion of Child Rights. They responded as follows:

Facilities at School

1. Need more number of bathrooms for girls, boys and teachers separately;
2. Running tap water in bathrooms;

3. Protected water supply;
4. Dining rooms for day students;
5. Regular medical facility and first aid kit;
6. Regular cleaning of school surroundings and water tanks;
7. Regular maintenance and repairs to the building and furniture.

Administrative Set-up

1. Interaction sessions with students;
2. Parent teacher association meetings;
3. Formation of a committee to ensure basic amenities at school;
4. Child Rights committee at school level.

The above indicates that the schools under study require improvement in basic facilities and conduct sessions and form committees to promote Child Rights at school level.

Child Rights Knowledge of School Teachers

The child Rights knowledge of school teachers is assessed using a Child Rights knowledge scale. The mean score of TTD and municipal school teachers are 32 and 35 respectively as against a maximum score of 38. A 't' test is conducted to know the difference between the men and women teachers. It is found that they did not differ significantly in their Child Rights knowledge ($t_e = 0.43$; $t_o = 1.96$).

Association Between the Child Rights Knowledge and the Independent Variables

Child Rights knowledge may be influenced by the teachers' Age, Sex, Educational status, Length of service, Orientation/ Training received during their service, Levels of awareness of Child Rights, Mass media and Preference for methods of child Rights education. Hence a chi-square test was done to know the association between child Rights knowledge of school teacher and the independent variables mentioned above.

Table 14.7

Association between Child Rights knowledge and independent variables

S. No.	*Independent Variables*	*Chi-square calculated value*	*Chi-square Table value*	*Significance at 5% level*
1.	Age	3.84	1.2	@
2.	Sex	3.84	1.3	@
3.	Educational Status	3.84	3.2	@
4.	Duration of Service	5.99	0.1	@
5.	Orientation/ Training Received	5.99	1.1	@
6.	Levels of Awareness of Child Rights	3.84	0.4	@
7.	Mass media	3.84	0.2	@
8.	Need for Manual on Child Rights	5.99	0.66	@

@ Indicates there is no significant difference at 5% level.

From the above table it is evident that none of the independent variables showed association with Child Rights knowledge of school teachers.

The school teachers under study have not undergone any formal training in Child Rights. Yet, their levels of awareness on Child Rights is good and their sources of knowing Child Rights was mass media. The teachers felt the need for publication of a Child Rights manual and its distribution to all school teachers. The teachers suggested provision of facilities for children and improvements in administrative setup to promote Child Rights.

The teachers' knowledge on Child Rights is good and they did not vary in their knowledge on the basis of their sex. And no association found between the Child Rights knowledge and the independent variables.

REFERENCES

Bhaskara Rao, D., (1997), *Care the Child, the Right to be a Child*, Discovery Publishing HousePvt. Ltd., New Delhi; pp. 174-176.

Khanna, S.K., (1999), *Children and the Human Rights*, Commonwealth Publishers; pp. 339-381.

Lakshmi Devi, (1998), *Policies and Programmes Relates to Child Development*, Anmol Publication Pvt. Ltd., New Delhi; pp. 57-80.

15

Ways and Means of Fulfilling Health and Nutritional Rights of Children

Dr. N. Rajani

INTRODUCTION

Childhood is irreversible, the Health and Nutrition inputs needed for proper growth and development have to be provided at the right time and right age. The articles 5, 6, 20, 24, 27 and 39 of United Nations convention on child rights, emphasise the role of family and the State in fulfilling the health and nutritional rights of children. A statement of child rights is a statement of adult responsibilities. It is the responsibility of all adults, of governments and International community to create and maintain the circumstances in which families themselves can protect the rights of the child.

Several welfare and development programmes were launched to provide health, nutrition and allied services to children and their families by various government departments in India. Notable percentage of people could not access these services effectively due to problems in delivery of these services and low accountability of service providers.

Poor people in most countries have the worst health outcomes. They are pushed further into poverty due to ill-health and they are often excluded from support networks that enhance the social and economic benefits of good health. Unlike education, health and nutrition outcomes of poor people are produced by households – with contribution from many services. Health and nutrition services contribute to other aspects of human welfare, such as protecting people from catastrophic health spending. They should thus be judged by the way they contribute to poor people's health outcomes, to protect citizens from improvising health expenditure and to help the poor breakout of their social exclusion.

The existing health and nutrition services delivered to children and their families by the government departments and their programmes include Integrated Child Development Services (ICDS), Primary Health Centres (PHC) and District Primary Education Programme (DPEP). An effort is made to examine the quality, adequacy, consistency and coverage of these services in Chittoor district of Andhra Pradesh.

1. Methodology

The data such as aim, objectives, package of Health and Nutrition Services, delivery system and coverage of beneficiaries of ICDS, PHC and DPEP was collected from the concerned departments using interview method, observation method and examination of records. The field level units of all the three programmes; Anganwadi centres, PHC/Sub centres and Primary schools were visited thrice (in the months of March, July and December) in the year 2006. the Health and Nutrition services rendered at the field level units; Anganwadi centres, PHC/Sub centres and Primary schools were observed and the observations were recorded on a checklist developed separately for each of the programme. The field level functionaries and beneficiaries of all the three programmes were interviewed using a interview schedule developed separately for each of the three programmes. The data thus collected were examined for quality, adequacy, consistency and coverage of services.

Study Design

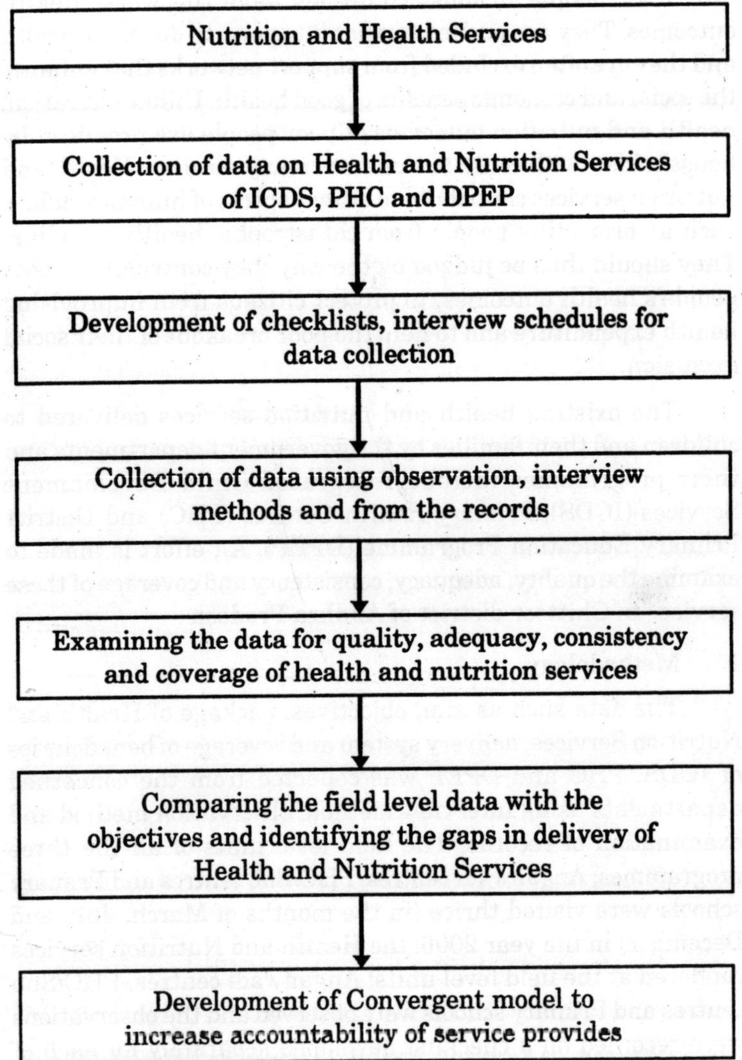

2. Sample Size

The Chittoor district of Andhra Pradesh consists of 3 revenue divisions and 66 mandals. From each revenue division one mandal was selected. From each mandal one project was selected for study of ICDS services. 30 Anganwadi workers and 30 Anganwadi children were selected. Thus the sample comprised of 90 Anganwadi workers and 90 Anganwadi children. For studying PHC services from each PHC, 30 PHC personnel and 30 patients were selected randomly. Thus comprising a total sample of 90 PHC/Sub centre staff and 90 patients. Similarly for studying DPEP services 30 primary school teachers and 30 primary school children were selected from each mandal. Thus comprising of a total sample of 90 primary school teachers and 90 primary school children.

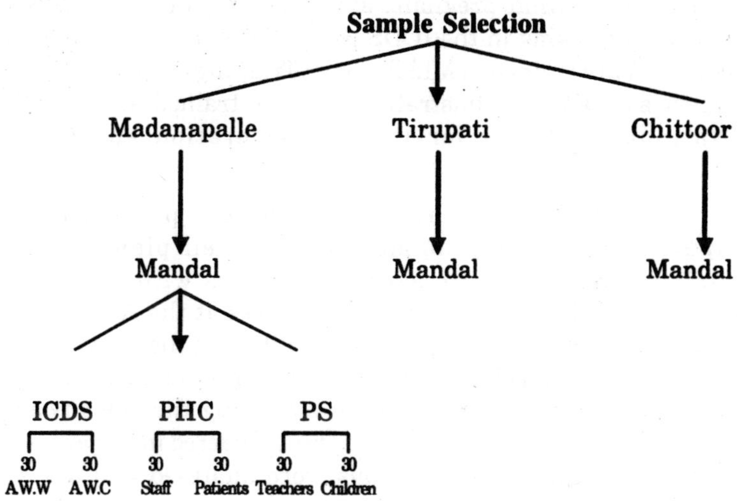

3. Results and Discussion

The data gathered was examined, analysed, interpreted and discussed.

(a) Health and Nutrition Services of ICDS Programme

The Integrated Child Development Service (ICDS) programme launched in the year 1975 is a national programme implemented throughout the country. The ICDS programme was initiated to provide a package of well integrated services such as nutrition communisation, early childhood education, referral services for children under six years of age and nutrition, health and education for pregnant and lactating mothers. The immunisation and health components was operated by the Health department through their Primary Health Centres (PHCs).

ICDS comes under the department of Women and Child Welfare. Each ICDS project is headed by Community Development Project Officer (CDPO). Under each CDPO four to five supervisors are there to supervise and monitor the work in Anganwadi centres. Each Anganwadi centre has a Anganwadi worker and an Ayah to deliver the package of services to children below 6 years and pregnant and lactating women. All the personnel working in the ICDS projects are trained. The field level staff are trained in Middle Level Training Centres and the supervisory and administrative staff are trained at NIPCCD (National Institute for Public Cooperation and Child Development).

Though the structure, delivery system, personnel and inputs of ICDS programme are very well planned and implemented, there are several problems with regard to utilisation of health and nutrition services at the Anganwadi centre. They include the physical facilities at the Anganwadi centre and the workload of Anganwadi worker and the ayah is not proportionate to the children attending the Anganwadi centre. The health and nutrition services rendered in Anganwadi centres of all the three mandals were analysed and are as follows:

- With regard to nutritional status (weight for age),. Majority of children in the age group 2 to 3 years and 4 to 5 years were normal. Around 14 per cent and 3 per cent of children in the age group of 2 to 3 years had mild and moderate malnutrition respectively. Similarly 15 per cent and 8 per cent of children in the age group of 4 to 5 years had mild and moderate malnutrition respectively. None of the children found to have grade-III and grade-IV malnutrition. This may be attributed to the nutritional services of anganwadi centres.
- A 79 per cent of children in the age group of 2-3 years and 61 per cent of children in the age group of 4-5 years were

found to be normal. Around 21 per cent of children in the age group of 2-3 years and 39 per cent of children in the age group of 4 to 5 years found to be stunted, that is their percentage heights for age of NCHS median values were less than two standard deviation (<2 SD). This shows that though majority of children had normal heights for their age, considerable percentage of children showed stunted growth.

- Majority of the children fell in the category of normal. Whereas 19 per cent of children aged between 2-3 years and 25 per cent of children aged between 4-5 years had grade-I malnutrition as their MUAC values were between 12.5 to 13.5 cms.
- The ratings for nutritional supplements indicate that 35 per cent of anganwadi centres were rated as very good, 55 per cent of anganwadi centres were rated as good and only 10 per cent of anganwadi centres were rated ass average.
- Health check-up was rated as very good in 45 per cent of centres as good in 30 per cent of centres and as average in 25 per cent of centres. This indicates that the health check-up, which is to be done at least once in three days is not done regularly in the anganwadi centres under study.
- The monthly monitoring reports should include vital statistics viz., Birth rate, still birth rate, infant mortality rate, under five mortality rate, maternal mortality rate, number of pregnant and lactating women in the anganwadi area. This responsibility of anganwadi workers was rated as very good (70%) and good (30%).
- Deworming tablets are provided to children once a year, the deworming of children was rated as very good in 90 per cent of centres and good in 10 per cent of centres.
- One of the prime duties of the anganwadi workers is to monitor the growth of children through monthly assessment of nutritional status. This service of anganwadi was rated as very good in all the anganwadi centres.

- The supplementary nutrition to children in anganwadi centres was rated as very good in all the twenty anganwadi centres.
- The supplementary nutrition given to pregnant and lactating women provides 500 K.Cals of energy and 20-25 g of protein per day. All the anganwadi centres under study distribute the supplementary nutrition regularly to the pregnant and lactating women enrolled. Hence this service of anganwadi were rated as very good for all the anganwadi centres under study.
- Supply of nutritional supplements viz., iron folic acid tablets and vitamin A for pregnant women and nursing mothers along with nutritional counselling was included in the package of services of ICDS. Only iron folic acid (IFA) was distributed to women as and when the supply was received. This service of ICDS was rated as very good (5%) and good (95%) centres.
- Health and nutrition education to adolescent girls and mothers in anganwadi centres were rated as very good in 20 per cent, good in 35 per cent, average in 15 per cent, poor in 20 per cent and very poor in 10 per cent of anganwadi centres under study.
- The anganwadi workers role in promotion of breast feeding in their anganwadi area was rated as very good in 35 per cent and good in 65 per cent centres.
- The ratings for the preschool education programme was very good in 15 per cent, good in 30 per cent, average in 30 per cent, poor in 15 and very poor in 10 per cent centres.
- The ICDS services for HIV/AIDS infected mothers and children were rated as very good in 80 per cent and good in 20 per cent centres.
- The health, nutrition and education services provided under ICDS programme at the anganwadi centres were assessed for their quality in selected anganwadi centres, which showed that immunisation and supplementary nutrition

to children and mothers were rated as very good for all twenty centres under study. Only the health and nutrition education services to women and adolescent girls and pre-school education programme to children found to be poor and very poor in 30 per cent and 35 per cent of centres respectively. The remaining seven services viz., health check-up, vital statistics, nutritional supplements, deworming, nutritional status assessment, screening of HIV/AIDS were rated as very good to average.

(b) Health and nutrition services of Primary Health Centres

The Primary Health Centres are field level units of Government health delivery system in Andhra Pradesh and in India. Each PHC covers a population of one lakh and above. For every 5000 population a sub centre is to be established; each sub centre consists of a Auxiliary Nurse Midwife (ANM), Multipurpose Health Worker (MPHW) and Dais. All the National and State Health programmes are complemented through the PHCs. The PHC services were not utilised by majority of families due to the following reasons:

1. The PHCs are located on the outskirts of the village and people have to walk long distance with children who are sick;
2. The Physical facilities such as toilets, running water facility are very poor;
3. The sanitation, hygiene and security in majority of PHCs are also poor;
4. The diagnostic services and medicines are not available always;
5. The health personnel including medical officers are not available in the PHCs on all days.
6. In order to access health services of PHC, the poor people have to forego their daily wages and in return the treatment rendered were also inadequate and incomplete;

7. Majority of the respondents and the health personnel rated the maternal child health services as good. The treatment and medication for general health problems and emergencies were rated as average;
8. The school health services were rendered occasionally; it is confined to distribution of deworming tablets and iron and folic tablets once in a year or two years;
9. There are no regular, consistent health and nutrition services for children below 14 years from PHCs;
10. There is no health surveillance system to screen and treat communicable diseases prevalent among children and their families.

There is every need to channelling. The health services and nutrition supplements to poor children. Ill-health affects growth and development of children.

(c) The Health and Nutrition Services of Primary Schools

The District Primary Education Programme in Andhra Pradesh integrates the primary education programme with the mid-day meals programme and health services. Mid-day meals are provided to all children attending Primary Schools in order to meet one third of the total calories and protein requirement of young children. The mid day meals consisted of rice and dhal with vegetables. The preparation and distribution of mid-day meals was entrusted to local women Self Heal Groups. Almost all the children attending the primary schools received mid-day meal and the meals provided were inadequate in all the primary schools studied.

The health services rendered to primary school children by the PHC are very poor and inadequate. In every school one teacher was trained in first-aid and maintenance of children health records. The first-aid kits are not replaced when it is used up and health records are not verified by the PHC health personnel. In 90 per cent of the schools the health records are not maintained accurately and regularly.

Ways and Means of Fulfilling Health and Nutritional Rights of Indian Children

Although the objectives and programmes are well formulated, the service delivery is very poor due to the lacuna in the system itself.

- Channelling collective resources to poor people through multiple allocation mechanisms that combine targeting diseases of the poor, poor regions, service delivery providers close to poor people and vulnerable groups and individuals;
- Developing coalitions that bring poor people into the policy-making process through both elections and advocacy by civil society;
- Establishing accountability for progress on outcomes, particularly among poor people through increased information and citizen monitoring of health services.
- At the field level the community based organisations such as the youth groups Women Self Help groups and local committees should be involved in monitoring. The delivery of health and nutrition services of ICDS, PHC and DPEP. The accountability of the delivery system of all the three programmes will be greater if local community based organisations participation is ensured.

16

Status of Street Children (0-14 Years)

—Ms. K. Lalitha Kumari and Prof. D. Sarada

INTRODUCTION

The phenomenon of street children is an off-shoot of the complex interplay of various factors in India. The phenomenon seems to have acquired a gigantic dimension in the wake of rapid industrialisation and urbanisation. The large-scale presence of street children as a disease that is widespread due to an exploitative social structure, lopsided development and iniquitous resource ownership. Other parameters contributing to its presence in India are large-scale unemployment, rapid urbanisation, fast population growth, extreme poverty increasing disparities in wealth, high levels of children abuse by parents, society and a breakdown of traditional family and community structure. Human migrations from rural to urban areas have contributed significantly to a substantial increase in the number of street children. Migrants shift to cities in the unorganised or semi-organised, low-paid sector. Consequently, children are forced to live on the street and earn livelihoods for themselves and also support their families.

India has the larges population of street children in the world. A significant proportion of street children are working in the unorganised or informal service sector in every city, big or small, offering cheap labour, and catering to various needs of city-dwellers. The majority of children live or work on the streets of urban India labouring as porters at bus or railway terminals; as mechanics in auto-repair shops; or as vendors of food, tea and handmade articles. They work as street toilers or as rag-pickers, picking garbage and selling usable materials to local buyers. They are often seen polishing shoes in shopping and commercial centres, working as domestic servants or as vegetable sellers, milk carriers and car cleaners. They carry heavy loads and work in cycle and automobile repair shops. They are also engaged in several hazardous industries and processes throughout the country. May of them are also procured as sex workers. The parents/crime rings many a times use these children for begging around crossroads and places of worship.

These children suffer from the worst kind of deprivation and denial of basic necessities like education, health, food, shelter, physical protection, security and recreation.

From what proceeded, it is obvious that there is exodus of rural families to the cities, resulting in transformation of rural society into urban. Slums and shanty towns are emerging with startling speed. The urban poverty and the 'fourth world' living have become the common characteristics of the new human habitat. Trapped in poverty, children, girls and youth have become the most vulnerable group to the risks of urbanisation. Children in cities are now encountering several problems, including child labour and exploitation, sexual harassment, child abuse, neglect and abandonment, and a variety of unhealthy parent-child relationships. Multiplicity of factors are working against children.

To be sure, the phenomenon of 'street children' is not limited any particular country; in fact, it is a world-wide social reality. At least , two different types of appellations given to street children can be discerned: popular and official with overtones of euphemism. In the popular vocabulary, street children carry different nomenclatures. In the developed North, they are labelled "homeless youth", "runaways" or even "throwaways". In developing countries, they are called "parking boys" (Kenya), "pogey boys" (Philippines), "pivetes" (Brazil), "Ragpickers" (India), "gamines" (Bogata) or a variety of other names. In Naples, they are called "scugnizzo" (a spinning-top always on the move); in Peru, the "pajaro frutero" (fruit bird) looking out for the police in the market-place; in Columbia, "gamin" (kid having negative connotation). The same word appears in Rawanda in the form of "Saligoman" (sale gamin, nasty kid). In Zaire, street children are "moineau" (sparrows); in Cameroon, "poussins" (chicks) to field workers, "moustiques" (mosquitoes) to the police.

Euphemistically, the word "twilight children" is proposed to suggest their fragile and indefinite status. Officialdom, in contrast, tends to be more circumspect, and refers to street children euphemistically, for example, as "children in an irregular situation" or 'in difficult circumstances'.

Study of these children's status interns of quality of life is necessary to plan interventions and rehabilitative services. In this context the investigator made an attempt to study the status of street children of 0-14 years age group. The status of children also reflects the quality of life of street children.

METHODOLOGY

In the world today the process of urbanisation has become an inevitable phenomenon. Street children is growing urban phenomenon all over the world, with increasing industrialisation. The process of rural, urban migration ahs caused the disintegration of the family, leading to many social problems, including juvenile vagrancy. The main reason which prompts children to run away from their home is not mere poverty, but also unhappy home conditions, parental neglect and cruel treatment by step parents, the place of abode for these children arc platforms, basements of flyovers, subways, temple premises, Darghas, Bazaars and railway and bus stations. With this background, the investigator undertook a project work to design a methodology for the study of street children.

Locale of the Study

The study was conducted in Tirupati urban mandal for the following reasons:

Tirupathi is one of the biggest pilgrim city with a floating population of around one lakh. Tirupathi has a large number of street children next to Hyderabad and Vijayawada. Moreover Tirupati is located in the border district of Chittoor, which has two metropolitan cities next to it – Chennai and Bangalore.

Sample Selection

The investigator surveyed the public places and identified street children who were below 14 years of age. Thus the sample comprised of 10 girls and 25 boys aged below 14 years.

Selection of Variables

A review of available literature on street children lead to identification of independent variables which may have influence on the status of street children, they are:

Family size, Family type, Family literacy index, Family income, Birth order and Age were included in the present study.

Working Definition of Independent Variables

1. **Family size**: The number of Family members residing in the respondent's family is considered as family size, determines the demand for available resources and also the amount of time allocated in the parents for the children. Hence it was included as available.

2. **Family type**: The type of family determines the amount of leisure time available and the level of interaction among the family members. Further it also determines the decision-making opportunities of women.

3. **Family literacy index**: To total years of education the family members underwent is calculated and its mean is considered as the family literacy index. The educational aspirations of the child, hence it was included as a variable in the present study.

4. **Family income**: The family income is the total amount of money earned by the family in a year.

5. **Birth order**: The chronological age of respondents and his position among his/her siblings in the family is birth order. Birth order determines the child's expose to various family activities and the attention received by his/her family members. Hence it was included as a variable in the present study.

6. **Age**: The chronological age of the subjects in completed years is taken as age in years.

7. **Occupation**: Occupation is the nature of work done to make a living. It depends on the person's education training, personal capabilities and interests. The street children parents' occupation was also.

Dependent Variables

Status of street children – assessment of the education, health, occupation, basic needs and the quality of life.

TOOLS FOR MEASUREMENT OF VARIABLES

In order to measure the variables chosen for the study, the following tools and research methods were used:

1. Questionnaire
2. Child Rights, Scale
3. Interview
4. Observation

Questionnaire

A questionnaire was developed to collect information on personal profile, family profile and the status of street children, understudy. Relevant questions were formed to collect information from the street children, which were arranged order of familiarity (more familiar to less familiar) and recollection to analytical type.

The questions are presented under headings:

1. Personal profile of the street child
2. Family profile of the street child
3. Reasons for child streetism
4. Health and nutrition profile
5. Hygiene and sanitation practices
6. Educational status
7. Work and working conditions
8. Income and serving
9. Recreation
10. Accommodation

Thus the questionnaire framed covers information needed to assess the status of the street child.

Child Rights Scale

A child rights scale developed (Sarada 2000) in the Department of Human Development and Family Studies, was used to assess the child rights knowledge and attitudes of street children under study. The scale consisted of twenty six questions under child rights knowledge, rated on a Yes/No type. The child rights attitudinal scale consisted of seventeen statements related on a three point scale (Strongly agree/Agree/Disagree). The child rights knowledge and attitudinal scales prepared both in English and Telugu (Local language) were administered to the street children.

Interview Method

As the street children's reading skills were not adequate to fill in the questionnaire and scales, the investigator used interview method to collect information using the questionnaire and child rights scales. Each street child understudy was interviewed separately and the responses were recorded.

Observation Method

In order to validate the information given by each street child, their place of residence, work places were visited by the investigator. Observation method was used to verify the responses of the street children.

Statistical Analysis

The data collected were pooled, tabulated and subjected to statistical analysis: Mean, Standard Deviation, 'Z' Test, χ^2 Test.

RESULTS AND DISCUSSION

The results of the study was analysed and interpreted and discussed as under:

Personal Profile of Street Children

The personal information about the street children was gathered in order to understand their personal background. They are as follows:

1. Majority of boys and girls belonged to 5-10 years of age group;
2. A good percentage of girls (40 per cent) were first born and a notable percentage of boys (44 per cent) were third born. Parental neglect, lack of attention, academic pressure were found to be the few reasons related to birth order;
3. Majority of street children belonged to scheduled tribe, scheduled caste and backward castes. Only a small percentage of street children belonged to other castes;
4. Around 28 per cent of boys and 40 per cent of girls belonged to small families of less than four members. Around 72 per cent of boys and 60 per cent of girls came from families of 5-8 members. None of the subjects belonged to families above 8 members. This shows that small and medium size families are in vogue in present society;
5. 64 per cent of boys and 60 per cent of girls belonged to extended families. A good percentage of boys (24 per cent) and girls (40 per cent) belonged to nuclear type of families. Only 12 per cent of boys had come from single parent families. None of the street children had joint families. This shows that in contrary to the general observation, majority of the subjects belonged to extended families;

6. Majority of boys and girls belonged to low income group of 12001 to 24000 rupees per annum;
7. Majority of street boys (64 per cent) and street girls' (90 per cent) fathers were daily wage earners. Only 12 per cent of boys' fathers were employed in Govt. sector, 24 per cent of boys and 10 per cent of girls' fathers were self employed. This indicates that the occupation of most of the street children were not of permanent nature and has less job security;
8. In contrary to the general observation in the present study, majority of mothers of boys (64 per cent) and girls (60 per cent) were house wives, only 24 per cent of boys and 40 per cent of girls' mothers were working as daily wage earners;
9. Majority of the girls were illiterates and a good percentage of boys (48 per cent) and girls (30 per cent) had only primary education, only 28 per cent of boys were in high schools, the data complies with the general finding;
10. Majority of boys (72 per cent) and all the girls (100 per cent) fathers were illiterates. A 24 per cent of boys' fathers had primary education and only 4 per cent of boys fathers had high school education. None of the street children fathers had college or professional education;
11. A 88 per cent of boys and 10 per cent of girls' mothers were illiterates. Around 12 per cent of boys' mothers had only primary education. None of the mothers of street children studied upto high school and college education.

CAUSES OF CHILD STREETISM

Age of Streetism

The age at which the child came away from home was gathered in order to know the age of streetism. Several studies were conducted on child streetism in which the age of streetism was studied along with reasons which showed that unpleasant. Home and school environment were one of several reasons for child streetism. In the present study the age at which the child came away was gathered and presented in Table 16.1.

Table 16.1

Distribution of children according to their age of streetism

S. No.	Age in years	Street children		Percentage	
		Boys	Girls	Boys	Girls
1.	<5	–	–	–	–
2.	6-10	14	8	56	80
3.	11-14	11	2	44	20
	Total	**25**	**10**	**100**	**100**

Figure 16.1

Distribution of children according to their age of streetism

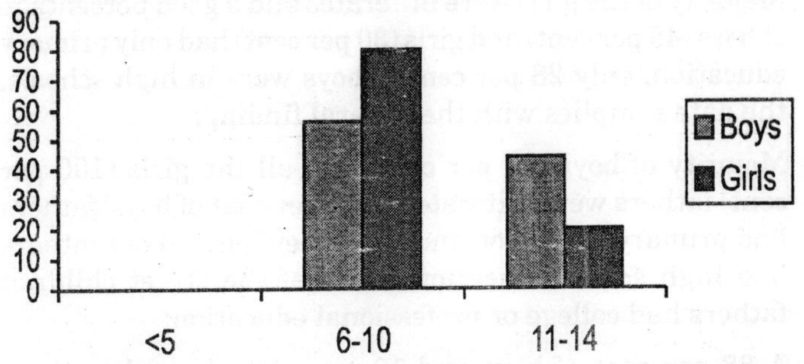

The above table shows that majority of boys (56 per cent) and girls (80 per cent) came away from home when they were 6 to 10 years age. Around 44 per cent of boys and 20 per cent of girls given to streetism at the age of 11 to 14 years. None of the children belonged to less than 5 years. This shows that almost all the children come away belong to school going age.

The Reasons for Coming Away

The responses of the children to a question what are the reasons for coming away was recorded and presented in Table 16.2.

Table 16.2

Distribution of children according to their reasons for coming away

S. No.	Reason for coming away	Street children		Percentage	
		Boys	Girls	Boys	Girls
1.	Academic	10	10	40	100
2.	Family conflicts	8	–	32	–
3.	Discipline by parents	2	–	8	–
4.	Father's drinking habit	5	–	20	–
	Total	**25**	**10**	**100**	**100**

Figure 16.2

Distribution of children according to their reasons for coming away

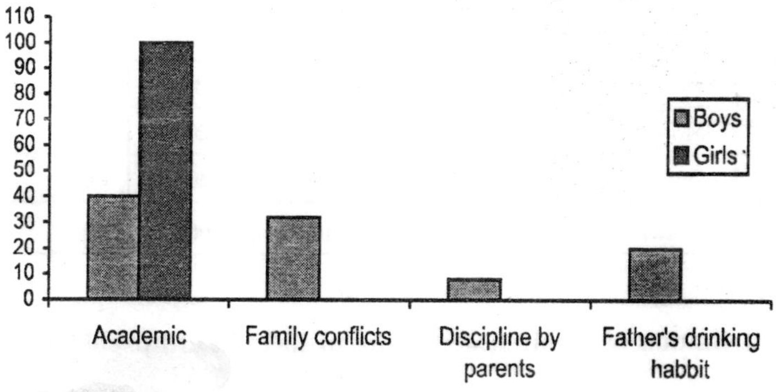

The Table 16.2 shows that children have academic problems (school environment) which is the main reason expressed by 40 per cent boys, 100 per cent of girls. Around 32 per cent of boys indicated family conflicts as reason for streetism. A 20 per cent attributed their coming away from home to father's drinking habit. Only 8 per cent of children expressed parents strict discipline as reason for streetism.

The above table shows that majority of children stated school environment as the main reason; 40 per cent of boys indicated family conflicts as reason for coming away. A 20 per cent attributed their coming away from home to abusive and alcoholic fathers; only 8 per cent of children expressed parents disciplinary methods as reason for streetism.

HEALTH AND NUTRITION PROFILE

Health is dependent on nutrition and hygiene, health and nutrition problems affect one's health and nutritional status.

Health Problems

The prevalence of health problems and their frequency of occurrence was collected as shown in Table 16.3.

Table 16.3

Distribution of children according to their health problems

S. No.	*Reason for coming away*	*Street children*		*Percentage*	
		Boys	*Girls*	*Boys*	*Girls*
1.	Daily	5	–	20	–
2.	Weekly	5	2	20	20
3.	Monthly	5	6	20	60
4.	Occasional	10	2	,40	20
	Total	**25**	**10**	**100**	**100**

Figure 16.3

Distribution of children according to their health problems

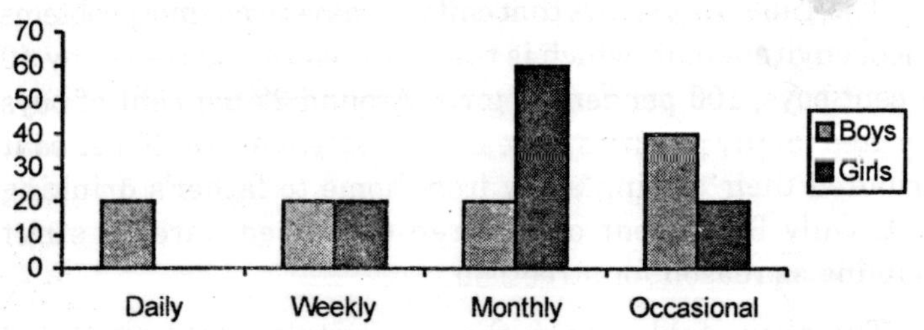

The above table shows that the street children varied with regard to frequency of occurrence of health problems. A 20 per cent of boys regularly had some health problem or the other. Around 20 per cent of boys and girls suffered from health problems weekly, whereas majority of girls (60 per cent) and 20 per cent of boys had health problems monthly; only 40 per cent of boys and 20 per cent of girls had health problems occasionally.

Source of Seeking Medical Advice

The street children hesitate to go to a medical officer when they have health problems. This may be due to their general appearance and fear of ill-treatment. This stigma makes them seek medical advice from less reliable source which may lead to other health consequences.

Table 16.4

Distribution of children according to their source of seeking medical advice

S. No.	*Whom do you consult when you have health problem*	*Street children*		*Percentage*	
		Boys	*Girls*	*Boys*	*Girls*
1.	Medical doctor	5	–	20	–
2.	Medical shopkeeper	10	4	40	40
3.	Friends	–	2	–	20
4.	Self medication	5	4	20	40
5.	Any other	5	–	20	–
	Total	**25**	**10**	**100**	**100**

Figure 16.4

Distribution of children according to their source of seeking medical advice

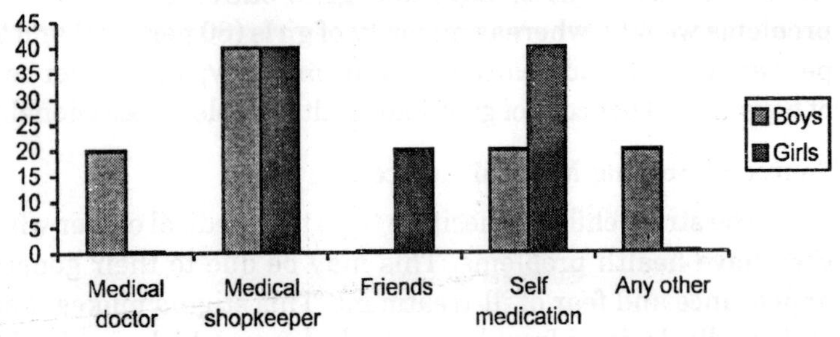

The Table 16.5 shows that 40 per cent of street boys and girls seek medical advice from shop keepers; a 20 per cent consult friends; a 40 per cent depend on self medication. Around 20 per cent try other methods, which include indigenous healthcare techniques; only 20 per cent of street children consult a medical doctor.

Types of Health Problems

Almost all the children had all the health problems listed in the Table 16.5. Besides these health problems, almost all the subjects suffered from problems like cuts, wounds month boiler, prices/cramps, amoebiasis, loose motions, constipation etc.

Table 16.5

Distribution of children according to their health problems

S. No.	*Health problems*	*Street children*		*Percentage*	
		Boys	*Girls*	*Boys*	*Girls*
1.	Fever and headache	25	10	32	40
2.	Cold and cough	25	10	16	20
3.	Stomach pain	25	10	24	40
4.	Allergy	25	10	8	–
5.	Eye infection	25	10	8	–
6.	Any other	25	10	12	–
	Total	**25**	**10**	**100**	**100**

Figure 16.5

Distribution of children according to their health problems

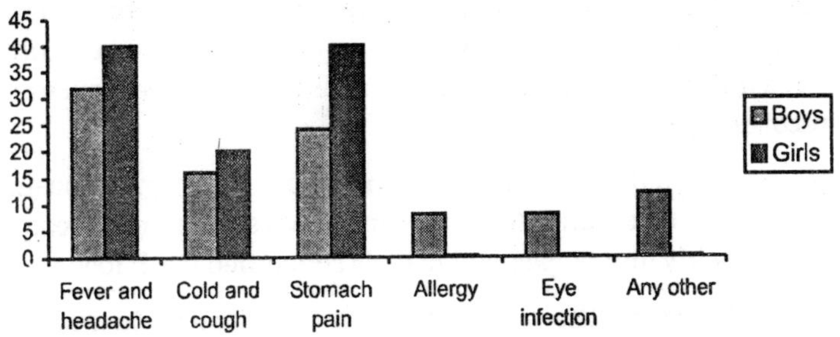

This shows that street children regularly suffer from minor ailments, which may affect their health status. During sickness the street children get help from their own friends. None of the Government health systems, non-governmental organisations helped any of these street children.

Nutritional Adequacy of Diets Consumed by Street Children

Dietary intake of street children is not consistent as the food intake depends on availability of food and income of the street children. It is difficult to make reliable dietary assessment of street children. Even then an attempt was made to know the nutritional adequacy of diets consumed by street children.

The dietary intake of street children was collected using 24 hours recall method and a set of standardised vessels. Through which the menu and approximate quantities of food consumed by each child was collected based on the food items and their quantity consumed by each child. Nutritive value of the diet was computed using nutritive value of Indian foods (ICMR, 1990). The actual nutrient intake of each child was compared with the recommended dietary allowances (RDA), in order to know whether the diets are adequate or not adequate which showed that 90.9 per cent of street boys diets were adequate nutritionally; only 10 per cent of street boys diets were not adequate.

Quality of Food Consumed by the Street Children

Quality of food consumed by the street children was gathered. The street children do not have a regular place of eating. The food consumption of these children depends on their earnings and also on the availability of food. The street children were interviewed about their eating pattern. The responses were recorded which indicate that:

(a) Around 60 per cent of boys and 20 per cent of girls consumed fresh food daily. A 40 per cent of boys consumed fresh food weekly and 80 per cent of girls consumed fresh food weekly.

(b) Almost all the street children consume plate waste and stale food occasionally.

The reasons for consumption of plate waste and stale food include inability to set food due to ill-health (20 per cent of girls and 40 per cent of boys), lack of money to purchase and lack of availability of food during strikes and Bandhs.

Hygiene and Sanitation

To be hygienic and sanitation requires minimum facilities such as water, toilet, bathrooms and materials like soaps, shampoo, broom, cleaning agents, which are expensive for the children living on streets without a shelter and very difficult to maintain hygiene and sanitation.

Table 16.6

Distribution of street children according to their levels of hygiene

S. No.	*Hygiene cleanliness*	*Percentage of Boys*			*Percentage of Girls*		
		Good	*Average*	*Poor*	*Good*	*Average*	*Poor*
1.	Work spot	40	32	28	30	40	30
2.	Clothes	32	48	20	10	10	20
3.	Hair	20	52	52	20	20	60
4.	Nails	8	8	40	-	20	80
	Total	**100**	**100**	**–**	**100**	**100**	**100**

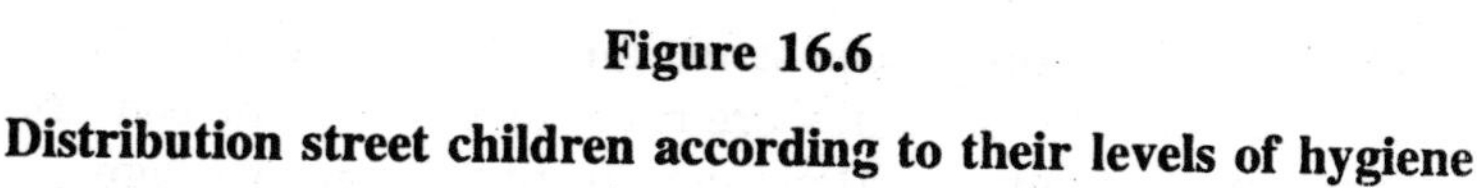

Figure 16.6

Distribution street children according to their levels of hygiene

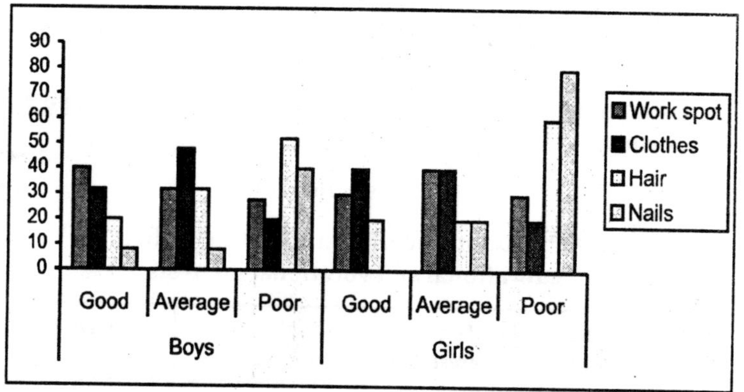

The levels of hygiene was rated on a three point scale as poor, average and good. The cleanliness of children at work place shows that a 40 per cent of boys and 30 per cent in girls were rated as good, a 32 per cent of boys and 40 per cent of girls were rated as average and 28 per cent of boys and 30 per cent of girls were rated as poor.

Cleanliness of clothes worn by the street children was observed, which showed that 32 per cent of boys and 40 per cent of girls were rated as good; 40 per cent of boys and 40 per cent of girls were rated as average; and 20 per cent of boys and 20 per cent of girls were rated as poor with regard to cleanliness of clothes.

The condition of street children's hair was rated on a three point scale. The findings indicate that a 20 per cent of boys and 20 per cent of girls had clean hair, whereas 52 per cent of boys and 20 per cent of girls were rated as average and 60 per cent of girls had shabby hair. This shows that boys had average to good hair when compared to girls.

Cleanliness of nails was also observed. The street children nails was rated on a three point scale. Among boys only 12 per cent had clean nails, whereas 48 per cent of boys nails were rated as average and 40 per cent had very shabby nails (rated as poor). Among the street girls none of them had clean nails; 80 per cent of them were rated as poor for the condition of their nails, whereas 20 per cent were rated as average.

Thus the present study reveals that boys were comparatively hygienic when compared to girls.

EDUCATION AND VOCATIONAL INTERESTS OF STREET CHILDREN

Table 16.7

Distribution of children according to their educational and vocational interests

S. No.	*Educational and vocational interests of street children*	*No. of street children*		*Percentage*	
		Boys	*Girls*	*Boys*	*Girls*
1.	Yes	18	3	72	30
2.	No	6	7	24	70
	Total	**25**	**10**	**100**	**100**

Figure 16.7

Distribution of children according to their educational and vocational interests

Among the sample studied, 38 per cent of boys and all the girls are illiterates; only 12 per cent of boys had primary school education. Around 72 per cent of boys and 30 per cent of girls showed interest in education. A 24 per cent of boys and 70 per cent of girls are not interested in education.

In response to a question "If you are provided an opportunity will you continue education"? Around 44 per cent of boys and 30 per cent of girls were willing to continue education. Majority of children (56 per cent of boys and 70 per cent of girls) were not interested in continuing education. Among those willing to continue education, majority preferred vocational education followed by non-formal education; none of them preferred recently formal education.

Educational Status of Street Children

Street children are working children, who form a part of child labour; these children are employed in various types of works. If given a vocational training along with relevant education, these children can improve their skills and become eligible for better employment in their adulthood.

Table 16.8

Distribution of street children according to their vocational training

S. No.	*Kind of vocational training*	*Street children*		*Percentage*	
		Boys	*Girls*	*Boys*	*Girls*
1.	Electrical works	8	–	32	–
2.	Mechanical work	2	–	8	–
3.	Tailoring	6	6	24	60
4	Food and cookery	2	2	8	20
5	Printing and binding	2	–	8	–
6	Any other	5	2	20	20
	Total	**25**	**10**	**100**	**100**

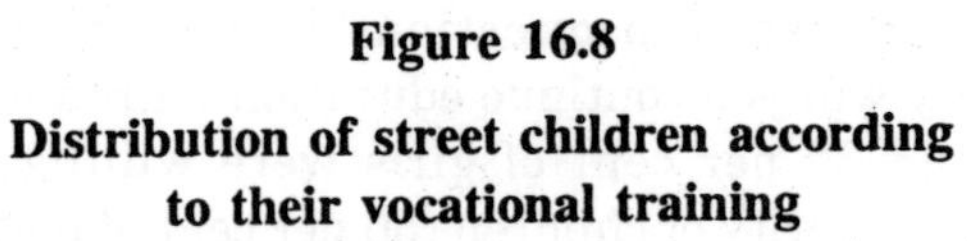

Figure 16.8

Distribution of street children according to their vocational training

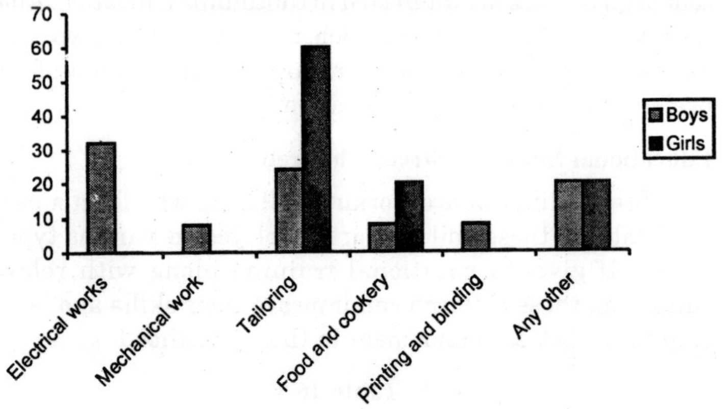

The vocational interests of street children are as shown in Table 16.8 which indicates that among the boys (32 per cent) showed interest in electrical works; a 20 per cent showed interest in other types of works. Only small percentage (8 per cent) showed interest in mechanical, cookery and printing and binding respectively. Among the girls 20 per cent of them showed interest in other types of work, 20 per cent showed interest in cookery and a 60 per cent showed interest in tailoring.

Work and Working Conditions

All the street children do work for their living and the nature of work done by street children is given in Table 16.9.

All the street children do work for their living and the nature of work done by street children is given in Table 16.9, which indicates that 32 per cent of boys and 20 per cent of girls had interest in manual work; only 20 per cent of boys had interest in field work.

Table 16.9

Distribution of street children according to their work and working conditions

S. No.	Health problems	Street children		Percentage	
		Boys	Girls	Boys	Girls
1.	Manual work	8	2	32	20
2.	Skilled work	5	–	20	–
3.	Errand work	4	2	16	20
4.	Any other	8	6	32	60
	Total	25	10	100	100

Figure 16.9

Distribution of street children according to their work and working conditions

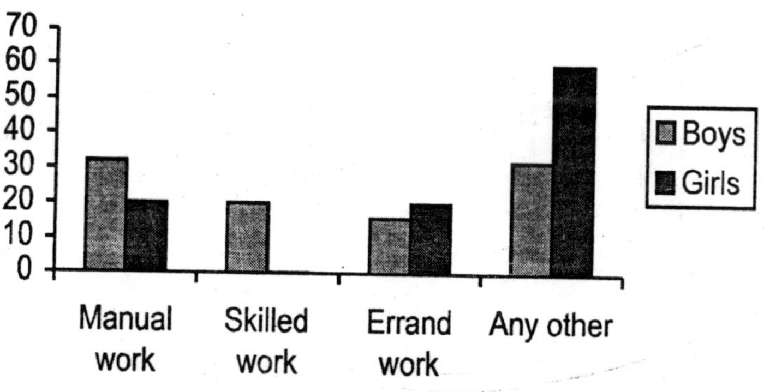

Which indicates that 32 per cent of boys and 20 per cent of girls were engaged in manual work; only 20 per cent of boys were doing skilled work. A 6 per cent of boys and 20 per cent of girls were doing errand work. Around 32 per cent of boys and 60 per cent of girls were engaged in other types of work.

Skills of Street Children

Table 16.10

Distribution of street children according to their work skills

S. No.	Possess skills for any specific work	Street children		Percentage	
		Boys	Girls	Boys	Girls
1.	Electrical work	8	–	32	–
2.	Mechanical work	12	–	48	–
3.	Tailoring	2	6	8	60
4.	Any other	3	4	12	40
	Total	**25**	**10**	**100**	**100**

Figure 16.10

Distribution of street children according to their work skills

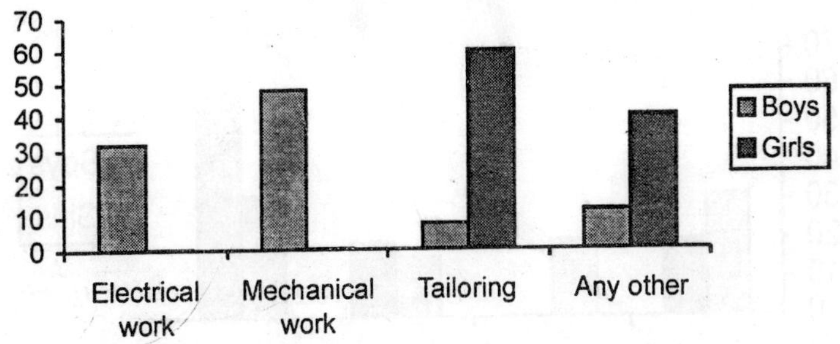

The skills of street children specific to work was gathered. Among the girls 60 per cent have stated that they have skills in tailoring and 40 per cent in other types of works; among the street boys 32 per cent had skill in electrical work, and 48 per cent in mechanical work, 8 per cent of boys had skill in tailoring and 12 per cent had skills in other types of works.

Income and Savings

The street children are also child labourers as they make a living for themselves by working. The money earned by these children are not safeguarded for use on non-work days. Mainly due to lack of a safe place to keep the income, lack of proper address and identity deprives them from using available safe saving services such as post office, banks etc.

Table 16.11

Distribution of children according to their income

S. No.	*Monthly income of street children in rupees*	*No. of street children*		*Percentage*	
		Boys	*Girls*	*Boys*	*Girls*
1.	<150	12	8	48	80
2.	151-300	9	2	36	–
3.	301-450	4	–	16	–
4.	>450	–	–	–	–
	Total	**25**	**10**	**100**	**100**

Figure 16.11

Distribution of children according to their income

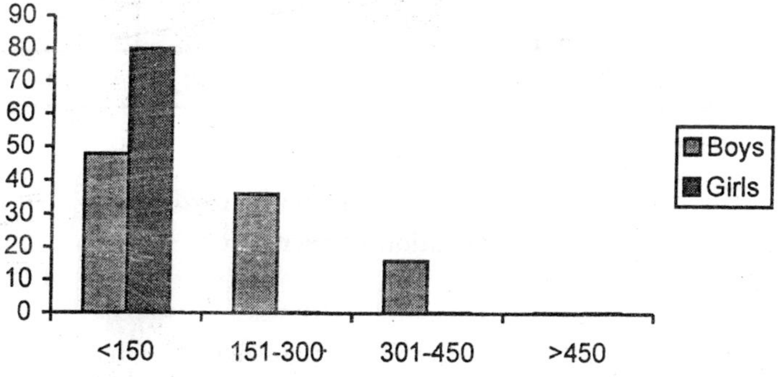

The income of street children is not consistent. It was found that their income ranged from less than rupees 150 to 450 per month. Around 48 per cent of boys and 80 per cent of girls had less than 150 rupees as their monthly income. A 36 per cent of boys and 20 per cent of girls had monthly income between 151 to 300; only 16 per cent of boys had a monthly income between rupees 301 to 450.

Almost all the children saved some money which they usually keep with a known person. There savings are not regular. The street children showed interest in saving their daily income in post offices.

Recreation

Recreation is the only source of happiness and relief for street children. Almost all the street children watch movies, television. All the street children has access to television sets in railway station and bus stations.

Table 16.12

Distribution of street children according to their duration of recreation

S. No.	*Recreation*	*Street children*		*Percentage*	
		Boys	*Girls*	*Boys*	*Girls*
1.	One hour	6	4	24	40
2.	Two hours	3	2	12	20
3.	3 hours	4	4	16	40
4.	4 hours	12	–	48	–
	Total	25	10	100	100

Figure 16.12

Distribution of street children according to their duration of recreation

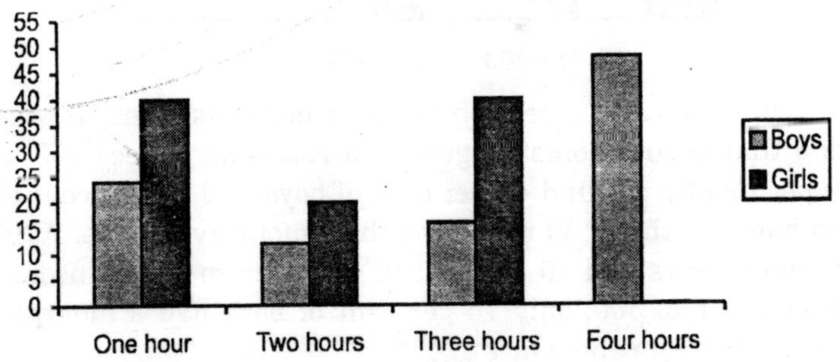

Table 16.12 shows that among the girls 40 per cent watch television for one hour, 20 per cent for two hours and 40 per cent for three hours. Among the boys 24 per cent watched television for one hour, 12 per cent watched for two hours and 16 per cent watched for three hours.

All the street children watch films every week; the street children learn most of the things from films on various aspects was gathered (showed that 40 per cent of boys and girls learnt about family aspects from films; 20 per cent of boys and girls come to know about marriage and sex from films. 20 per cent gained awareness about religion, epics and culture from films; 20 per cent come to know about legal provisions law government from films. The data reflects that films and television have become main source of information for street children.

Physical Facilities

Physical facilities availability and access to physical facilities such as shelter, toilet, water are the basic amenities needed for any human being. Deprivation of such basic amenities make human life miserable and poor.

The street children are highly independent and are on their own. This often exposes them to exploitation and are subjected to abuse. Lack of safe night shelter is the biggest problem the children face. An attempt was made to gather information on the place of living of street children.

Table 16.13

Distribution of street children according to their place of living

S. No.	*Place of living*	*Street children*		*Percentage*	
		Boys	*Girls*	*Boys*	*Girls*
1.	Group living	–	6	–	60
2.	Sharing a small house	–	–	–	–
3.	Sleeping someone's house	–	–	–	–
4.	Platform	25	4	100	40
	Total	**25**	**10**	**100**	**100**

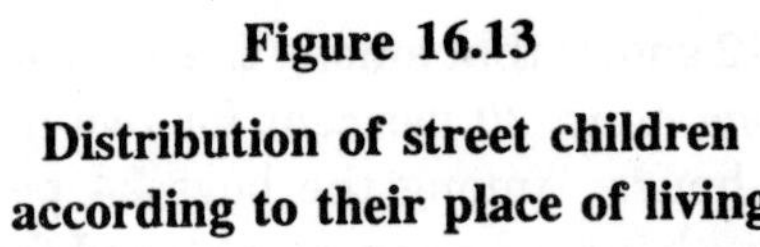

Figure 16.13

Distribution of street children according to their place of living

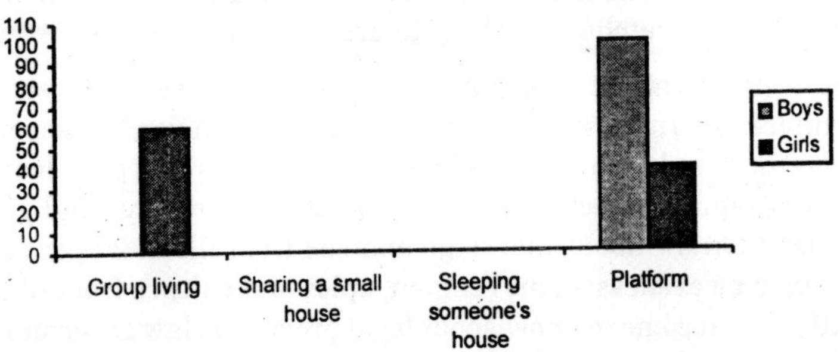

The Table 16.13 shows that majority of street children (60 per cent) lived together in groups. Around 40 per cent lived on platforms. None of the street children understudy shared a house or slept in someone's house.

The street children depend on public water facility for bathing and for completion of their daily courses. None of the street children had toilet facility, storage place and also some kind of bedding or blanket for sleeping. This indicates that their living conditions are very poor.

Child Rights Knowledge and Attitudes of Street Children

Using the child rights scale the knowledge and attitudes of street children (0-14 years) was measured. The mean knowledge scores of boys was 18 and girls was 15.8, which shows that boys mean child rights knowledge scores of boys was slightly higher than that of girls.

From the Table 16.14 it is clear that the knowledge of boys is significantly higher than the knowledge of girls.

In order to know the difference between boys and girls child rights knowledge scores 't' test was done, which showed that the girls and boys significantly differed with regard to child rights knowledge, that is the knowledge of boys is significantly higher than the girls child rights knowledge (i.e., $t_o = 2.52$, $t_e = 1.96$).

Table 16.14

Difference between boys and girls with regard to child rights knowledge

H_o	*Mean score*	*Sample size*	*t_o*	*t_e*	*Inference*
There is no significant difference between mean score of boys (x) and mean score of girls (y) regarding knowledge	x = 18 y = 15.8	$N_1 = 25$ $N_2 = 10$	2.52	1.96	Rejected

Table 16.15

Difference between boys and girls according to their child rights attitudes

H_o	*Mean score*	*Sample size*	*t_o*	*t_e*	*Inference*
There is no significant difference between mean score of boys (x) and mean score of girls (y) regarding attitude	x = 17.72 y = 16.5	$N_1 = 25$ $N_2 = 10$	1.64	1.96	H_o is accepted

From the above table it is clear that there is no significant difference between the attitudes of boys and girls.

With regard to child rights attitudes the mean scores of boys was 17.72 and girls was 16.5; here again the boys scored slightly higher scores than the girls.

The calculated 't' values for child rights attitudes was 1.64 and the table value is 1.96 as the t_0 is less than the t_e, the null hypothesis is accepted, which means the boys and girls did not differ with regard to their child rights attitudes.

Table 16.16

Difference between child rights knowledge and attitudes of street children

H_o	χ_o^2	χ_e^2	Inference
Knowledge and attitude are non associated	0.7	3.841	H_o is accepted

It is clear from the above table that knowledge and attitudes are non-associated.

There is no association between the child rights knowledge and attitudes of boys and girls that is the null hypothesis is accepted. The calculated chi-square value (0.7) is less than the chi-square table value (3.841). This shows that knowledge and attitudes are not associated.

Conclusion

The study allows to conclude that the reasons for streetism lie in the families, schools and society, where the child's needs are perceived in the context of child rights. The families need to be oriented and supported in handling the problems of children, although efforts are made to send back the children to their homes where if same conditions prevail they do not remain there and come back to streets once again.

The study further arrives at a conclusion that the quality of life and status of street children are very low and pathetic. The efforts of Government and Non-Government Organisations continue to be sporadic, irregular, and are not reaching there children in difficult circumstances. The community involvement in the form of vigilance groups and some amount of concern and commitment from every citizen will go a long way in integrating street children into their local societies.

REFERENCES

Agnelli, S.: Street Children—*A Growing Urban Tragedy Report for the Independent Commission on International Humanitarian Issues (ICIHI)*, Geneva 1986.

Bellamy, C.,: *The State of World's Children. Focus on Child Labour 1997*, UNICEF, Oxford Univ Press.

Delhi NGO Forum: *Street and Working Children*, Vol. No.1 – 1995. Child Country Report India, Ministry of Human Resource Development, February 1997.

Pandey, R.: *Street Children of Kanpur—A Situational Analysis*, National Labour Institute (UNICEF study) India 1992.

Panicker, R. and Nangia P.: *Working and Street Children of Delhi*, National Labour Institute (UNICEF study) India 1992.

Convention on the Right of the Child. India First Periodic Report – 2001. Published by Department of Women and Child development, Ministry of Human Resource Development with Assistant from UNICEF, India.

17

Child Rights and Street Boys (15-18 Years)

—**Ms. A. Sowmya** and **Prof. D. Sarada**

INTRODUCTION

Problems of Street Children

The mental make-up of an adult is to a substantial extent the product of the environment in which he or she has grown as a child. Differences in attitudes to life, personal traits, value systems and even skills can often be traced to the physical and socio-economic milieu surrounding the child in its formative years. Factors like the availability or lack of protective family care and affection, of various necessities and luxuries and access to various facilities like education, health-care, recreation etc., all have a contribution to make towards the growth of a person's personality and shape his or her future life. Different components of the environment in the childhood leave their indelible impression on the person in some form or the other, physical or psychological.

Life on the street does many things to children living in an atmosphere devoid of all the affection, love, care and comfort of a family life. Street children are compelled by force of circumstances to struggle for the basic daily needs like food and shelter at a very tender age. Such a compulsion arises in the case of normal children much later in life, if at all it does arise. Street children are deprived of all the things they covet in early childhood, including access to education. They are also aware and jealous, of the gap that exists between them and the normal children. Thus, street children learn to survive in a hostile environment. They learn early in their lives to take their own decisions on matters that affect them vitally since there is no one to help them or guide them in taking such decisions. Street life leads to different kinds of development in different children. On one hand it encourages positive traits like independence and ability to face antagonism and on the other it leads to undesirable and socially unacceptable habits like crimes and vices.

Certain things are done best at an appropriate age. It is too early for and too cruel on a child to be worn down by need and concern to make a living, to look for shelter and to feed oneself and often others. In the case of street children, thus, there is a total imbalance between what is normal for their age and what they are compelled to do by the peculiar circumstances in which they find themselves. This chapter makes an attempt to discuss the impact of these peculiar circumstances on the personality of street children.

The causes that drive children to streets away from the loving care and security of their homes are varied but in all cases beyond their control. They are a victim of cruel circumstances and social compulsions for no fault of their. While they pine for a loving hand or even moments of affectionate concern, the world around them goes on with little care for the unfortunate children who are creatures of the same God. It is not enough that we know why they are on the streets. Social conscience must assert itself to ensure that these children are helped to join the mainstream and contribute to social good in a meaningful way of which they are certainly capable.

In the present study an attempt was made to study the status of street boys of 15-18 years of age. The turbulent adolescences is the period which requires empathy, guidance and support to travel through this phase status also reflects of life.

METHODOLOGY

Street children are a growing phenomenon of modern times, especially in the urban areas in developing countries, which are faced with the process of rapid and unplanned urbanisation. The process of urbanisation though common to all countries is very rapid in developing world.

Whatever may be the activity pursued by the street children they have one thing in common; lack of parental care, love, protection, supervision and separation from the general stream of education and basic needs, which are their legitimate right of that age. They enter the adolescent period with the problems. The deprivations in childhood the children and leads to delinquency the investigator undertook a project work to design a methodology for the study of street children.

Locale of the Study

The study was conducted in Tirupati urban mandal for the reasons stated as under. Tirupati is one of the famous pilgrims city with a floating population of around one lakh. Tirupati has a large number of street children next to Hyderabad and Vijayawada. Moreover Tirupati is located in the border district of Chittoor, which has two metropolitan cities next to it -- Chennai and Bangalore.

Sample Selection

The investigator surveyed the public places and identified street boys who were above 15 years of age. Thus the sample comprised of 35 boys aged above 15 to 18 years.

Selection of Variables

A review of available literature on street children led to identification of independent variables which may have influence on the status of street children; they are:

Independent Variables

Family size, Family type, Family literacy index, Family income, Birth order and age were included in the present study.

Working definition of Independent Variables:

1. **Family size:** The number of Family members residing in the respondent's family is considered as family size, determines the demand for available resources and also the amount of time allocated in the parents for the children. Hence it was included as available.

2. **Family type:** The type of family determines the amount of leisure time available and the level of interaction among the family members. Further it also determines the decision making opportunities of women.

3. **Family Literacy Index:** To total years of education the family members underwent is calculated and its mean is considered as the family literacy index. The educational aspirations of the child, hence it was included as a variable in the present study.

4. **Family income:** The family income is the total amount of money earned by the family in a year.

5. **Birth order:** The chronological age of respondents and his position among his/her siblings in the family is birth order. Birth order determines the child's expose to various family members. Hence it was included as a variable in the present study.

6. **Age:** The chronological age of the subjects in completed years is taken as age in years.

7. **Occupation:** Occupation is the nature of work done to make a living. It depends on the person's education training, personal capabilities and interests. The street children parent's occupation was also.

TOOLS FOR MEASUREMENT OF VARIABLES

In order to measure the variables chosen for the study, the following tools and research methods were used.

1. Questionnaire
2. Child rights scale
3. Interview
4. Observation

Questionnaire

A questionnaire was developed (see to collect information on personal profile, family profile and the status of street children under study. Relevant questions were formed to collect information from the street children, which were arranged in order of familiarity (more familiar to less familiar) and recollection to analytical type.

The questions are presented under headings:

1. Personal profile of the street child
2. Family profile of the street child
3. Reasons for child streetism
4. Health and nutrition profile
5. Hygiene and sanitation practices
6. Educational status
7. Work and working conditions
8. Income and serving
9. Recreation
10. Accommodation

Thus the questionnaire framed covers information needed to assess the status of the street child.

Child Rights Scale

A child rights scale developed (Sarada, 2000) in the Department of Human Development and Family Studies, was used to assess the child rights knowledge and attitudes of street children under study. The scale consisted of twenty six questions under child rights knowledge, rated on a yes/no type. The child rights attitudinal scale consisted of seventeen statements related on a three point scale (strongly agree/Agree/Disagree). The child rights knowledge and attitudinal scales were prepared both in English and Telugu (Local language) were administered to the street children.

Interview Method

As the street children's reading skills were not adequate to fill in the questionnaire and scales. The investigator used interview method to collect information using the questionnaire and child rights scales. Each street child under study was interviewed separately and the responses were recorded.

Observation Method

In order to validate the information given by each street child, their place of residence, work places were visited by the investigator. Observation method was used to verify the responses of the street children.

Statistical Analysis

The data collected were pooled, tabulated and subjected to statistical such as Mean, Standard Deviation, t-test and chi-square test.

RESULTS AND DISCUSSION

Personal Profile of Street Children

1. The children under study are divided into two groups age that is 15 to 16 years and 17 to 18 years. Majority of boys (65.75 per cent) belonged to 15 to 16 years age group, the remaining 34.2 per cent belongs to 17 to 18 years.

2. In the present study a good percentage of boys (51.4 per cent) were second born, followed by 34.2 per cent of first born and 11.4 per cent were third born. A 2.85 per cent of street children had birth order above three.

3. Majority of street children belonged to backward castes and scheduled castes; only a small percentage (8.5 per cent) of children were scheduled tribes.

4. Around 77.1 per cent of boys belonged to small families of less than four members; around 22.8 per cent of boys came from families of 5 to 8 members. None of the subjects belonged to families above 8 members.
5. Majority of children 74.2 per cent belonged to nuclear families. A good percentage of boys 22.8 per cent belong to extended families; only 2.85 per cent of boys had come from single parent families. None of the street children has joint type of families. This data complies with the general observation of the majority of street children belonged to nuclear type of families.
6. A good per cent of street children (42.9 per cent) had come from families with an annual income 24001 to 36000 annual income of 12001 to 24000 rupees. Only 17.1 per cent of street children had family income above 48,001. Although family income of the boys were low, they were not below the poverty line.
7. The occupation of most of the street children fathers were not of permanent nature and has less job security.
8. Majority of mothers of boys were daily wage earners. 17.1 per cent of boys mothers were employed in Government sector and only 11.4 per cent of boys mothers were self employed.
9. Majority (48.5 per cent) boys had high school education followed by 37 per cent of boys who have had primary school education; only 14.2 per cent of boys were illiterates.
10. It is interesting to note that a good percentage (40 per cent) of boys fathers were illiterates; 31.4 per cent of boys fathers had high school education and 22.8 per cent of boys fathers had primary education and only 5.7 per cent of boys fathers had college professional education. The data reflects that majority of the fathers of street children had low levels of education, that is less than high school education.
11. Mother's education positively contributes to children's development. A 60 per cent of mothers were illiterates.

A 28.5 per cent of mothers had only primary education. A small percentage (11.4 per cent) had high school education. School studies on childcare and development revealed that the capabilities of mothers in childcare is influenced by her levels of education.

Child Streetism

The responses of street boys to a question "When did you come away from home" was gathered to know age at which the child came away from home.

Table 17.1

Distribution of children according to their age of streetism

S. No.	*Age at which the child came away*	*Street children*	*Percentage*
1.	<5	0	0
2.	6-10	2	5.7
3.	11-15	16	45.7
4.	16 to 18	17	48.5
	Total	**35**	**100**

Figure 17.1

Distribution of children according to their age of streetism

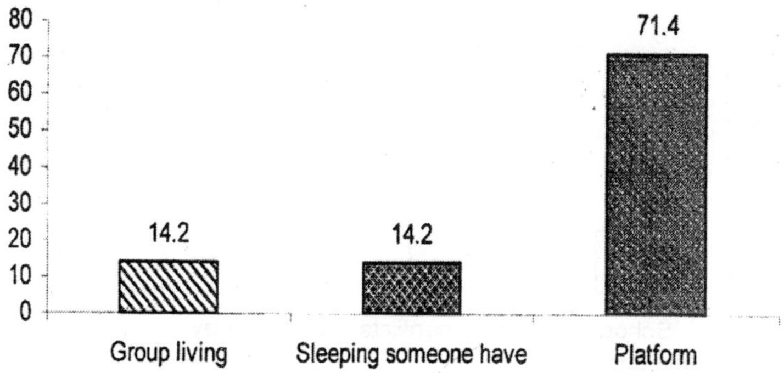

The Table 17.1 shows that the majority (48.5 per cent) understudy left their homes at the age of 16 to 18 years. A good percentage (45.7) of children given to streetism at the age of eleven to fifteen years. Only 5.7 per cent of children left their homes at the age of six to ten years. The study reveals that majority of the sample given to streetism during adolescence.

What are the reasons for coming away

The responses of the children to a question "What are the reasons for coming away" was recorded and presented in Table 17.2.

Table 17.2

Distribution of street children according to their reason for coming away from home

S. No.	*Reason for coming away from home*	*Street children*	*Percentage*
1.	School environment	5	14.2
2.	Family conflicts	10	28.5
3.	Discipline by parents	4	11.4
4.	Alcoholic fathers	16	45.7
	Total	**35**	**100**

Figure 17.2

Distribution of street children according to their reason for coming away from home

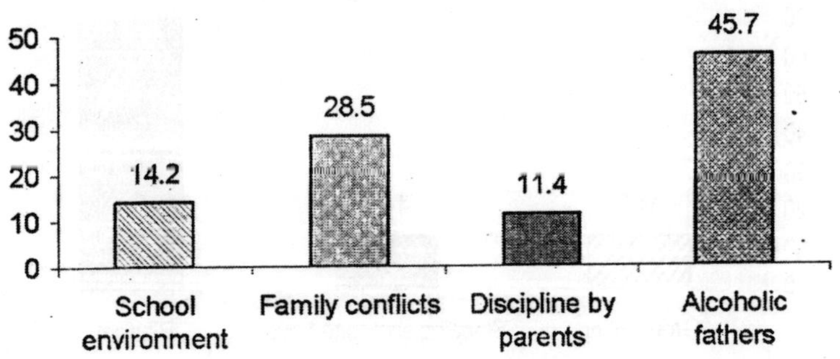

The Table 17.2 shows that child abuse by alcoholic father were found to be the main reason expressed by 45.7 per cent of children. Around 28.5 per cent of children indicated family conflicts as reason for streetism. A 14.2 per cent attributed their coming away from home to school environment. Only 11.4 per cent of children expressed parents strict discipline as reason for streetism.

The responses of street children to a question "Do you like to go back to your home" was gathered, which showed that 62.8 per cent did not want to go back; only 37.2 per cent stated that they like to go back to their home.

The response to a question "can you recognise your parents/family members", 90 per cent of the children said that they can recognise their parents whereas 10 per cent of the children did not feel confident about recognizing their parents.

It was found that 14.2 per cent made an effort to go back to their parents, which include sending word through their relatives, friends and writing letters.

Health Problems of Street Children

The prevalence of health problems and their frequency of occurrence was collected as shown in Table 17.3.

Table 17.3

Distribution of children according to the frequency of Health problems

S. No.	*Frequency of Health problems*	*Street children*	*Percentage*
1.	Daily	5	14.2
2.	Weekly	6	17.1
3.	Monthly	5	14.2
4.	Occasionally	19	54.2
	Total	**35**	**100**

Figure 17.3

Distribution of children according to the frequency of Health problems

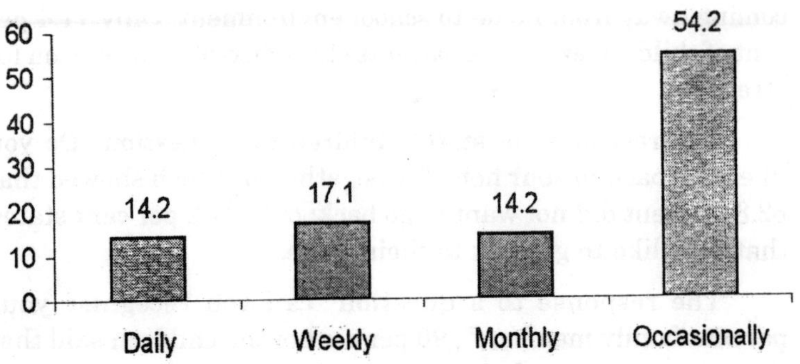

Which indicates that a good percentage of children suffered from health problems every month and 54.2 per cent of children occasionally suffered from health problems.

Sources of Seeking Medical Advice

Street children hesitate to go to a medical officer when they have a health problem. This may be due to their general appearance and fear of ill-treatment. This situation makes them seek medical advice from less reliable sources, which may lead to other health consequences.

Table 17.4

Distribution of children according to their source of seeking medical advice

S. No.	*Whom do you consult when you have a health problem*	*Street children*	*Percentage*
1.	Medical officer	4	11.4
2.	Medical shopkeeper	6	17.1
3.	Friends	15	42.8
4.	Self medications	10	28.5
5.	Any other	0	0
	Total	**35**	**100**

Figure 17.4

Distribution of children according to their source of seeking medical advice

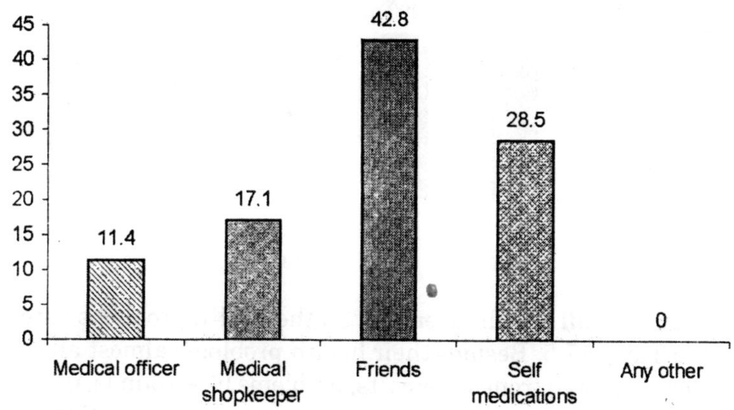

Table 17.4 shows that 42.8 per cent of street children seek medical advice from friends, followed by 28.5 per cent depend on self medication. A 17.1 per cent consult medical shopkeeper and only 11.4 per cent go to a medical officer.

Table 17.5

Health problems of street children in a year

S. No.	*Health problems*	*Street children*	*Percentage*
1.	Fever and Headache	35	100
2.	Eye infection	35	100
3.	Allergy	35	100
4.	Stomach ache	35	100
5.	Cold and cough	35	100
6.	Any other	35	100
	Total	**35**	**100**

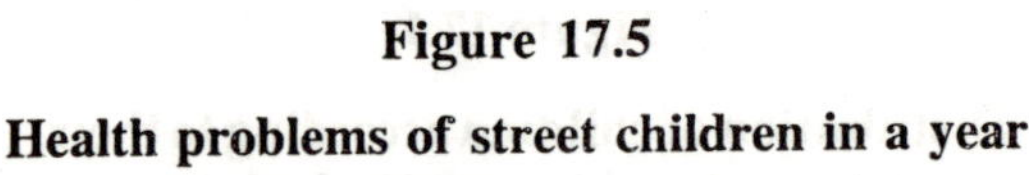

Figure 17.5

Health problems of street children in a year

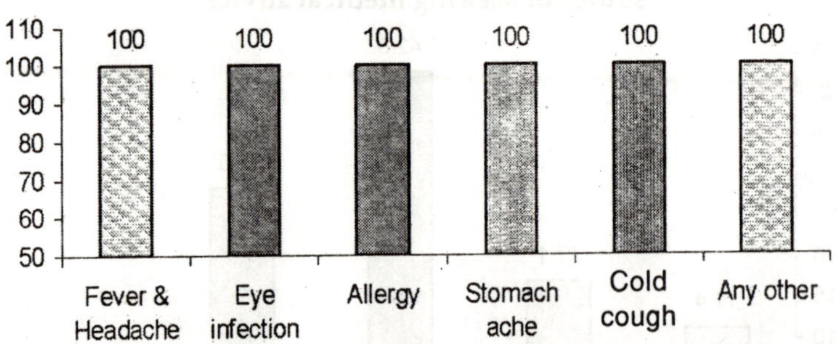

Almost all the children had all the health problems listed in the Table 17.5. Besides their health problems almost all the subjects suffered from other cults, problems like wounds, mouth boiles, bruises, cramps amoebiasis, loose motions, constipation etc.

This shows that street children regularly suffer from minor or major ailments, which may affect their health status.

During sickness the street children get help from their own friends. Any of the Government and Non-Government Organisations health service did not help any of these children.

Nutritional Adequacy of Diets Consumed by Street Children

Dietary intake of street children is not consistent as the food intake depends on availability of food and income of the street children. It is difficult to make reliable dietary assessment of street children. Even then an attempt was made to know the Nutritional adequacy of diets consumed by street children.

The dietary intake of street children was collected using 24 hour recall method and a set of standardised vessels through which the menu and approximate quantities of food consumed by each child was collected based on the food items and their quantity consumed by each child. Nutritive values of the diet was computed, using Nutritive Value of Indian Foods (ICMR, 1990). The actual Nutrient intake of each child was compared with the Recommended Dietary's Allowances (RDA), in order to know whether the diets are adequate, not adequate, which showed that 90.9 per cent of street boys' diets were adequate nutritionally; only 10 per cent of street boys diets were not adequate.

Quality of Food Consumed by the Street Children

Quality of food consumed by the street children was gathered. The responses indicated that 71.4 per cent consumed fresh food daily, only 28.5 per cent consumed fresh food occasionally.

It was also found that 14.2 per cent consumed stale food, followed by 14.2 per cent consuming plate waste. This data reflects that notable percentage of children are consuming stale food and plate waste.

Table 17.6

Quality of food consumed by the street children

S. No.	*Did you consume*	*Street children*	*Percentage*
1.	Stale food	5	14.2
2.	Plate waste	5	14.2
3.	Spoiled food	0	0
4.	Fresh food	25	71.4
	Total	**35**	**100**

Figure 17.6

Quality of food consumed by the street children

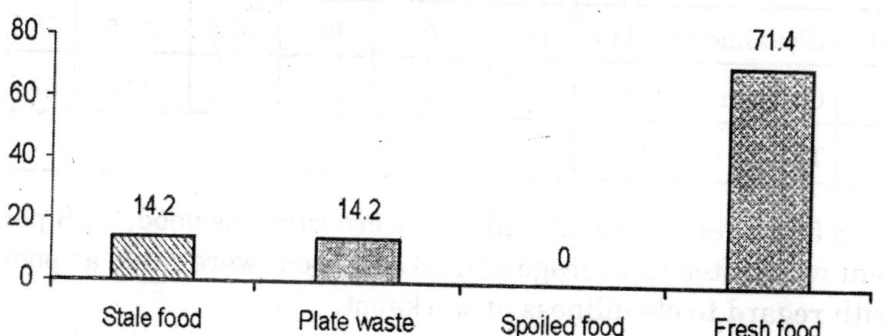

The reasons for consuming poor quality of food is inability to get food due to ill-health (14.2 per cent), lack of money to purchase food (71.4), lack of availability of food due to strikes/ Bandh.

Levels of Hygiene

Hygienic practices both at work and personal levels are necessary for good health. The street children have a greatest problem in keeping themselves hygienic. The kind of work they engage in and the lack of minimum facilities to keep themselves clean makes them unclean. An attempt was made to know the levels of hygiene in street children through observation and interview method.

Hygiene and Sanitation

The levels of hygiene was rated on a three point scale as poor, average and good. The cleanliness at workspot was rated, which shows that.

Table 17.7

Distribution of street boys according to their levels of hygiene

S. No.	*Hygiene*	*Number of street boys*			*Percentage of street boys*		
		Good	*Average*	*Poor*	*Good*	*Average*	*poor*
1.	Cleanliness at workspot	10	15	10	28.5	42.8	28.5
2.	Clothes worn by street children	5	10	20	14.2	28.5	57.1
3.	Cleanliness of Hair	15	10	10	42.8	28.5	28.5
4.	Cleanliness of nails	10	5	20	28.5	14.2	57.1
	Total		**35**				

A 28.5 per cent of street children were rated as good, 42.8 per cent were rated as average and 28.5 per cent were rated as poor with regard to cleanliness at workspot.

Cleanliness of clothes worn by the street children: A 14.2 per cent were rated as average and 57.1 per cent were rated as poor with regard to cleanliness of clothes worn by the street child.

Levels of Hygiene Among Street Boys

Cleanliness of hair: A 42.8 per cent of children were rated as good, 28.5 per cent were rated as average and 28.5 per cent were rated as poor with regard to cleanliness of hair.

Cleanliness of nails: A 28.5 per cent of children were rated as good, 14.2 per cent were rated as average and 57.1 per cent were rated as poor with regard to cleanliness of nails.

The data on the personal chores of street children with regard to hygiene and cleanliness was gathered which showed that 42.8 per cent of children take bath everyday, 28.5 per cent take bath once in two days and 28.5 per cent take.

Figure 17.7

Distribution of street boys according to their levels of hygiene

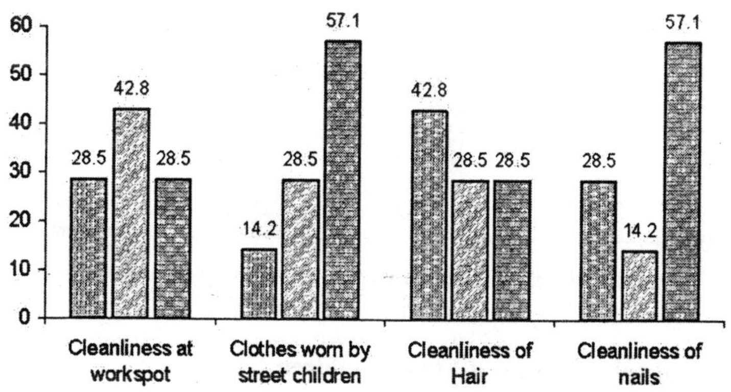

Educational and Vocational Interests of Street Children

The street children's interests in education and vocational training was collected which showed that only 14.2 per cent of children are interested in education; the remaining 86.8 per cent were not interested in education. If an opportunity is provided to continue education then 14.2 per cent of children are willing to continue their education. The type of education preferred was as follows:

A 60 per cent preferred vocational education, 40 per cent preferred formal education. None of the children preferred non-formal education or National Child Labour Programme Schools.

Table 17.8

Education and vocational interests of street children

S. No.	Type of education	Street children	Percentage
1.	Formal schools	5	14.2
2.	Vocational education	20	57.1
3.	Non-formal education	9	25.2
4.	Any other	1	2.85
	Total	**35**	**100**

Figure 17.8

Education and vocational interests of street children

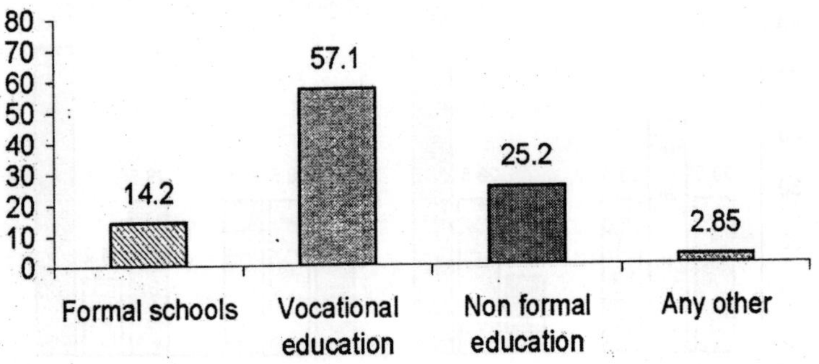

Vocational Interests of Street Children

The vocational interests of street children are as shown in Table 17.9 which indicate that 28.5 per cent showed interest in learning electrical works, 42.8 per cent wanted to learn mechanical work, 14.2 per cent preferred training whereas 8.5 per cent showed interest in cookery and bakery and 5.7 per cent wanted to learn printing and binding works.

Table 17.9

Vocational interests of street children

S. No.	*Kind of vocational training*	*Street children*	*Percentage*
1.	Electrical works	10	28.5
2.	Mechanical work	15	42.8
3.	Tailoring	5	14.2
4.	Cookery and bakery	3	8.5
5.	Printing and binding	2	5.7
6.	Any other	–	–
	Total	**35**	**100**

Figure 17.9

Vocational interests of street children

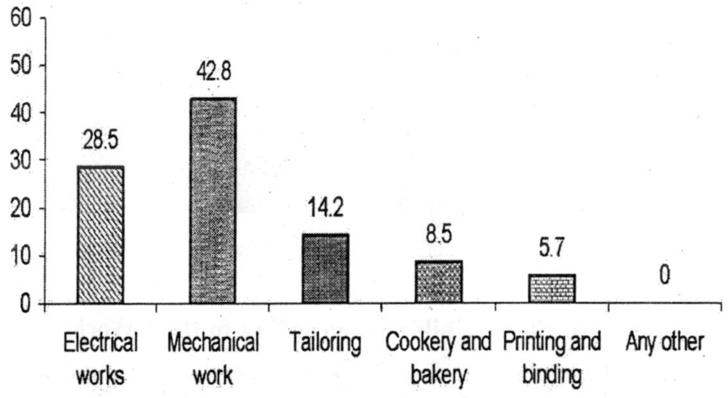

Work and Working Conditions of Street Children

All the street children do work for their living. The nature of work done by street children is given in Table 17.10 which indicates that 17.1 per cent of street children are doing manual work, 22.8 per cent are engaged in skilled work, 14.2 per cent to ground work and 45.7 per cent do any work depending on availability; they are not specifically engaged in one type of work.

Table 17.10

Distribution of children according to their nature of work

S. No.	*What is the nature of work*	*Street children*	*Percentage*
1.	Manual work	6	17.1
2.	Skilled work	8	22.8
3.	Errand work	5	14.2
4.	Any other	16	45.7
	Total	**35**	**100**

Figure 17.10

Distribution of children according to their nature of work

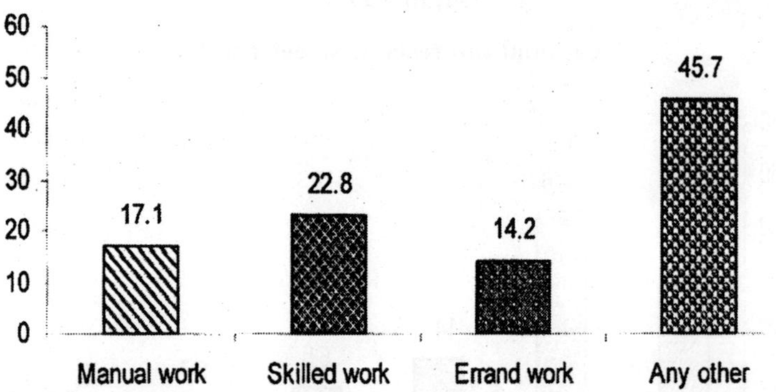

Distribution of Street Children According to their Work Skills

The skills of street children specific to work was gathered (see Table 17.11) which showed that 28.5 per cent of children said they have skills in electrical work, 57.1 per cent said they have skills in mechanical work and 14.2 per cent said they can do any work.

Table 17.11

Distribution of street children according to their work skills

S. No.	*Possess skills for any specific work*	*Street children*	*Percentage*
1.	Electrical work	10	28.5
2.	Mechanical work	20	57.1
3.	Tailoring	–	–
4.	Any other	5	14.2
	Total	**35**	**100**

Figure 17.11

Distribution of street children according to their work skills

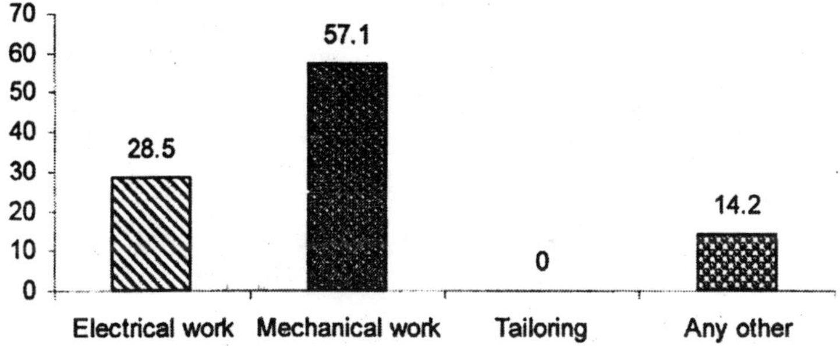

Income and Savings

The street children are also child labourers, as they make a living for themselves by working. The money earned by these children are not safeguarded for use on non-work days mainly due to lack of a safe place to keep the income. Further lack of proper address and identity deprives them from using available safe saving services such as post office, banks etc.

The monthly income of street children was less than 150 rupees. This income is also not consistent. Almost all the children saved some money, which they keep with the person known to them. But their savings are not regular; the savings are done for a week or so and then used. None of the children had accounts in bank or post offices; but they showed interest in saving in post offices.

Recreation

Recreation is the only source of happiness and relief for street children. Almost all the street children watch movies, television.

Table 17.12

Distribution of street children according to their duration of TV viewing

S. No.	*Do you watch T.V. in hours*	*Street children*	*Percentage*
1.	One hour	–	–
2.	Two hours	5	14.2
3.	3 hours	5	14.2
4.	4 hours	25	71.4
	Total	**35**	**100**

Figure 17.12

Distribution of street children according to their duration of TV viewing

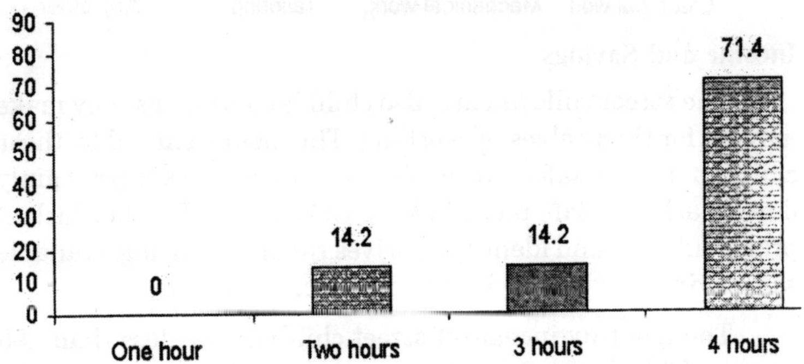

Table 17.12 shows that 14.2 per cent of street children watch television for 2 hours, 14.2 per cent watch television for 3 hours and 71.4 per cent watch television for 4 hours.

All the street children watch films every week. The street children learns most of the things from films. Street children knowledge received from films on various aspects was gathered and presented in Table 17.13.

Table 17.13

Distribution of street children according to their message from films

S. No.	*Type of message learnt from movies*	*Street children*	*Percentage*
1.	About religion	5	14.2
2.	About family	5	57.1
3.	Legal	5	57.1
4.	Health	20	14.2
5.	Marriage and sex	10	28.5
6.	Exploration	10	28.5
	Total	**55**	**199.6**

Figure 17.13

Distribution of street children according to the message from films

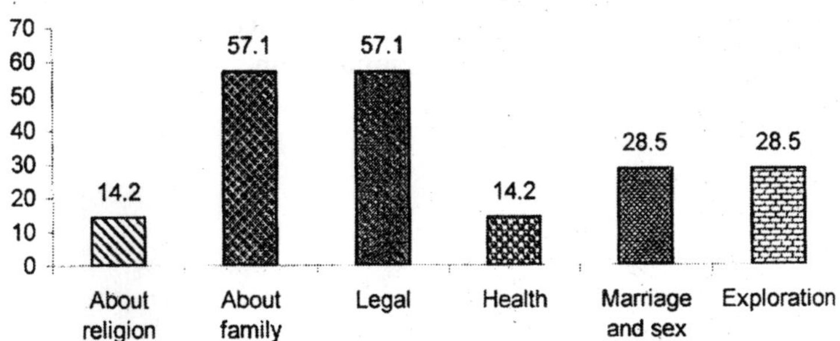

Which showed that 57.1 per cent learnt about family aspects from films. 14.2 per cent came to know about religion and related issues from films. Around 57.1 per cent learnt about legal aspects from films. 14.2 per cent came to know about health issues from films. 28.5 per cent came to know about marriage and sex from films. And 28.5 per cent children learnt about exploitation from films. The data reflects that cinemas/films are one of the important sources of knowledge of street children.

Distribution of Children According to Their Accommodation

The street children's greatest problem is a place of living. They do not have a safe and comfortable shelter to keep their things and take rest. In the present study the type of accommodation of street children collected, which is presented in Table.

Table 17.14

Distribution of street children according to their accommodation

S. No.	*Accommodation*	*Street children*	*Percentage*
1.	Group living	5	14.2
2.	Sleeping someone have	5	14.2
3.	Platform	25	71.4
	Total	**35**	**100**

Figure 17.14

Distribution of street children according to their accommodation

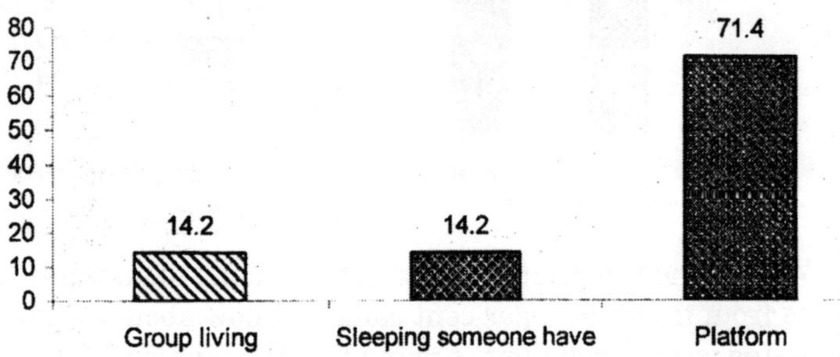

The above table shows that 14.2 per cent of children lived in a small house with other children, a 14.2 per cent slept in someone's house, 71.4 per cent lived on pavements. This shows that majority of street children lived on platforms/pavements.

Conclusion

Through the study "Status of Street Boys (15-18 years)" an effort was made by the investigator to assess the quality of life of street boys who are also adolescents. The study reveals that the street boys are leading a poor quality of life in terms of basic needs, facilities. They have no access to learn for their livelihoods and life skills. As children of this country, as any other children it is their right to have all the minimum facilities, amenities to fulfill their basic needs, which is ultimately the responsibility of the State Government. The families from which these children are coming need to be helped through appropriate family support systems or local Government and Non-Government units. There are lot of funds available with the Government, Non-Government Organisations, International agencies exclusively meant for street children. Even if these funds are used to extend regular constant services for these street boys it will go a long way.

REFERENCES

Mishra, Sudha, (1998), *Street Children. A Strategy for an Institutional—Plus Programmes,* Paper Presented in the National Workshop on Street Children Organised by the National Institute of Social Defence, Ministry of Welfare, Government of India.

Panicker R and Nangia, (1992), *Working and Street Children of Delhi,* National Labour Institute of India.

Pinto, G., (1994), *Street Children: Problems and Responses* CEDC, UNICEF, New Delhi (July).

Ritapanicker and Kalpana Desai, (1993), *Street Girls of Delhi*, Institute of Social Service, Probhatara, New Delhi.

Rashmi Agarwal, (1999), *Street Children—A Socio-psychological Study.*

Rajendra Panday, (1993), *Street Children of Kanur—A Situational Analysis.*

18

Status of Children (8-12 Years) in Government Observation Home, Tirupati (A.P.)

—Ms. T. Manju Bhargavi and Prof. D. Sarada

India's commitment to the cause of children is as old as its civilisation. It has been a time honoured belief in our culture that the child is a gift of God. A gift that must be nurtured with care and affection within the family and the society. Unfortunately, over the years in the pre-independence period, due to socio-economic and cultural changes, the code of child centeredness got replaced by neglect, abuse and deprivation, particularly in the poverty afflicted sections of the society. From being advantaged, children plummeted into disadvantaged group.

Children who are not privileged to attend schools and enjoy their childhood like their counterparts within their own society spend their valuable childhood in making a living to feed themselves and their family members. These children sometimes have to work day and night wasting their health and growth, such a situation may bitter their feelings towards their family and society. These negative feelings may affect their attitudes towards their family and society. Such children easily fall prey to anti-social elements and indulge in criminal activities.

The children belonging to poor families, yet privileged to attend schools could not cope up with the school system due to its rigid rules, unfriendly and strict disciplinary methods. In addition to the formal school system the children have a very poor home environment which is not helpful in assisting children to cope up with the academic work. The poor physical facilities at school further discourages these children. Finally it makes children to stay away from school. Any pressure from parents and teachers may force these children to run away from home.

The above situations are placing children in the hands of traffickers and middle men, who exploit these children and use them for their selfish means. It is these children who are brought to observation homes as under trials, delinquents, child Criminals, runaways etc. The observation homes are established under Juvenile Justice Act. Juvenile means a boy or a girl who has not attained the age of 18 years.

Observation Homes Contribution Towards Rehabilitation of Children

It is well accepted fact that children are the wealth of a nation. They have an important place in the family and family ties are reinforced with the presence of children and than other hand children became a liability if they are subjected to cruelty, harassment and exploitation. This leads them to anti-social and criminal behaviour. In order to overcome this melody the United Nations had declared the chapter of right for children.

In order to provide proper care, protection treatment development and rehabilitation of neglect and delinquent Juveniles the Government established the observation homes.

The main objective of observation home is to observe the activities of the Juvenile (neglected and Delinquent). Observation homes are established by the Government for the temporary reception of the Juveniles during the tendency of the case against them. The observation home shall provide the juvenile with accommodation, maintenance and facilities for medical examination and treatment and for useful occupation. The State Government may make rules for the management including the nature of services maintained by observation homes.

The Government Observation Home is one of the institutions under the aegis of social welfare department which caters to the needs of children undergoing trial for crimes, for being in crime situation and involving in delinquent activities. There are separate institutions for boys (Tirupati) and girls (Kadapa). These institutions provide remedial services in the form of education, recreation and vocational activities to some extent. As the period of stay of children is uncertain, there is no specific curriculum for their education. After the completion of the trial period the children are integrated into their community. In this context, it is essential to have a relook on: (i) the factors such as acceptance of these children in their cultural milieu; (ii) levels of integration into the mainstream; (iii) magnitude of children who have drifted back into allied antisocial activities; (iv) role of Government Observation Homes in rehabilitation of these children. Study entitled status of children (8-12 years) in government observation home was carried out in Tirupati (A.P.).

The hypotheses framed were:

1. The services provided in government observation homes are inadequate;
2. The factors contributing to delinquency mostly remain unchanged;
3. The efforts of observation home staff changing home environment of children are inadequate;
4. The children released from observation home allowed to live in almost same environment;
5. The rehabilitative efforts of observation home are inadequate.

The study was carried out on the children released from the government observation home, Tirupati during 2002 to 2004 and aged between 8 to 12 years and belonging to Tirupati surrounding areas were selected. Thus the sample comprised of 35 boys aged between 8 to 12 years.

The variables selected for the study were Age of children, Birth order, Educational status of child, Educational status of mother and father, Occupation of mother and father, Annual income of family, Family type, Family size, Place of residence as independent variables and the Dependent variables selected for the study are Home environment, School environment.

A questionnaire was developed to collect data on personal profile, family profile, school profile and observation home. Care was taken to include all the variables selected for the study. The questionnaire developed was a structured one. The investigator visited the government observation home and obtained official permission to collect information from records and staff. Interview and observation methods were used to collect information about physical facilities, programme and administration of observation home. The records such as staff and children's attendance registers, case registers, reports and provisions issue records were analysed and information was collected. The investigator made several visits to children's houses, as they were not available easily. Using interview and observation methods, data on family structure and environment, school environment and child's behaviour was gathered from the parents and also children. The data was pooled and tabulated.

The nature of the topic requires discussion and interpretation of observed information meaningfully, the numerical data gathered through questionnaire was presented only in percentages. Mostly qualitative analysis was used.

RESULTS AND DISCUSSION

Personal and Family Profile of Street Children

- A major percentage 54.28 of children belonged to 11 to 12 years of age and 37.14 per cent were of 9 to 10 years of age. Only 8.58 per cent were of less than 8 years of age. This indicates that majority of children belonged to late childhood period.

- A major percentage of children are second born that was 48.57 per cent, 31-42 per cent were first born, 14.29 per cent were third born and 5.72 per cent were found to be only child.
- 42.86 per cent of boys were school dropouts. Around 28.57 per cent of boys had primary education. A 14.29 per cent of boys were attending high school. Around 14.28 per cent of boys were illiterates. This shows that the majority of children under study were school dropouts and illiterates. The reason for poor educational status was the poverty and unappealing educational system, as expressed by the respondents.
- A major percentage of boys (57.14 per cent) had normal heights. Around 28.58 per cent of boys had heights below normal and 14.28 per cent of boys had heights above normal. It shows that majority of boys were normal and above normal.
- A major percentage of boys 51.43 per cent had normal weights. Around 34.29 per cent of boys had weights below normal. Only 14.28 per cent of boys had weights above normal. It shows that majority of boys were normal and above normal with regard to their weights.
- The majority of the sample (42.86 per cent) belonged to urban slum. A (34.28 per cent) belong to urban area and (22.86 per cent) belonged to rural area.
- Majority of children have come from nuclear families (45.72 per cent), a 17.14 per cent boys came from joint families and 25.71 per cent of boys were from extended families. Around 11.43 per cent of boys belonged to other types of families such as single parent families and co-habitation of single parent and children with a father figure or substitute. Majority of children belonged to nuclear type of families.
- A major percentage of boys (62.86 per cent) had families of 5 to 8 members. A 37.14 per cent of boys had small families of less than 4 members. None of the children had family sizes above 8 members.

- 71.42 per cent of mothers were illiterates. Around 25.72 per cent of mothers had primary school education and 2.86 per cent had high school education. The mothers of most of the children were illiterates and had low levels of education.
- 51.43 per cent of fathers were illiterates. Around 22.86 per cent of fathers had primary school education, and 22.85 per cent of fathers had high school education. Only 2.86 per cent of fathers have studied up intermediate. The reasons for poor educational status was the poverty as expressed by the respondents.
- A major percentage (45.71) of fathers were daily wage earners, followed by 25.72 per cent of fathers engaged in petty business and 25.72 per cent of fathers were employed in private sector. Only a small percentage of (2.85 per cent) fathers were employed in government. The pattern of occupation of fathers shows that majority of them are underemployed and do not have a security of regular income or job, who deprives their families of a steady income.
- 42.85 per cent of mothers were daily wage earners. Around 25.72 per cent of mothers were housewives and 17.15 per cent were engaged in other occupations such as seasonal, part-time works; 14.28 per cent of mothers were engaged in Petty business. This shows that a major section of the sample are working in unorganised sector, where there is no guarantee of employment and uniform wages.
- 25.73 per cent of families had annual income below 11,000 rupees, which is Below Poverty Line. Around 71.42 per cent of families had annual income between 11,001 to 24,000 per annum, which is not an adequate income for urban families. Only 2.85 per cent of families had annual income above 24,000 rupees.

Home Environment

Conditions in the family are probably the most important factors in producing delinquency; this applies to both sexes. One of the commonest factors among delinquents is friction with parents and the school which leads to stressful conditions and adjustment problems. Conditions at home, especially the mother's influence, seem to have more causal relationship to girls delinquency than boy's.

In the present study the home environment of children was assessed in rating the areas, parenting, family cohesion, psycho-social needs fulfillment and physical facilities available at home. The rating was done on a five point scale as very good, good, average, poor, very poor. The rating was done by the children themselves, after receiving a detailed instruction from the investigator.

Table 18.1

Home Environment of Children of Observation Home

S. No.	*Area of Home Environment*	*Rating by Children*					*Total*
		Very good	*Good*	*Average*	*Poor*	*Very poor*	
1.	Parenting	0	11.42	34.29	42.86	11.43	100
2.	Family cohesion	5.71	11.43	25.71	40	17.15	100
3.	Psycho social needs fulfillment	0	17.14	34.28	28.58	20	100
4.	Physical facilities	0	11.42	20	37.15	31.43	100
	Total	**5.71**	**51.41**	**114.28**	**148.59**	**80.01**	

Parenting

Although theoretically several parenting styles have been described by experts of parent education. In the present study the children's perception of their parents functions and behaviour in relation to what is expected of parents was considered for rating. The Table 18.1 indicate that a majority of children (42.86 per cent) had poor parenting, 34.29 per cent had average parenting, 11.42 per cent had good parenting and 11.43 per cent had very poor parenting. These perceptions of children comply with the findings of perceptions of empirical studies on this topic.

Family Cohesion

The children were asked to rate their family cohesion on a five point scale based on the strength of family relationships and levels of interactions. This was explained to children how close are your parents to each other and to you (children). Do you feel free to express yourself to parents and sibling, do you tell everything at home, do your parents consult each other on family issues, tasks, decision by consulting each other etc.

The children's ratings on family cohesion (as shown in Table 18.1) indicate that majority of children (40 per cent) had poor family cohesion, 25.71 per cent rated their family as average for cohesion, 17.15 per cent rated their family as very poor in cohesion. Only 5.71 per cent and 11.43 per cent rated their family cohesion as very good and good respectively.

Psycho-social Needs Fulfillment

Recognition, approval, empathy, reward, love and affection, appreciation were considered as psycho-social needs of children. Children based on their experiences at home rated their parents for provision of psycho-social needs which are as shown in Table 18.1.

Around 17.14 per cent children rated good, 34.28 per cent rated as average, 28.58 per cent rated their parents as poor and 20 per cent rated their parents as very poor. None of the children rated their parents as very good for psycho-social needs fulfillment. Deprivation of psycho-social needs leads to dissatisfaction and may manifest into delinquent behaviour.

Physical Facilities

The basic facilities needed to complete daily chores in privacy were considered as physical facilities, place to keep things, sleep and toilet facilities etc. The children were asked to rate the physical facilities available at home on a five point scale. The ratings were tabulated (see Table 18.1.).

Around 37.15 per cent have rated the physical facilities as poor and 31.43 per cent as very poor. A 20 per cent rated the physical facilities as average and 11.42 per cent as good. The ratings indicate that the physical facilities available at home are poor and inadequate.

School Environment

The school is less influential than the home in its bearing on delinquency, but it does play a part in evoking incipient anti-social tendencies. A delinquent's deficiencies in school achievement seem to be related not so much to their inability to do school work as to their non-conforming to the standards set by the school. Since lower class standards are typically represented as undesirable by middle-class teachers, the lower class child feels that he is being devalued or held up as a bad example. His feelings of inferiority are further accentuated by patronising attitudes, slurs and taunts from his peers.

The children were asked to rate their school environment prior to their stay in observation home. The rating was done on a five point scale as very good, good, average, poor and very poor. The areas of school environment rated include physical facilities, teaching, access to school material, disciplinary methods and peer group. The data was tabulated shown in Table 18.2.

Table 18.2

School Environment of Children of Observation Home

S. No.	*Area of School Environment*	*Rating by Children*					*Total*
		Very good	*Good*	*Average*	*Poor*	*Very poor*	
1.	Physical facilities	0	0	42.85	42.86	14.29	100
2.	Teaching	0	28.57	34.28	22.86	14.29	100
3.	Access to school material (books, pencils, bag, test books)	0	34.29	42.86	11.43	11.42	100
4.	Acceptability of disciplinary methods	0	0	17.14	25.72	57.14	100
5.	Peers	11.43	45.72	34.28	8.57	0	100
	Total	**11.43**	**108.58**	**171.41**	**111.44**	**97.14**	

The children have rated the physical facilities that were available at their school as average (42.85 per cent), poor

(42.86 per cent) and very poor (14.29 per cent). This shows that the physical facilities at school were inadequate.

The teaching at school were rated by children as good (28.57 per cent), average (34.28 per cent), poor (22.86 per cent) and very poor (14.29 per cent). This shows that only a small percentage have perceived teaching as good and the rest of the sample have felt the teaching at school to be average to very poor.

The children's access to school material (such as books, note books, pencils, bag etc.) for attending the school is also important as it makes children feel confident and adequate. the sample have rated this area of school environment as good (34.29 per cent), average (42.86 per cent), poor (11.43 per cent) and very poor (11.42 per cent). This shows that a good percentage of sample had access to school material and only a small percentage had poor access.

The disciplinary methods followed at school influences the children's attendance. Harsh and unpleasant disciplinary methods such as abuse, canning, beating, punishing, drive away children from school. When compelled by their parents to attend school the children may resort to running away from home. The children have rated the disciplinary methods in terms of acceptability as average (17.14 per cent), poor (25.72 per cent) and very poor (57.14 per cent).

Conclusion

The study on "Status of Children (8-12 years) in Government Observation Home, Tirupati" indicates that the factors responsible for children's deviant and delinquent behaviour, have their roots in poverty, poor living conditions, inadequate home environment, unappealing school environment. The facilities at observation home were also inadequate and the programmes are not really addressing the needs of the children. The follow-up activities are also negligible. The total programme needs to be reorganised to and made relevant to the children of observation home.

REFERENCES

Mitra, Dr. N.L., (1988), "*Juvenile Delinquency and Indian Justice System*", Deep and Deep Publications, New Delhi.

Misra, B.N., (1991), *Juvenile Delinquency and Justice System*, New Delhi. Ashish Publishing House; pp. 15-22.

Pramila Pandit, Barooah, (2000), "*Handbook on Child*" (*with Historical Background*) Concept Publishing Company, New Delhi, pp. 22, 60-62.

Paras Diwan and Peeyushi Diwan, (1994), "*Children and Legal Protection*", Deep and Deep Publications, F-159, Rajouri Garden, New Delhi.

Rajendra Pandey, (1993), "*Street Children of Kanpur*", Publication of the Child Labour Cell, National Labour Institute, NOIDA has been founded by UNICEF, New Delhi.

Suneetha, B. and Rayalu, T.R., (2002), Conducted a Study on the Psycho-social Profile of the Juvenile Delinquent Children. *Journal of Psychological Research*, Vol. 46, No. 1 and 2, pp. 79-85.

19

Status of Children (13-18 years) in Government Observation Home, Tirupati (A.P)

—**Ms. S. Anuradha** and **Prof. D. Sarada**

INTRODUCTION

Children who are not privileged to attend schools and enjoy their childhood like their counterparts within their own society spend their valuable childhood in making a living to feed themselves and their family members. These children sometimes have to work day and night wasting their health and growth. Such a situation may bitter their feelings towards their family and society. These negative feelings may affect their attitude towards their family and society. Such children easily fall prey to anti-social elements and indulge in criminal activities.

The children belonging to poor families, yet privileged to attend schools could not cope up with the school system due to its rigid rules, unfriendly and strict disciplinary methods. In addition to the formal school system the children have a very poor home environment which is not helpful in assisting them to cope with the academic work. The poor physical facilities at school further discourages children. Finally it makes children to stay away from school. Any pressure from parents and teachers may force these children to run away from home.

The above situations are placing children in the hands of traffickers and middle men, who exploit these children and use them for their selfish means. It is these children who are brought to observation homes as delinquents, child criminals, under trails, runaways etc.

The observation homes are established under juvenile justice Act. Juvenile means a boy or a girl who has not attained the age of 18 years. In 1908, the Prevention of Crime Act has authorised the courts to order special treatment for young delinquents and introduced the Borstal system as part of the National Penal Programme. Under the Children's Act of 1912 Juvenile Courts and Probation Services were established. Borstal Institutions grew in number and became more specialised in the nature of their methods of education, vocational guidance and occupation training. The age of young offenders who might be admitted to Borstal Institutions was raised to 23 years and maximum time of institutional treatment in Borstal Schools is four years. The commissioner of the Borstal Institutions was a member of the National Prison Commission. He or she decides on the recommendation of his or her staff, how long the individual young offender shall remain in the institution. Education was entrusted to teacher, housemasters and matrons who under a cottage system, live together with the youngsters. Disciplinary officers were separated from the other educational staff. A preliminary observation of each offender in a clinical setting enables the governor of the Borstal Institution to select the specific school, the type of vocational training and the personnel that best suit the needs of the individual delinquent. Tho vocational training in Borstal schools is directed towards practical skill. Competition with free labour on the general market has been avoided by manufacturing goods approved by labour unions. After the young offender is released, he or she remains under parole supervision, which was carried out by trained parole officers or by volunteers instructed by the Borstal association.

In their work of protection and adjustment of children and young people the Juvenile courts depend on the aid of public and private Child Welfare Agencies, Child Guidance Clinics and Probation Services. Probation for minors is widely used in Great Britain. If it is necessary to remove the child from his or her family, foster homes are selected and supervised by child protective agencies or by chapters of the Borstal association. There are also hostels and probation homes for young offenders who cannot be placed in a foster family and Recently Attendance Centers as day institutions for the adjustment of difficult and seriously delinquent children and adolescents, the Borstal institutions and approved schools are used. The values of preventive services such as recreation and youth group activities is well recognised, and these clubs and recreation groups receive financial support from private organisations, the countries, and the national government. The approved schools, in contrast are classified according to their special training, equipment and their staff skills. There are separate schools for girls and boys and the various age groups and particular difficulties of the children are taken into consideration. After release from a Borstal institution the young offender remains for two years under the supervision of an after care officer.

In India the Borstal homes were run under the Department of Police and Jails. The name "Borstal Home' was replaced by observation home and was shifted to social welfare department.

The detention home, or juvenile hall receives children who may be classified into 3 main categories; children in need of protection such as dependent, neglected and abused children without proper care, lost children in need of emergency shelter, mental defectives awaiting commitment and habitual truants who are being returned to their parents. Children in temporary custody such as children who are runaways from their natural or foster families and from children's institutions; and children who must serve as witness to secure their presence in court; and juveniles expecting trial before the juvenile court and children awaiting transfer to a training school or another institution after court decision.

In some detention homes, dependent and neglected children are kept separate from delinquent children. Many children remain only a day or a night in the detention home until they return to their families. But for 3 types of children longer placement in the detention home is frequently necessary; children and youngsters beyond the control of their parents, foster parents and guardians, who cannot be prevented from committing new delinquencies such as serious assault, sexual attacks, burglary, armed robbery; children who are in physical or moral danger in their families (or) are without a home. And children whose attendance or uninfluenced testimony at a court hearing or whose placement in an institution can be assured only by detention.

Detention homes are administered by the Juvenile court (Sometimes the chief probation officer is superintendent of the home), the country authorities (Board of supervisors or commissioners), a local public welfare department, the state's department of social welfare, or a private children welfare agency.

Services to the child in the detention home includes physical and custodial care, medical and dental treatment, recreation, instruction according to the age of the child and the length of his or her stay, and religious services. Although a certain security against escape is necessary, detention homes try to avoid an atmosphere of fear and repression. More recently, the need of professional case work and clinical services for emotionally disturbed children has been acknowledged, as well as stimulating, cheerful group activities in workshops, play and recreation. However, many detention homes are still far from meeting these facilities, which require employment of trained personnel, a superintendent, teachers, case workers, group workers and supervisors. The observation in the detention home of the children's health, mental abilities and behaviour renders valuable information for the court, the probation staff and social agencies.

Because most children are held for only a few days or weeks in detention home, little systematic, academic or technical education and personality adjustment is possible. The children are of different age groups; most of them are sent home again or are placed in a foster home or another Children's Institution before they are well acquainted with the detention home staff.

With an accepting, friendly attitude toward the children the staff sometimes are able to break through the tearful or hostile defence that most children bring to the detention home after they have been arrested. The establishment of contact between the child and the case worker, group worker or counsellor may be the beginning of a treatment process. An intensive influence on corrective adjustment of the children can seldom occur during such a short period. But the child is protected against the destructive influences, is well cared for physically and the family and society are protected against the child's delinquent action for the period of detention. Whenever children feel that the staff take a sincere interest in their well-being and are willing to help them, a start in treatment may be made in the detention home.

In the observation home the delinquents runaway children, children under trial are brought and provided boarding and accommodation. The children are confined to the observation home, where the children are given Non-formal Education, Vocational Training and provided Indoor Facilities for games and recreation. Every child is given four pairs of dresses per annum. Government provides 25 lakhs of rupees per annum to take care of 50 to 60 children in observation home for boys, Tirupati. The diet provided for these children includes a cereal breakfast, lunch and rice, dhal, curry and curds and the dinner with rice, dhal, curry and rasam. The staff of observation home include a superintendent, a probation officer, junior assistant, typist, cook,. sweeper and ayah.

A personal observation of Observation Home indicates that almost all the facilities available are inadequate and does not meet the minimum needs of children who are growing adolescent boys. It is astonishing to note that no efforts are made to change the existing situation.

The children coming out of observation homes are expected to be followed up by observation home staff. The follow-up activities include correctional behaviour, counselling to parents and children, provision of rehabilitative services. The follow-up activities are not effectively implemented in majority of the observation homes.

Thus the observation homes aim at sheltering young offenders and also sheltering young offenders and also reorient and retrain them through counselling and vocational training to lead normal life when they go back to their parents or homes. In this context the present study was undertaken to know the children's personal and family profile and appraise the services rendered in observation home in order to arrive at appropriate suggestions to rehabilitate children coming out of observation homes.

METHODOLOGY

The Government Observation Home is one of the institutions under the aegis of social welfare department which caters to the needs of children undergoing trial for crimes, for being in crime situation and involving in delinquent activities. There are separate institutions for boys (Tirupati) and girls (Kadapa). These institutions provide remedial services in the form of education, recreation and vocational activities to some extent. As the period of stay of children is uncertain, there is no specific curriculum for their education. After the completion of the trial period the children are integrated into their community. In this context, it is essential to have a relook on: (i) the factors such as acceptance of these children in their cultural milieu; (ii) levels of integration into the mainstream; (iii) magnitude of children who have drifted back into allied anti-social activities; (iv) role of Government Observation Homes in rehabilitation of these children.

In light of the above, this study intends to develop appropriate strategies for convergence (Government and Non-Governmental) of efforts towards the rehabilitation of children coming out of Observation Home.

Statement of Problem

A study on "Status of Children (13 to 18 years) in Government Observation Home".

Research Design

- All the children availing the services in the Government Observation Home, Tirupati during the period 2002-2004 were will be considered for the study.
- Depending on the available number of children adequate size of the sample were selected randomly.
- The methods of collection of data were questionnaires, interview, observation and case study.
- Tools for data collection was structured questionnaire prepared specifically for the study.
- Sources of data were personal visits, analysis of records and other secondary data.

Hypothesis

1. The services provided in Government observation homes are inadequate.
2. The factors contributing to delinquency mostly remain unchanged.
3. The efforts of observation homes in changing home environment of children are inadequate.
4. The rehabilitative efforts of observation home are inadequate.

Sample Selection

The children released from the Government Observation Home, Tirupati during 2002 to 2004 and aged between 13 to 18 years and belonging to Tirupati surrounding areas were selected. Thus the sample comprised of 35 boys aged between 13 to 18 years.

FLOW CHART – 19.1

Research design

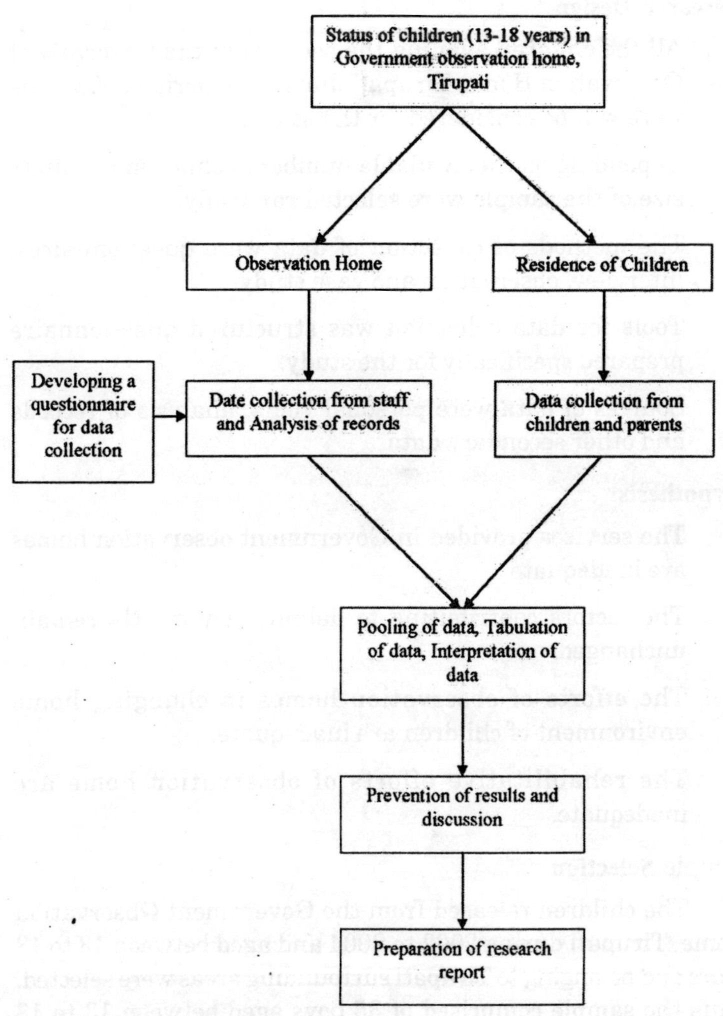

Selection of Variables

Based on the review of literature and a thorough discussion or research topic with the research supervisor, the following variables were selected for inclusion in the present study.

The independent variables selected for the study are:

1. Age of children
2. Birth order of the child
3. Educational status of the child
4. Educational status of mother and father
5. Occupation of mother and father
6. Annual income of family
7. Family type
8. Family size
9. Place of residence

The Dependent variables for the study

1. Home environment
2. School environment

DEFINITION OF VARIABLES

Working definitions for variables selected for the study were framed; they are as follows:

Independent Variables

1. Age of Children

The chronological age of the subjects in completed years is taken as age. The age of the respondents were collected from the admission records of observation home.

2. Birth Order

The chronological age of respondents and their position among their siblings in the family is considered as birth order. Birth order determines the child's exposure to various family activities and the attention received by their family members. Hence it was included as a variable in the present study.

3. Educational Status

The number of years of formal education received by an individual (child/father/mother) was considered as their educational status.

4. Occupation

The nature of work, undertaken to make a living is called occupation. A person's occupation usually depends on his/her educational status, training skills. The income earned depends largely on occupation. The amount of leisure time available also depends on the nature of occupation.

5. Mother's Occupation

The type of work that is done by mother to earn money is termed as occupation.

6. Father's Occupation

The type of work that is done to get income is considered as occupation.

7. Annual Income of Family

Annual income of family has an influence on the respondent's quality of life. Hence it was considered important to include this as variable. The total income earned by the family in a year is considered as the annual income of family.

8. Type of Family

The type of family determines the amount of leisure time available and the level of interaction among the family members. Hence it was chosen for inclusion in the present study.

9. Family Size

The number of family members residing in the respondent's family was considered as family size.

10. Place of Residence

The locality where the respondent resides with his family is considered as place of residence.

Dependent Variables

1. School Environment

The physical facilities available, the academic programme, disciplinary methods followed. The other activities organised at school has an influence on child's interest in school, his regularity and performance of schools. Hence it was included as a variable in the study.

2. Home Environment

Conditions in the family are probably the most important factors in producing delinquency. This applied to both sexes. One of the commonest factors among delinquents is friction with parents and the siblings. Conditions at home, especially the parents influence, seem to have more causal relation to delinquency.

Tools for Measurement of Variables

A questionnaire was developed to collect data on personal profile, family profile, school profile and observation home. Care was taken to include all the variables selected for the study. The questionnaire developed was a structured one.

Data Collection

The investigator visited the Government observation home and obtained official permission to collect information from records and staff. Interview, observation methods were used to collect information about physical facilities, programme and administration of observation home. The records such as staff and children's attendance registers, cases register, reports and provisions issue records were analysed and information was collected.

The investigator made several visits to children's houses, as they were not available in one or two units. Using interview and observation methods data on family environment, school environment and child's behaviour was gathered from the parents and also children. The data was pooled and tabulated.

Analysis of Data

The nature of the topic requires discussion and interpretation of observed information meaningfully, the numerical data gathered through questionnaire was presented only in percentages as they are simple with less scope for statistical analysis. Mostly qualitative analysis was used.

RESULTS AND DISCUSSION

The data on the topic "Status of Children (13 to 18 years) in Government Observation Home, (Tirupati)" was gathered from the sample and their family members and the authorities of observation home. An effort was made to present the data meaningfully reflecting the study results.

Personal Profile of the Sample

The personal information such as age, birth order, height and weight, educational status of the children was collected using a questionnaire specially developed for the purpose to facilitate better understanding of personal variables which are as follows.

Age of Children

The Chronological age of the children is useful in understanding the physical, psychological and social maturity of children. The Table 19.1 shows that a major per cent of children belonged to 13 to 14 years of age (48.6 per cent). 25.7 per cent were of 15 to 16 years and the 17 to 18 years of age respectively.

Table 19.1

Distribution of Children according to their age

S. No.	*Age in Years*	*Percentage*
1.	13-14	48.6
2.	15-16	25.7
3.	17-18	25.7
	Total	**100.0**

Fig. 19.1

Distribution of Children according to their age

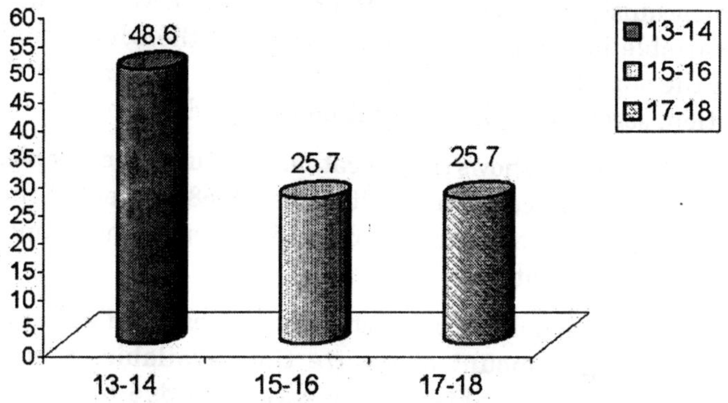

Birth Order of Children

The care and attention of parents on children partly depends on the birth order also. The Table 19.2 shows that a major per cent of children were second born (42.8 per cent). A 25.7 per cent were third born and 17.1 per cent were first born. Around 2.8 per cent were last born that is fourth born and the remaining 11.6 per cent were only (single) child in the family.

Table 19.2

Distribution of Children according to their birth order

S. No.	*Birth order of children*	*Percentage*
1.	First born	17.1
2.	Second born	42.8
3.	Third born	25.7
4.	Fourth born	2.8
5.	Only one/single child	11.6
	Total	**100**

Educational Status

The number of years of formal education received by the sample was considered as their educational status. Education exposes individual to selected knowledge and gives necessary skills in acquisition of knowledge. Hence, education was included as a variable in the present study. Based on the educational status the sample was classified as illiterates, primary school education, secondary school education and graduation.

The Table 19.3 shows the educational status of the sample. Majority (48.57 per cent) were illiterates, 28.58 per cent of the sample had primary education, and 22.85 per cent of the sample had secondary education.

The educational status of children of observation home also reflects the amount of leisure time available. School dropouts and non-entrants become way ward due to lack of productive engagement needed for a child.

Table 19.3

Distribution of Children according to their Educational Status

S. No.	*Educational Status*	*Percentage*
1.	Illiterate	48.57
2.	Primary education	28.58
3.	Secondary education	22.85
	Total	**100.00**

Height

Height indicates prolonged nutritional status. Malnourished or undernourished children may not have optimum growth required for the age.

The Table 19.4 shows the height of the sample. Majority of the children (51.43 per cent) were of normal height, a 28.57 per cent had heights below normal and 20 per cent had heights above normal.

The height of the children was measured using height scale in centimeters and compared with that of ICMR standards.

Table 19.4

Distribution of Children according to their Height

S.No.	*Height*	*Percentage*
1.	Above normal	20.00
2.	Normal	51.43
3.	Below normal	28.57
	Total	**100.00**

Weight

Weight gain is measured in kilograms using platform weighing scale. Body weight indicates the current nutritional status.

Table 19.5

Distribution of Children according to their Body Weights

S. No.	*Body weight of children*	*Percentage*
1.	Above normal	14.28
2.	Normal	60.00
3.	Below normal	25.72
	Total	**100.00**

The Table 19.5 shows the weights of the sample. A major percentage of sample (60 per cent) had normal weight, a 25.72 per cent had weights below normal. The remaining 14.28 per cent had weights above normal.

Family Profile of the Sample

The variables such as place of residence, education of father and mother, occupations of father and mother and family income were studied in order to understand the socio-economic background of the sample.

Place of Residence

The place where one resides has an influence on their exposure to mass media and other sources of information. The place of residence is usually determined by one's occupation and economic status. The sample were classified into three groups that is rural, urban, tribal and urban slum.

The Table 19.6 shows that a majority of children (51.42 per cent) belonged to urban area. A 37.16 per cent belonged to urban slum and 11.42 per cent belonged to rural areas.

Fig. 19.2

Distribution of Children according to their Place of Residence

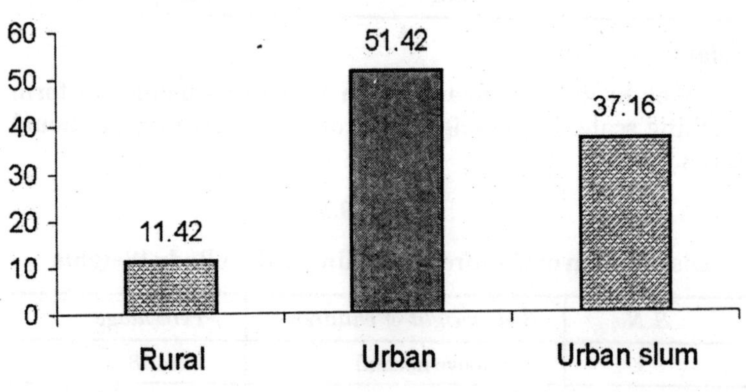

Table 19.6

Distribution of Children according to their Place of Residence

S. No.	*Place of Residence*	*Percentage*
1.	Rural	11.42
2.	Urban	51.42
3.	Urban slum	37.16
	Total	**100.00**

Type of Family

Depending on the type of family the sample was divided into three groups, that is nuclear family, extended family and joint family. A major percentage of the sample 82.85 per cent belonged to nuclear families, 11.42 per cent of the sample belonged to extended families and only 5.73 per cent of the sample belonged to joint families.

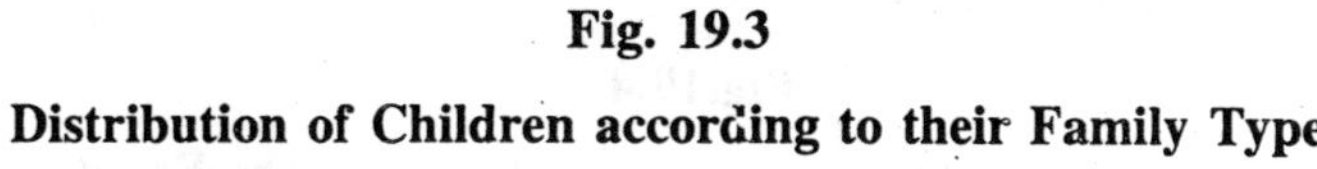

Fig. 19.3

Distribution of Children according to their Family Type

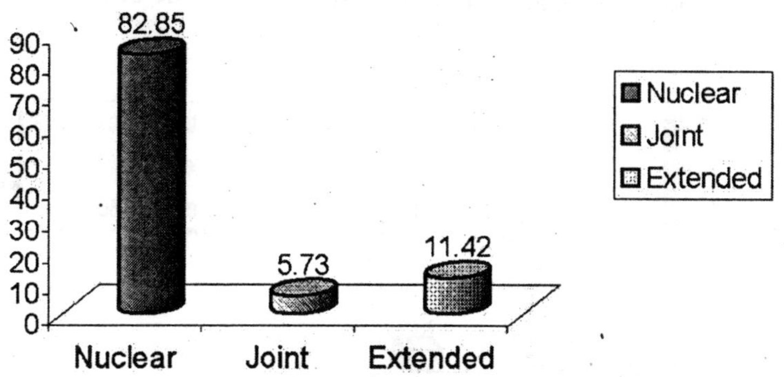

Table 19.7

Distribution of Children according to their Family Type

S. No.	*Type of Family*	*Percentage*
1.	Nuclear	82.85
2.	Joint	5.73
3.	Extended	11.42
	Total	**100.00**

Size of the Family

The number of members present in the family was taken as 'size' of the family. As the family members share the family resources available, the more the members, the greater will be the demand on resources and the poorer will be the quality of life. Depending on the size of the family the sample were grouped under three heads, that is less than 4 members, 4-8 members, above 8 members.

The Table 19.8 shows that a major percentage of the sample (65.72) had family sizes of less than 4 members, 28.57 had family sizes of 4-8 members and only 5.71 per cent had come from families of above 8 members.

Fig.19.4

Distribution of Children according to size of the Family

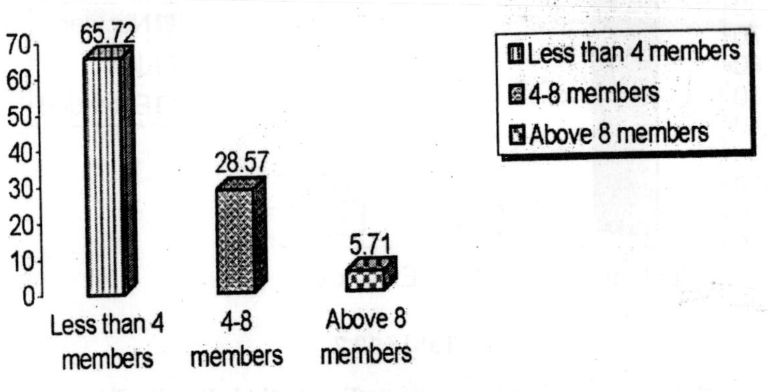

Table 19.8

Distribution of Children according to size of the Family

S. No.	*Size of the family in No. of members*	*Percentage*
1.	Less than 4 members	65.72
2.	4-8 members	28.57
3.	Above 8 members	5.71
	Total	**100.00**

Educational Status of Mother

Mothers education known to have a positive influence on children.

The Table 19.9 shows the educational status of the mothers. A major percentage of 62.85 children's mothers were illiterates; 25.73 per cent had primary school education and only 11.42 per cent had secondary school education.

Table 19.9

Distribution of mothers according to their Education

S. No.	*Educational status of Mothers*	*Percentage*
1.	Illiterate	62.85
2.	Primary school education	25.73
3.	Secondary school education	11.42
	Total	**100.00**

Educational Status of the Father

Education is essential as it develops the mental faculties of a person, acquaints him with the world around him and satisfies the need for the intellectual development.

The Table 19.10 shows the educational status of the respondents' fathers. A major percentage of fathers were illiterates (48.57 per cent). A 28.58 per cent had primary school education and 22.85 per cent had secondary school education.

Table 19.10

Distribution of Children according to their Educational status

S. No.	*Educational status of father*	*Percentage*
1.	Illiterate	48.57
2.	Primary school education	28.58
3.	Secondary school education	22.85
	Total	**100.00**

Occupational Status of the Father

The nature of work undertaken to make a living is called occupation. A person's occupation usually depends on his/her educational status and, training skills. The income earned depends largely on occupation. The amount of leisure time available also depends on the nature of occupation.

The Table 19.11 shows the occupational status of the father. A major percentage of children's fathers (68.57 per cent) were daily wage earners; 11.44 per cent were employed in private sector and 8.57 per cent were doing Petty business, and only 5.71 per cent were holding government jobs and 5.71 per cent of fathers were engaged in other types of works such as self employed artisans and skilled work.

Fig. 19.5

Distribution of Fathers according to their Occupational Status

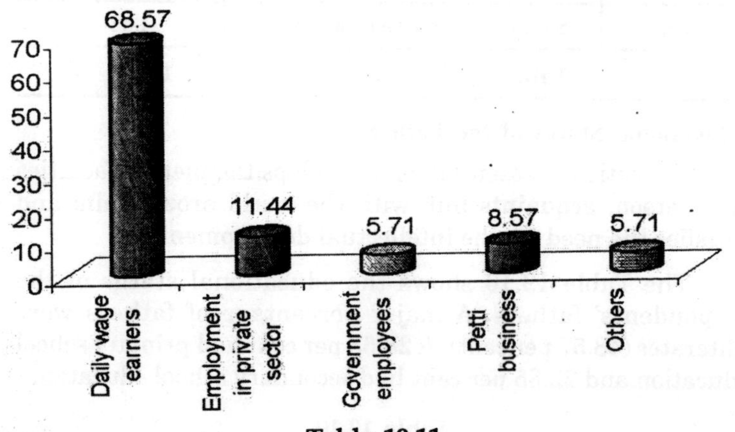

Table 19.11

Distribution of Fathers according to their Occupational Status

S. No.	*Occupational Status of Children's fathers*	*Percentage*
1.	Daily wage earners	68.57
2.	Employment in private sector	11.44
3.	Government employees	5.71
4.	Petty business	8.57
5.	Others	5.71
	Total	**100.00**

Occupational Status of the Mother

Women of today constitute a major section of workforce, especially in the un-organized sector. The occupation of mother affects the time available for care of children and also to herself.

It further exposes the mother to various experiences, which may influence her knowledge and attitudes. Based on the occupation the mother were grouped as follows: Daily wage earners, Employment in private sector, Petty business, Housewives.

The Table 19.12 shows the occupational status of the mothers. A major percentage (51.44) of children's mothers were daily wage earners; 40 per cent were housewives and 5.71 per cent were employed in private sector, and only 2.85 per cent were doing petty business.

Table 19.12

Distribution of Mothers according to their Occupational Status

S. No.	*Occupational status of Children's mothers*	*Percentage*
1.	Daily wage earners	51.44
2.	Employment in private sector	5.71
3.	Petty business	2.85
4.	Housewife	40.00
	Total	**100.00**

Family Annual Income

The total income earned by the family in a year is considered as the family's annual income. In the present study 'status of children in government observation home', family income at the time of their earning families was gathered.

Choudhary (1992) reported that because of the low income of parents and in order to compensate the demands of the family, the children are made to go for work.

The Table 19.13 shows that majority of the sample (61.0 per cent) had family income below poverty line. Around 36 per cent had family income between 11,001 to 24,000 and only 3 per cent had family income above 24,001. The family income of children reveals that it may also be a contributing factor for delinquency among children.

Fig.19.6

Distribution of Parents according to their Annual Family Income

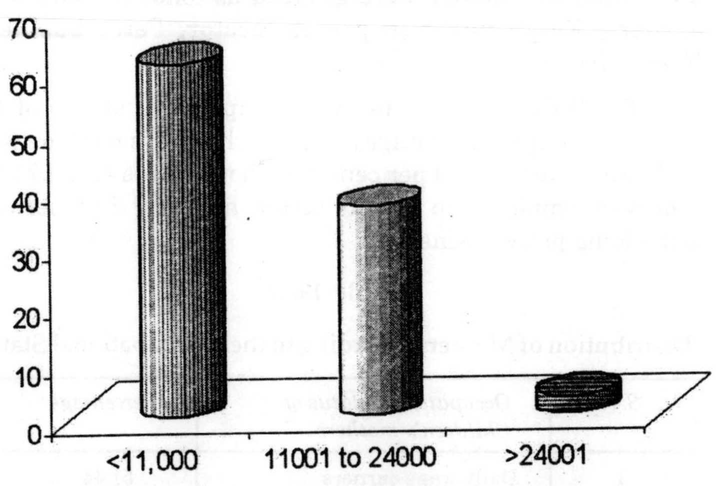

Table 19.13

Distribution of Parents according to their Annual Family Income

S. No.	*Annual income*	*Percentage*
1.	<11,000	61
2.	11001 to 24000	36
3.	>24001	3
	Total	100

CASE STUDIES OF CHILDREN OF OBSERVATION HOME

With regard to the case studies of children coming out of observation home, out of fifty addresses provided by the observation home the investigator could trace out only twenty five children at the given addresses. The case studies of the children were presented in order to understand the background of observation home children.

11. Occupation of mother : Housewife
12. Educational status of father : 6th class
13. Educational status of mother : 4th class
14. Monthly income of father : 3000/-
15. Monthly income of mother : Nil

Seenu at the age of two years was left to work in a hotel, in Guduru (Nellore district) by his parents, where he works as a server for thirteen years. He came to Tirumala along with his friends for a visit, where got separated from his friends and missed them. He was questioned by police about his address; he could not give a satisfying reply. Hence, he was taken to observation home and kept there for a year and then he was allowed to go away. He came to Muthyalareddypalli of Tirupati, approach a house, who offered shelter to the boy. From then onwards the boy is living with the family.

5. **Case Study**

1. Name of the child : Jayaprakash
2. Residence Address : Jayaprakash
S/o Venkateswara Rao
Maruthi Nagar
Tirupati
3. Age : 14 years
4. Sex : Male
5. Educational Status : 5th class
6. Birth order : 1st born
7. Type of family : Nuclear
8. Size of family : 4
9. Place of residence : Rural
10. Occupation of father : Shop
11. Occupation of mother : Housewife
12. Educational status of father : 4th class

13. Educational status of mother : 3rd class

14. Monthly income of father : 3000/-

15. Monthly income of mother : Nil

Jayaprakash is a 14 year old boy studied fifth class. He is a first born in the family, having younger brother who is studying fourth class. The family is of nuclear type having a monthly income of 3000/- rupees. The boy's father Venkateswara Rao studied upto fourth class and mother has studied third class. Father is a shop runner. The family lives in Maruthi nagar, near west church, Tirupati.

The subject Jayaprakash having robbing and stealing behaviour in the early years of his life. One day he took 1500/- rupees and went away from home and enjoy well with friends and came back after a few days. The mother of Jayaprakash handed over the child to police station. The child is on custody in observation home. After he came back to home he still continued his stealing, his mother wanting once again to admit the child in observation home.

Availability of Services in Government Observation Home

The public services are meant for the welfare and development of the families living in a particular area. These are provided by the State through its local governments. The services in government observation home were health, nutrition, sanitation, education, utilities were included as they are also rights of children. Hence, availability and accessibility of these services were studied.

The basic services and utilities usually needed and made available for children or inmates of an institution were identified and listed. The sample were asked to rate these services on a four point scale as: very good, good, average and poor. The scores 3, 2, 1 and 0 were assigned respectively. The total score for each service was calculated based on the rating scores given by each subject. The total scores for each service is given in Table 19.14.

The total scores were interpreted as follows:

Very good = 45

Good = 30 – 44

Average = 15 – 20

Poor = 0 (zero)

Table 19.14

Total Scores of each Service available in the Government Observation Home

S. No.	*Type of Services*	*Total Scores*	*Rating*
1.	Education	23	Average
2.	Vocational Training	13	Average
3.	Accommodation	25	Average
4.	Provision for sleeping	24	Average
5.	Ventilation	35	Good
6.	Lighting	37	Good
7.	Mosquitoes and other insects control	18	Average
8.	Serving of diet	32	Good
9.	Diet	37	Good
10.	Toilet facilities	35	Good
11.	Clothing	33	Good
12.	Health care	20	Average
13.	Privacy	29	Average
14.	Recreation	35	Good
15.	Other services	18	Average

Fig. 19.7

Total Scores of each Service available in the Government Observation Home

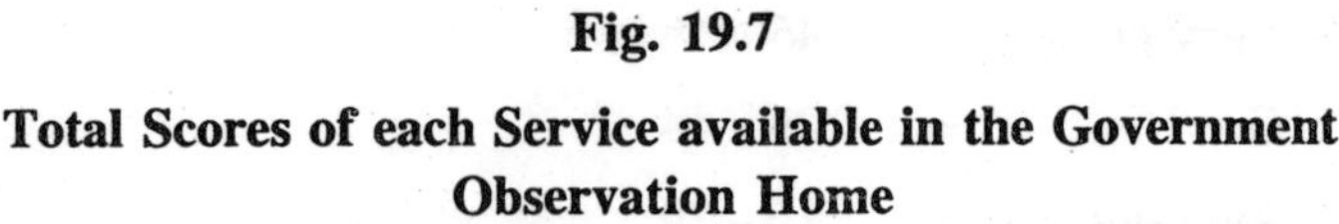

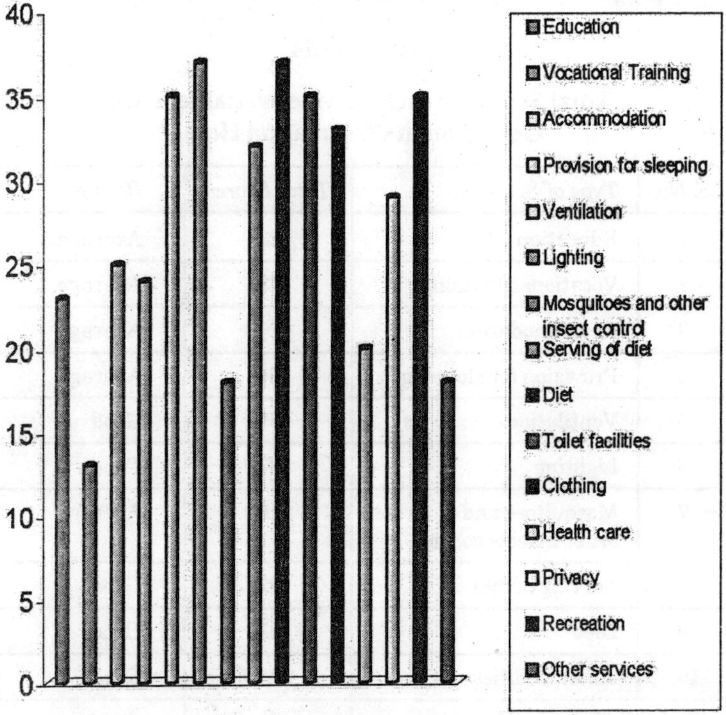

The ratings for each service as shown in Table 19.14 indicate that eight out of 15 services were good. None of the services were rated as very good and poor. This shows that children perceived the services available in observation home as average to good. This perception may also be influenced by their home environment.

Suggestions by Children for Improving the Government Observation Home

The children of observation home were asked to respond to questions on the services needed and the following activities to be undertaken by the observation home to alleviate the problems and facilities for rehabilitation of children coming out of observation home.

(a) Type of Education for the Children of Observation Home

The responses of the sample to a question "Do you suggest that there should be some kind of education programme for children of observation home", was "yes". This shows that all the children wanted some kind of education though majority of them were school dropouts and non-entrants.

The preference for type of education is as follows:

Table 19.15

Distribution of children according to their preference for type of education

S. No.	*Type of Education*	*Percentage*
1.	Formal Education	42.88
2.	Informal Education	11.40
3.	Vocational Education	45.72
	Total	**100.00**

The Table 19.15 indicates that around 45.72 per cent of children preferred vocational education, followed by 42.85 per cent preferred formal education and only 11.40 per cent of children preferred informal education. The responses indicate a strong preference for some kind of education.

(b) Vocational Training

The responses of children to a question "Do you think vocational training should be given to children of observation home so that they can be rehabilitated", revealed that almost all the children felt there should be some kind of vocational training for children of observation home, so that they can be rehabilitated productively.

(c) National Child Labour Schools

The responses of children to a question "Do you think children of observation home can be sent to Child National Labour School (NCLP), so that they can reenter the formal education", indicate that all the children know about Child Labour Schools and felt that they should be placed in Child Labour Schools, so as to continue their studies by re-entering formal education system.

Table 19.16

Distribution of Children according to their Opinion to go to Nation Child Labour Schools

Yes	*No*
62.86	37.14

(d) Children's Perception of their Future activities at when they return home

When asked about, what will they be doing when they go back to their homes from observation home. the children responded as follows:

Table 19.17

Distribution of children according to their responses

S. No.	*Future activity*	*Percentage*
1.	Continue studies	45.72
2.	Have to go to work	51.43
3.	Have to come on to the street	2.85
	Total	**100.00**

The Table 19.17 shows that 51.43 per cent of children expected to be engaged in some kind work. Around 45.72 per cent expected to continue their studies, only 2.85 per cent were expected to that they will be on the streets.

(e) Utilization of Child Labour School Facility

The children's responses to a question, "Do you think you are provided an opportunity to attend a child labour school in your place you will be allowed", it showed that majority of children 71.42 per cent felt that they may utilise child labour school facility. Around 28.58 per cent children were not sure.

(f) Financial Assistance to Families of Children of Observation Home

The children's response to a question "Do you think financial assistance should be given to your family so that they will take care of you and your siblings in a better manner", showed that they wanted financial assistance for their family. With regard to the children's responses on the purpose of financial assistance and for whom, around 69.2 per cent of children felt that their fathers should be given livelihood opportunities through financial assistance whereas 30.8 per cent of children wanted livelihood opportunities for their mothers.

Table 19.18

Financial Assistance to Families of Children of Observation Home

S. No.		*Percentage*
1.	Livelihood opportunities for father	69.2
2.	Livelihood opportunities for mother	30.8
	Total	**100.0**

(g) Kind of help for improving the living conditions

The responses of children to the question "What kind of help do you think will be useful in improving your condition after going to your home", was gathered in a discussion session at observation home. The children felt that to improve their living conditions (present and future):

- They need some kind of wage earning occupation for mothers and also fathers;

- They need vocational training and job opportunities for themselves;
- They need monthly ration of provisions at low cost;
- They need free medical facilities;
- They need utilities such as electricity or fuel at low cost.

It is the responsibility of social welfare department which supervises the administration of observation homes to reshape and to strengthen existing programmes by coordinating with poverty alleviation programmes, to change the living conditions of children living below poverty line.

REFERENCES

Bharti Sharma (1990): "*Juvenile Delinquents and the Social Culture*", Uppal Publishing House, New Delhi.

Borroah, P.P., (1992): "*Handbook on Child*" (*with Historical Background*), Concept Publishing Company, New Delhi.

Chandana Sarkar (1987): "*Juvenile Delinquency in India*", Daya Publishing House, Delhi, pp. 1 to 55.

Dr. N.L. Mitra (1988): "*Juvenile Delinquency and Indian Justice System*", Deep and Deep Publications, New Delhi, pp. 130 to 133, 423, 426-430, 433-437.

Index

L

W

❑❑❑